TYNDALE HOUSE
and FELLOWSHIP

For Elaine, and for our daughters Catherine, Janet, Margaret and Elspeth in thanksgiving to God for the many friends we each made in the Christian Unions at Glasgow, Cambridge, Lancaster and Edinburgh

Research for the
Academy and the Church

TYNDALE HOUSE
and FELLOWSHIP

THE FIRST SIXTY YEARS

T. A. Noble

INTER-VARSITY PRESS
38 De Montfort Street, Leicester LE1 7GP, England
Website: www.ivpbooks.com
Email: ivp@ivp-editorial.co.uk

First published 2006

British Library Cataloguing in Publication Data
A catalogue record for this book is available from the British Library.

ISBN-13: 978-1-84474-095-6
ISBN-10: 1-84474-095-1

Set in Monotype Garamond 11/13pt
Typeset in Great Britain by Servis Filmsetting Ltd, Manchester
Printed and bound by Creative Print & Design (Wales), Ebbw Vale

*Inter-Varsity Press is the publishing division of the Universities and Colleges Christian
Fellowship (formerly the Inter-Varsity Fellowship), a student movement linking Christian
Unions in universities and colleges throughout Great Britain, and a member movement of the
International Fellowship of Evangelical Students. For more information about local and
national activities write to UCCF, 38 De Montfort Street, Leicester LE1 7GP, email us at
email@uccf.org.uk, or visit the UCCF website at www.uccf.org.uk.*

CONTENTS

APPENDICES

FOREWORD

The Rt Revd John B. Taylor

My first acquaintance with Tyndale House was when I was an undergraduate in Cambridge in 1948. The then Warden, known to us only as Colonel Anderson, issued an open invitation to members of the CICCU to meet and hear the well-known Australian scholar Archdeacon T. C. Hammond, who was visiting Cambridge. I have no recollection of either the subject or the content of his talk, but a by-product for many of us who crammed into the lounge that evening was to be reassured that it was possible to be both an Evangelical and a member of the Church of England. Rumour had it that the only true Evangelicals were either Baptists or members of the Plymouth Brethren, so this was a comforting experience for us. Now here was a stout defender of the evangelical faith, author of such hard-hitting and scholarly IVF books as *Reasoning Faith* and *In Understanding Be Men*, and a convinced churchman to boot, proclaiming an evangelical, scriptural message that no-one could gainsay. Now I realize that this effect was not one of the primary functions of the newly established biblical research library known as Tyndale House. The venue was chosen simply because it was the Andersons' home and they were hosting a private gathering, but as far as I was concerned it put Tyndale House on the map, to my everlasting benefit.

So, when I graduated in Classics and Theology in 1950 and was awarded a Lady Kay scholarship to Jesus College for two further years of concentrated work on Hebrew and the Old Testament, an invitation to spend it as a Tyndale resident was too good an opportunity to resist. I spent those years under the kindly and solicitous eye of the Lady Bursar, Mrs Lilian MacLean (the legendary 'Mrs Mac'), and in company with Leon and Mildred Morris, Bruce and Mary Reed, Kenneth Howkins, Peter Schneider, Elizabeth Lloyd-Jones, Percy Hammond, Alan Weir and a number of other good friends, all of whom in later life became distinguished in Christian service. For my part this was the beginning of a life of indebtedness to Tyndale House and all that it has stood for.

While my recollections of Tyndale House go back therefore almost to its foundation, and I might have been expected to know roughly most of its history through my continuing involvement with its activities, I nevertheless have discovered through the reading of Dr Tom Noble's masterly chronicle what a treasury of background information he has been able to put together in this book. He leads us through the cut and thrust of debate surrounding its initial establishment, the differing viewpoints of the founding fathers (all familiar names to me from my youth), the behind-the-scenes stresses and strains that never came to the public eye, the financial pressures, the doctrinal and political issues and sensitivities; but through it all there are the triumphs and achievements, the mini-miracles, the answers to prayer, the quiet and lasting work of the Spirit in reviving and renewing the Evangelical movement through the 'signs and wonders' of painstaking scholarship, biblical study and intellectual integrity.

The story of Tyndale House is one that could have been penned by a religious journalist, telling the world of one of the most influential means of grace that the church of the latter half of the twentieth century has known. Instead we are given a historian's measured account drawn from the primary sources of committee minute books and archival material, livened occasionally with personal reminiscences from members of the cast. I have found it gripping reading, not just because most of the actors have been known to me, but because behind the story we are shown the thinking, the vision, the mental strivings that have undergirded all that has gone on in Tyndale House and in the Tyndale Fellowship over these past sixty years.

But there is more to this story than the undoubted achievements of a growing institution in a university city and a worldwide fellowship of like-minded scholars. I look back at the astonishing changes that have taken place in the churches, not least in the Church of England (which is the only communion I can really assess), and in university theological faculties over the past sixty years. Today evangelicals are not derided as they used to be; there are so many more of them, and they include respected scholars in their ranks. There is much less antagonism towards conservative scholarship. The publications of the Inter-Varsity Press and other similar publishing houses are read and appreciated far more widely than within their own constituencies. The climate is much more accepting of biblical viewpoints. The resurgence of evangelical life within all the churches cannot fail to be noted and commented upon, even by those who may be dismayed by it. Evangelicals in the Anglican Communion are stronger in numbers and in influence than they have ever been. And if we attempt to identify the causes for this transformation, I am not alone in coming to the conclusion that, among many influences that have been brought to bear on the church, the one key contributing factor has been the establishment of Tyndale House and the concentric circles of influence that have rippled out from there. Yes, there have been outstanding personalities and movements of the Spirit, from Billy Graham to the charismatic movement, but revivals and surges of interest that are not grounded in serious, continuing biblical study, preaching and research do not stand the test of time. I believe that what has come out of the library and fellowship of 36 Selwyn Gardens and has percolated the worldwide church in every continent has been crucially responsible under God for the climate change that we see in the church today.

The words that came to my mind when I reached the end of Tom Noble's book were those that my wife and I had printed on the little cards that notified all our friends of the safe arrival and birth-weights of our firstborn twin daughters: 'The Lord hath done great things for us, whereof we are glad' (Psalm 126:3). May Tyndale House and the Tyndale Fellowship, the twins born to the former Inter-Varsity Fellowship, continue to grow and flourish and fulfil the purposes God intended when he brought them into the world.

PREFACE

Research for this history of Tyndale House and the Tyndale Fellowship began when I was secretary of the Tyndale Fellowship in the early 1990s. Being rather curious about the constitutional relationship of the Tyndale Fellowship Committee to other committees of the UCCF (Universities and Colleges Christian Fellowship), and becoming aware that senior members of the committee were guided by past debates and decisions, and that these were not codified anywhere, I realized that these things could only be understood by reading the old minute books. Those had their own fascination. In the discussions and decisions of such pioneering figures as G. T. Manley, Douglas Johnson, Martyn Lloyd-Jones, W. J. Martin, F. F. Bruce and A. M. Stibbs contained in those dusty old minute books I soon saw a fascinating seam of evidence of significance for modern church history, and specifically for the history of the Evangelical movement and of the discipline of Biblical Studies in the late twentieth century. But I do not believe that I realized just how much time would be required to distil a history from the raw material of the minutes of several committees meeting over so many decades!

By the time of the Jubilee Conference of the Tyndale Fellowship in 1994, I had written enough to read a paper on the prehistory of the House and Fellowship, substantially what is now in the first two chapters. I was also able to enter into correspondence with the Revd John Wenham, who, as a student, had argued that the Inter-Varsity Fellowship (as it then was) should convene the Biblical Research Committee, and with Sir Norman Anderson, the first

Warden of Tyndale House, both of whom have since passed to their reward. New responsibilities and other pressing demands kept the history languishing thereafter, but the imminence of the sixtieth anniversary of the House and Fellowship brought the project to the top of the list of priorities and prompted me to complete the task.

The history is built on the framework of the minutes of the IVF Biblical Research Committee (which, when IVF had become UCCF, became the Tyndale House Council) and the committee of the Tyndale Fellowship, supplemented by other sources, both written and oral. I have deliberately kept as close as possible to the chronology of events revealed in the minutes, since I have always felt that careful historical chronology is essential to understanding the unfolding of any 'story'. But often the slightly different stories of the House and the Fellowship have been presented in parallel. Clearly, too, the closer the story comes to the present day, the more the confidentiality of committee work has to be respected.

I emphasize that this is intentionally a history: that is to say, a *narrative*, a *story*. As a narrative, it aims to work at several levels. First, I have tried to include the contribution of staff at the House without whose service it could not exist. Secondly, I have thought it important to mention the succeeding groups of research students who have lived together there over six decades as part of a formative community. These have emerged into a new generation of biblical scholars and teachers, and so I have detailed their first appointments to teaching posts in universities and colleges – thus emphasizing the vital role of Tyndale House and Fellowship in nurturing the Evangelical scholars who have nurtured the pastors and preachers who now in turn nurture hundreds of thousands of Christians in congregations throughout this country and abroad. The narrative also traces the emergence of significant publications of this school of biblical scholarship, from the initial works written for the general reader, such as the *The New Bible Commentary*, to the later joint projects of scholarship such as the Acts Project. Even then it cannot list the flood of works of scholarship coming from all the leading scholars associated through the years with Tyndale House and Fellowship.

Thirdly, the practicalities of finance and building projects and the organization, development and use of the library had to be included. That means that honest disagreements in business affairs have to be recorded, but there is no shame in those, and without the commitment of the 'business men' – the accountants, the bursars, secretaries and practical people – nothing would ever have been accomplished.

Fourthly, the theological discussions and debates and the differing priorities shaped by academic discipline and ecclesiastical tradition are part of the story, particularly the story of the Tyndale Fellowship. The Evangelical tradition never has been monolithic, and the very variety of traditions – Reformed, Anglican, Baptist, Brethren, Methodist – with the attendant debates, is part of its vigour and strength. Again and again the relationship of biblical inspiration and authority to honest biblical criticism was a matter for debate and discussion. It is a tribute to the open-minded honesty of those who participated in these many discussions that they wrestled with the paradox of these divine-human books, refusing to resolve it either by denying their humanity in rationalistic fundamentalism or by denying their divine inspiration with humanistic liberalism. The result has been a truly creative tension.

Fifthly, it is important to emphasize that the narrative is not just an account of the House and its residents, nor just of the Fellowship and its publications, but is the story of *committees*, mainly the IVF Biblical Research Committee and its later successors, the Tyndale House Council and the Tyndale Fellowship Committee. That is precisely what makes the history of value: namely, that it is the inside story of how theologically committed Evangelicals in the second half of the twentieth century wrestled with the promotion of biblical and theological research and the practicalities of running a research library. As Douglas Johnson well knew (for he committed his life to this), it is through the patient, dogged pursuit of *committee work* that joint ventures are undertaken and prosecuted. The committees whose histories are given here are surely worthy successors of the committees set up by their Evangelical predecessors in the so-called Clapham Sect who campaigned in their day to abolish slavery abroad and to abolish corruption from British national life. I have therefore deliberately tried to show the slow achievement of aims and objectives through successive *committee meetings*. I believe that the resulting record will be valuable for those who carry on their work in the future, but those who wish are welcome to skip the mundane details.

Finally, I have tried to bear in mind the wider context, for the work of Tyndale House and the Tyndale Fellowship has had wide significance for the Evangelical movement and for the church as a whole, both through publications and through the encouragement of future professors and lecturers. These in turn have had a deep and widespread influence on the church, both in the United Kingdom and throughout the English-speaking world.

Sadly, this is not appreciated as it should be by many Evangelical Christians. A superficial understanding of the mission of the church fails to see how scholarship and research and the consequent teaching ministries have been at the heart of the growing strength of Evangelical Christianity in the last fifty years. But surely the Spirit works not only (as he surely does) through the face-to-face work of evangelism – through the immediate and the spontaneous – but also through the patient backroom labours of the scholar and the theologian. Indeed, since the revelation of God in Christ comes to us in and through the holy Scriptures, it is only through the diligent work of dedicated biblical and theological scholarship that the mission of the church may be furthered not just sporadically in 'revivals' and 'renewal', but consistently and cumulatively over decades and centuries. Only through the biblical and theological *teaching* which is the fruit of *scholarship* is the church built solidly with gold and silver and precious stones and not with wood and hay and stubble.

My hope is therefore that the history will fulfil in the first place the objective which first inspired it, by providing a background and context to inform and guide the policy decisions of those who sit on the Tyndale House Council and Tyndale Fellowship Committee and other UCCF committees in the years ahead. No movement suffering from amnesia can maintain its sense of direction. Much of the detail has been included precisely to fulfil that purpose of informing the decision-makers of today and tomorrow. The history will also be of particular interest to all members of the Tyndale Fellowship and all residents and staff at Tyndale House and all who use or have used the library. But more generally, the research embodied here is offered as a contribution to the serious study of twentieth-century church history. Together with the worldwide Evangelical missionary movement of the nineteenth century, and particularly the student missionary movement from the 1880s onward, the academic development of a school of Biblical Studies through Tyndale House and the Tyndale Fellowship has had a significant impact not only on the church in the United Kingdom, but on the growth of Evangelical Christianity in the Americas and in the two-thirds world. No other institution anywhere in the world has provided such a service to the growth of evangelical Christian faith.

To comment briefly on two points of punctuation: the word 'Evangelical' normally appears in this narrative with a capital, since its denotation is not usually the original one, 'that which has to do with Christian gospel' (which appears without a capital), but with a specific historical tradition or movement within the Christian church. Occasionally exceptions to this are made in quotations where the writer could intend either meaning (and deliberately eight lines above!). Similarly, 'biblical' is not capitalized, except where it forms part of the academic discipline known as 'Biblical Studies'.

I am grateful for the encouragement of Prof. David F. Wright and Prof. Alan R. Millard, who respectively chaired the Tyndale Fellowship Committee and the Tyndale House Council when I began the project, and who have both read and commented on drafts of the book. It was Alan Millard who pointed out to me at an early stage that I had to extend my study of the Tyndale Fellowship to include Tyndale House, since both institutions had developed together. He also provided me with a copy of Douglas Johnson's unpublished history of Tyndale House, written in 1980. I am also grateful for the cooperation of all who have contributed orally or in writing, or who have read all or part of the book at various stages of its development and/or have made valuable suggestions and corrections. These include the late Sir Norman Anderson; the late Revd J. W. Wenham; Prof. Donald J. Wiseman; Prof. Geoffrey W. Bromiley; Prof. Andrew F. Walls; the late Prof. James B. Torrance; Canon Peter Cook; Prof. I. Howard Marshall; Bishop John B. Taylor; Prof. Kenneth Kitchen; Mr T. C. Mitchell; Mr J. P. U. Lilley; and the former wardens, the Revd F. D. Kidner, Dr R. T. France and Dr Murray J. Harris. Needless to say, the inaccuracies and misunderstandings which remain (and in such a mass of material there are bound to be some) are entirely my responsibility, and I shall be glad to be told of these, and to receive letters from residents of the House and members of the Fellowship whose memories have been stirred. I have to admit too that, given the amount of material generated by such a literate group over sixty years, it has been impossible to cover everything, and much more could have been written about (for example) the enormous number of research and discussion papers generated by the annual study groups of the Tyndale Fellowship.

I must express my gratitude too to my predecessor as TF secretary, the late Dr Martin J. Selman, who commented on a draft of the book and was helping me with the appendix on the Tyndale Lectures when he took his final illness. I am grateful also to the staff at Tyndale House, particularly for the appendices written by Dr Elizabeth Magba and Dr David Instone-Brewer, and for the continuing help and encouragement of the Warden, Dr Bruce W. Winter. The Tyndale House Council under their new chairman, Dr Andrew Clarke, have also been supportive. My thanks must also be expressed to my wife, Elaine, and to my daughter and son-in-law, Janet and Timothy Shea, for their work on the index, and particularly to the Theological Books Editor of Inter-Varsity Press, Dr Philip Duce, for his advocacy and continued guidance and support during the long final stage of preparation for production.

T. A. N.
Didsbury
June 2005

ABBREVIATIONS

BAC	Business Advisory Committee (of IVF/UCCF)
BCCU	British College Christian Union
BCMS	Bible Churchmen's Missionary Society
BRC	Biblical Research Committee of the IVF
BTI	Bible Training Institute (Glasgow)
CICCU	Cambridge Inter-Collegiate Christian Union
CMS	Church Missionary Society
CNAA	Council for National Academic Awards
CSSM	Children's Special Service Mission (Scripture Union)
EQ	*Evangelical Quarterly*
GF	Graduates' Fellowship (later Professional Groups)
IBR	Institute for Biblical Research
IFES	International Fellowship of Evangelical Students
IVF	Inter-Varsity Fellowship (now UCCF)
IVP	Inter-Varsity Press
JSOT	*Journal for the Study of the Old Testament*
LBC	London Bible College (now London School of Theology)
LIFCU	London Inter-Faculty Christian Union
LIHCU	London Inter-Hospital Christian Union
NICOT	New International Commentary on the Old Testament
OICCU	Oxford Inter-Collegiate Christian Union
OUBU	Oxford University Bible Union (temporary name of OICCU)
RAF	Royal Air Force

RTSF	Religious and Theological Studies Fellowship (previously TCPF, then TSPU, then TSF)
SBET	*Scottish Bulletin of Evangelical Theory*
SNTS	Society for New Testament Studies
SOTS	Society for Old Testament Studies
SCM	Student Christian Movement
SVMU	Student Volunteer Missionary Union
TCPF	Theological Colleges' Prayer Fellowship (now RTSF)
TF	Tyndale Fellowship
TFC	Tyndale Fellowship Committee
THC	Tyndale House Council
TSF	Theological Students' Fellowship (now RTSF)
TSPU	Theological Students' Prayer Union (now RTSF)
UCCF	Universities and Colleges Christian Fellowship (previously IVF)
WSCF	World Student Christian Federation

1. ORIGINS

G. T. Manley in the chair, 1938–42

Tyndale House and the Tyndale Fellowship have their origins in the Biblical Research Committee set up by the Inter-Varsity Fellowship of Evangelical Christian Unions in 1938. The IVF itself had been organized by Evangelical university students only ten years previously, but its roots go deeper into the history of the Evangelical movement in Britain. To explain the objectives of the founding of Tyndale House and the Fellowship in 1944, and to set them in their historical context, we must first therefore undertake a brief selective review of the Evangelical student movement and the emergence of the IVF.

Evangelical students

The history of Evangelicalism in Britain is linked at key points with students and universities. The Evangelical faith is essentially the faith and theology of the Protestant Reformation, and Luther's identification of the gospel with 'justification by faith' first gained a foothold in England among the scholars of Cambridge. William

Tyndale, whose name was adopted in 1944 for the House and the Fellowship, was himself a student at Oxford and is thought to have lectured at Cambridge. Two centuries after Tyndale, it was among the Oxford students nicknamed 'The Holy Club', 'Bible Moths' or 'Methodists' that the outstanding leaders of the eighteenth-century Evangelical revival – John and Charles Wesley and George Whitefield – first became 'earnest' Christians. Their fresh grasp of 'justification by faith', along with a new accent on the 'new birth' and assurance, came a little later. For Whitefield and his Calvinist brethren the major influence for this was the Puritan tradition; for the Wesleys, it was the Lutheran Pietism of the Moravians which revolutionized the Arminian 'High Church' tradition in which they had been nurtured. Together, their Evangelicalism revived the emphases of the Reformation – *sola fide, sola gratia, a solo Christo* and *sola scriptura* – but now in a different context and with a new emphasis on 'conversion' or the 'new birth'. It was no longer the opposition of the Roman Church they faced, but that of Enlightenment Deism and the broad tolerance of a formally ortho-dox Establishment.[1] Later in the eighteenth century Charles Simeon underwent an evangelical conversion as a student at Cambridge. Then as a Fellow of King's College he influenced hundreds of stu-dents during his long ministry as vicar of Holy Trinity from 1782 to 1836, and his influence lived on after his death until the Cambridge Inter-Collegiate Christian Union (CICCU) was formed in 1877.[2]

---

1. David W. Bebbington, in *Evangelicalism in Modern Britain: A History from the 1730s to the 1980s* (London: Unwin Hyman, 1989), famously defined Evangelicalism by four distinctives – conversionism, activism, biblicism and crucicentrism – and took the view that the movement arose only in the eighteenth century. However, *theologically* it is by no means clear that a satisfactory definition of 'Evangelicalism' can be taken from its 'distinc-tives', and while there were new features of the eighteenth-century revival, *theologically* it was a 'revival' of the Evangelical faith of the Reformation. Cf. the discussion of this in Oliver Barclay, *Evangelicalism in Britain, 1935–1995* (Leicester: IVP, 1997), 9ff.

2. See Oliver R. Barclay and Robert M. Horn, *From Cambridge to the World* (Leicester: IVP, 2002). This is an extended version of the centenary

The Student Volunteer Movement

In the succeeding few decades, CICCU was to be at the forefront of a remarkable movement of students volunteering for missionary service overseas. CICCU invited the American evangelist D. L. Moody to conduct a mission to the university in 1882, and in 1884 the 'Cambridge Seven', most notably the cricketer C. T. Studd, created something of a national sensation when they offered themselves for missionary service with Hudson Taylor's China Inland Mission.[3] Studd's brother, J. E. Kynaston Studd, who had been CICCU president and university captain of cricket, in 1885 undertook a speaking tour of American colleges at the invitation of D. L. Moody, and had a decisive influence upon the young Cornell student John R. Mott.[4] Mott and Robert Wilder became the leading figures in the Student Volunteer Movement, which adopted the famous watchword 'The evangelization of the world in this generation.' In the United Kingdom, the Student Volunteer Missionary Union (SVMU) was formed at a conference in Edinburgh in 1892 at which there were delegates from Aberdeen, Belfast, Cambridge, Edinburgh, Glasgow, London and Oxford.[5] Annual conferences, held at Keswick in the week following the Keswick Convention, led to the formation of the British College Christian Union (of which the SVMU became a department). An office was established in London, travelling secretaries were employed and a publishing department begun. In 1895, the World Student Christian Federation (WSCF) was formed, with

history of CICCU by Oliver Barclay, *Whatever Happened to the Jesus Lane Lot?* (Leicester: IVP, 1977).

3. For the remarkable effect of Moody's mission to Cambridge and the later impact of the 'Cambridge Seven', see Barclay and Horn, *From Cambridge*, 27ff. and 41ff.

4. C. Howard Hopkins, *John R. Mott 1865–1955* (Grand Rapids: Eerdmans, 1979), 19f. Oliver Barclay refers to this as Mott's conversion (*From Cambridge*, 47), but Clarence Shedd (according to Hopkins) calls it his 'second conversion'.

5. Douglas Johnson, *Contending for the Faith: A History of the Evangelical Movement in the Universities and Colleges* (Leicester: IVP, 1979), 64.

Karl Fries of Sweden as Chairman and John R. Mott as General Secretary. In keeping with Evangelical practice, the BCCU and the WSCF, like the Keswick Convention and many of the Evangelical societies of their day, were thoroughly interdenominational. To fulfil the purposes of evangelization and missions, the worldwide Evangelical student movement united those of differing church-manship around the essentials of the Christian gospel and the Christian faith.

By 1905, when the BCCU was renamed the Student Christian Movement (SCM), it had attracted the support of the leading churchmen of the day. But in order to fulfil the great aim of the watchword, its leaders had begun to broaden its appeal beyond its Evangelical base to include an even wider spectrum of theological opinion. In 1910, Mott, the leading figure in the World Student Christian Federation, was chairman of the epoch-making World Missionary Conference in Edinburgh, which is regarded as the beginning of the ecumenical movement. But the leadership of the WSCF and of its British component, the SCM, had passed from student hands, remaining with the students of twenty-five years earlier, such as Mott and Tissington Tatlow of the British SCM. Now recognized as ecclesiastical statesmen, they advanced beyond the interdenominationalism of the Evangelical movement to an ecumenism embracing shades of Liberal Protestantism.

But in broadening the base of the Student Christian Movement with their inclusivist policy, Mott, Tatlow and others had created unease in the Evangelical tradition which had given it birth. In 1910, the SCM Basis of Membership was identical to that of CICCU: 'I desire in joining this Union to declare my faith in Jesus Christ as my Saviour, my Lord and my God.' But objections were now raised to this clear declaration of faith in the deity of Christ, and in 1913 it was altered. The argument was that doubters should be included in membership in order to be helped towards faith. Whereas the Reformers had faced the opposition of Rome to 'justification by faith', and the eighteenth-century Evangelicals had faced the opposition of Deism and 'dead orthodoxy', Evangelicals at the beginning of the twentieth century believed that they were facing a so-called 'Liberal' theology which saw itself as 'Protestant' and could still speak of religious 'experience', even of 'conversion', but in fact called in question the classic Christianity of the creeds and the authority of the Bible.

Already, in 1910, the same year as the Edinburgh World Missionary Conference, CICCU, with a membership of 200, had disaffiliated from the SCM and the World Student Christian Federation with its 150,000 members.[6] The SCM and WSCF seemed to them to be compromising the original clear position on the deity of Christ, the doctrine of the atonement and the authority of the Bible. The London Inter-Hospital Christian Union (LIHCU) was formed by Evangelical medical students on similar lines to CICCU in 1912.

The Inter-Varsity Fellowship

The end of the First World War in 1918 brought a new generation of students, including ex-servicemen, to the universities. Captain Godfrey Buxton (whose father, Barclay Buxton, missionary to Japan, had been converted at the Moody mission organized in 1882 by CICCU under J. E. K. Studd) became president of CICCU, and Noel Palmer launched the Oxford University Bible Union.[7] The presidents of CICCU, OUBU and LIHCU presided at the first Inter-Varsity Conference, arranged at the initiative of Norman P. Grubb in 1919 (and so named, apparently, since it began on the evening of the Oxford and Cambridge 'Inter-Varsity' rugby match!).[8] In the succeeding years eight other Christian

---

6. Barclay and Horn, *From Cambridge*, 77.

7. Johnson, *Contending*, 99. According to Johnson, the Oxford SCM branch would not allow Noel Palmer at first to revive the original title of the Oxford Inter-Collegiate Christian Union. Palmer later married a daughter of Catherine Booth-Clibborn, 'La Maréchale' (see M. Pawley, *Donald Coggan: Servant of Christ*, London: SPCK, 1987, 31).

8. Barclay and Horn, *From Cambridge*, 95. See also Geraint Fielder, *Lord of the Years* (Leicester: IVP, 1988), 19ff. Norman Grubb and Alfred Buxton (brother of Godfrey) each married a daughter of C. T. Studd (cf. Norman Grubb, *Once Caught, No Escape*, London: Lutterworth, 1969). Grubb became the leader of WEC, the Worldwide Evangelization Crusade, after Studd's death.

Unions were formed by Evangelical students unhappy with SCM: Dublin (1920), Aberdeen (1921), Bristol (1921), Belfast (1922), Edinburgh (1922), Cardiff (1923), Glasgow (1923) and Londonderry (1925). By 1923 LIHCU had expanded into LIFCU, the London Inter-Faculty Christian Union, and was by far the strongest numerically.[9] Three further CUs were formed in Manchester, Reading and St Andrews in 1927, and the fourteen CUs which thus formed the Inter-Varsity Fellowship of Evangelical Unions in 1928 were joined by another eleven by 1934.[10] Over the next decade, Howard Guinness, a former president of LIFCU, toured the British Empire – Canada, Australia, New Zealand, India, South Africa – and various European countries as a roving ambassador. From Canada, the movement spread to the USA, leading to the formation of the Inter-Varsity Christian Fellowship there. Eventually this was to lead to the formation of the International Fellowship of Evangelical Students (IFES) at a conference in Boston in 1947.[11]

Not surprisingly, in view of the doctrinal trend which had developed in the Student Volunteer Movement, the Inter-Varsity Fellowship had a greater concern with safeguards against the loss of Evangelical identity. Chief among these safeguards was its Doctrinal Basis, which, in the context of the contemporary debates, was particularly clear in its affirmation about holy Scripture: 'The divine inspiration and infallibility of Holy Scripture, as originally given, and its supreme authority in all matters of faith and conduct.'[12]

---

9. Johnson, *Contending*, 101ff.

10. Johnson, *Contending*, 132, 150.

11. For these international developments, see Johnson, *Contending*, 144, 164 and 173–196.

12. Johnson, *Contending*, 109–114 and 359. This affirmation has been misinterpreted by some as extreme fundamentalism, but Robert M. Horn gives a helpful interpretation in *Ultimate Realities: Finding the Heart of Evangelical Belief* (Leicester: IVP, 1995), 38–47. 'Infallible' (which is an ancient term going back to Augustine) is to be taken to mean that 'If Scripture comes into conflict with any other writing, then the other must give way and Scripture must teach us and rule. It is the final arbiter' (43). 'As originally

There was also a considerable wariness about cooperation even
with 'Liberal' Evangelicals, who could not subscribe to this, but
were doctrinally orthodox and engaged in evangelism. But while
wishing to maintain a strictly Evangelical identity, the IVF continued to embody the interdenominationalism or 'catholic spirit' long
evident in Evangelical unity on the fundamentals of the Christian
faith.

'Conservative' and 'Liberal' Evangelicals

The background to this split in the Student Christian Movement
lay in the theological developments at the turn of the century. The
classic 'Liberal' theology of the Ritschlian school had been given
popular expression in Harnack's lectures of 1900, *Das Wesen des
Christentums (The Essence of Christianity)*, published in English in
1901. The teaching of Jesus, according to Harnack, concerned the
coming of the kingdom of God, the universal Fatherhood of
God and the infinite worth of the human soul, and the later
doctrines of Incarnation and Trinity were to be regarded as meta-
physical Greek speculation. Controversy was provoked in Britain
too by the pantheism of R. J. Campbell's *The New Theology*, published in 1907. Many Christians in the predominantly Evangelical
Christianity of the English-speaking world also tended to associate biblical criticism with Liberal theology, largely because of their
common German origin. The German critics were seen to inform
their biblical criticism with the presuppositions of Liberal theology, and popular opinion found it difficult to disentangle the two.

To counter theological Liberalism and defend and proclaim
Christian beliefs, a series of twelve booklets, *The Fundamentals*, was
published in Chicago between 1910 and 1915. The booklets
included articles by James Orr of Glasgow, B. B. Warfield of
Princeton, Bishop H. C. G. Moule of Durham (formerly Norrisian
Professor of Divinity at Cambridge) and Campbell Morgan of
Westminster Chapel, London. The articles on biblical criticism
rejected the conclusions of the 'Higher Critics', but attributed

---

given', a phrase subject to some carping, simply affirms the validity of
textual criticism (45 f.).

them generally to their 'rationalistic' presuppositions and accepted the validity of the critical method as such.[13]

By the 1920s a fierce debate raged in the United States between 'Fundamentalists', so named from the booklets, and those who were dubbed 'Liberals' or 'Modernists'. But it must be emphasized that the writers of the original booklets included several prominent scholars and were not 'Fundamentalists' in the later sense of the term. 'Fundamentalism' was an American development of the 1920s, characterized by a more extreme, anti-intellectual stance than the original booklets, and conducted a populist campaign against 'Liberalism', Darwinism and 'Higher Criticism'. The writers of the original booklets were not opposed to biblical criticism as such, and significant figures such as Warfield were quite prepared to accept evolution. Certainly there were those in Britain who took the position of a more hard-line opposition to biblical criticism and whose position was akin to the American Fundamentalists (including their premillenialism),[14] but generally, British Evangelical leaders took a more moderate stance. Stuart Holden, Russell Howden, Graham Scroggie, Rendle Short, Harold Earnshaw-Smith and Clarence Foster, for example, who were all on the Advisory Committee appointed by IVF in 1928,[15] affirmed the infallibility of Scripture

---

13. See, for example, Canon Dyson Hague in Vol. I; J. J. Reeve in Vol. III; W. H. Griffith Thomas in Vol VIII; James Orr in Vol. IX. These should be consulted in the original edition, not in the later abbreviated edition.

14. See Bebbington, *Evangelicalism*, 187, on the Bible League.

15. Johnson, *Contending*, 159f. Dr Stuart Holden was vicar of St Paul's, Portman Square, and had been chairman of the council of the Keswick Convention; J. Russell Howden was also an Anglican clergyman; Graham Scroggie was minister of Charlotte Chapel, Edinburgh, and later of Spurgeon's Metropolitan Tabernacle, and a leading Keswick speaker; A. Rendle Short, a Bristol surgeon, was a member of the Christian Brethren; Harold Earnshaw-Smith had been one of the first IVF travelling secretaries and was the rector of All Souls, Langham Place; and Clarence Foster of Scripture Union was secretary of the Keswick Council. See Timothy Dudley-Smith, *John Stott: The Making of a Leader* (Leicester: IVP, 1999), 593ff. for an engaging character sketch of Earnshaw-Smith.

without becoming embroiled in debates about detailed inerrancy. They repudiated the conclusions of biblical critics whom they regarded as being influenced by 'rationalist' assumptions, but accepted the validity of biblical criticism as such.[16] The emergence of another school of 'Liberal Evangelicals' (so named from a publication of 1923, *Liberal Evangelicalism: An Interpretation*) led to the epithet 'Conservative' being attached to what was eventually to emerge as the Evangelical mainstream.[17]

Liberal Evangelicalism (not to be confused with the classic Liberalism of the Ritschlian school) was orthodox in its subscription to the creeds and the classic doctrines of the Christian faith and genuinely concerned with evangelism, but, in reaction possibly to Fundamentalism, it moved away from the infallibility of Scripture. Yet it was the position of the IVF which was to prove definitive for the Evangelical tradition in the long run. The insistence on the infallibility of Scripture was its safeguard against repeating the SCM's loss of Evangelical identity, but the acceptance of the validity of biblical criticism differentiated it from Fundamentalism. It was precisely the compatibility of the doctrine of the infallibility of Scripture with the validity of biblical criticism which the Inter-Varsity Fellowship was affirming in effect in 1938 when it set up the Biblical Research Committee.[18]

---

16. See Bebbington, *Evangelicalism*, 222. See also David F. Wright, 'Soundings in the Doctrine of Scripture in British Evangelicalism in the First Half of the Twentieth Century', *Tyndale Bulletin*, 31 (1980), 87–106, esp. 97ff. on 'believing criticism'; and Mark A. Noll, *Between Faith and Criticism: Evangelicals, Scholarship and the Bible* (Leicester: Apollos, 1986), 78ff. There are two minor inaccuracies in Noll (84): it was not the TSF which organized the Tyndale Lectures in 1942 but the BRC; and secondly, Tyndale House was bought by the IVF in 1944, not 1943.

17. Bebbington, *Evangelicalism*, 201f.

18. For a fuller analysis of the distinction between 'Conservative' Evangelicalism and 'Liberal' Evangelicalism on the one hand and Fundamentalism on the other, see Chapter 6 of Bebbington, *Evangelicalism*, 181–228.

Johnson and Wenham

Douglas Johnson had been a medical student in London (where
he also studied theology at King's College) when, as secretary
of LIFCU, he was thrust into the secretaryship of the Inter-
Varsity Conference in 1924. When this became the Inter-Varsity
Fellowship in 1928, he became the first General Secretary. At the
end of his second hospital appointment in 1932 he decided in consultation with Professor Rendle Short (who acted as a senior
adviser to the infant Inter-Varsity Fellowship) not to proceed to
medical missions overseas, but to devote himself to the development of IVF.[19] John Wenham later recalled Douglas Johnson
like this:

> He had an almost boundless energy, working from morn till night six
> days a week and filling his home with visitors (often from abroad) on
> Sundays. He had a wonderful brain – reading to him whether in
> theology, philosophy, science, history or biography was a means of
> relaxation. He mercilessly scored his books and he retained most of
> what he read. He had a world vision; though his calling was to work
> amongst students and in the universities, it was all in the interest of
> church renewal and world evangelization. He had a remarkable sense of
> humour – at leisure times at conferences, wherever Douglas was there
> would be peals of laughter.[20]

In 1935, John Wenham, a Cambridge graduate studying theology
at Ridley Hall, became secretary of the Theological Colleges'
Prayer Fellowship (now the RTSF).[21] This had been formed in 1933
with F. H. Wynne of Assembly's College, Belfast, as secretary.
T. F. Torrance, a student at New College, Edinburgh, served as

19. Johnson, *Contending*, 190f.
20. John Wenham, *Facing Hell: An Autobiography 1913–1996* (Carlisle:
    Paternoster, 1998), 75.
21. The Religious and Theological Studies Fellowship. In 1938, the TCPF
    became the TSPU (Theological Students' Prayer Union); in 1946, the TSF
    (Theological Students' Fellowship); and in 1988, the RTSF (Religious and
    Theological Studies Fellowship).

secretary for 1934–35. Elected as student chairman of the IVF
Executive Committee the following year (1936), John Wenham's
deepest concern remained theological students. In January 1937
he organized the first TCPF conference at Digswell Park, north
of London, at which twenty students were present. Jack Cobb, a
former CICCU president who was now on the staff at the London
College of Divinity, Leo Stephens-Hodge, a contemporary of
Wenham's in CICCU and a student at Ridley Hall, Cambridge, and
John Wenham himself read papers.

Led by John Wenham, the TCPF pleaded for an Evangelical
return to scholarship. Evangelicalism had become quite anti-
intellectual in the inter-war years, particularly afraid of
theological studies, which were perceived to have destroyed the
faith of many. But Wenham argued that Evangelical students,
particularly theological students, needed older classics reprinted
and needed current publications. The initiative did not only come
from the students, however. In 1961, Douglas Johnson recalled in
a memorandum that it was the Revd G. T. Manley who took the
initiative:

> Following the completion of the IVF Study Course *Search the Scriptures*,
> the two chief draftsmen (G. T. Manley and H. E. Guillebaud, later
> returning as Archdeacon to Rwanda) began to urge the need for more
> scholarly work and pointed to the dearth of any new basic work on the
> Scriptures by Evangelicals. This was heartily seconded by John Wenham
> who was developing the Theological Students' Fellowship, as he badly
> needed up-to-date Evangelical books for his ordinands. The advocates
> were especially keen on Introductions to the OT and NT and separate
> Bible books and, particularly, on commentaries for theological students
> (including the Greek text).[22]

22. DJ wrote this memo for the day conference of the Biblical Research
    Committee held in the Waverley Hotel on 29 May 1961 (see below,
    Chapter 4, 'The Waverley Hotel conference'). That at least is the conclu-
    sion I draw from the fact that the memo was found folded into the agenda
    for the day conference in a collection of correspondence belonging to
    Noel Pollard. The memo is not in the BRC minute book.

This was what Johnson called the 'Phase I: The Germ'. Phase II was 'The Proposal and Result':

> G. T. Manley in a characteristically terse letter and memo proposed that 'an *ad hoc* committee for the investigation of the publishing of scholarly theological literature (particularly commentaries) be set up and that Mr Guillebaud be appointed first secretary.' An honorarium of £200 p.a. for two years from an anonymous friend (suspected by the General Secretary of the IVF to have been Mr Manley himself) was offered, provided that H. E. Guillebaud would undertake the secretaryship.

Acting on behalf of the IVF Literature Committee, chaired by Manley, Douglas Johnson invited the Revd A. M. Stibbs, Norval Geldenhuys (a South African student) and J. W. Wenham to an informal meeting at Manley's home, St Luke's Vicarage, Hampstead, in June 1938 to consider the publication of Bible commentaries. From this emerged the IVF Biblical Research Committee, which held its first formal meeting on 8 September in the IVF offices at 39 Bedford Square, London.[23] Manley, Stibbs, Guillebaud, Wenham and Johnson were present.

The Biblical Research Committee

G. T. Manley, who also chaired the new committee, was one of the IVF's senior advisers. A student at Christ's College, Cambridge, and one of the original leaders of the SVMU in 1892, Manley's intellectual prowess was demonstrated when he became

---

23. Minutes of the Biblical Research Committee. Douglas Johnson (*Contending*, 209) lists F. F. Bruce and H. E. Guillebaud as present at this June meeting and omits A. M. Stibbs, but the minutes give the names listed here. Norval Geldenhuys was a South African student introduced to CICCU by John Wenham. This and the preceding paragraph also draw on Chapters 9 and 10 of Wenham, *Facing Hell*.

ORIGINS: 1938–42   31

Senior Wrangler (top mathematical graduate) in 1893. Bertrand
Russell came sixth equal![24] After some years as a Fellow of
Christ's, Manley had become a missionary of the Church
Missionary Society in India, and had remained with the CMS
when some Conservative Evangelicals broke away in 1922 to
form the Bible Churchmen's Missionary Society.[25] On visits
home, he had encouraged CICCU to stand firm in its Evangelical
convictions, and after his return from India had been the
major proponent of the group Bible studies which became such
a feature of university Christian Unions. Along with H. E.
Guillebaud, he wrote the first edition of *Search the Scriptures* published by IVF in 1934, a publication which was very influential in
encouraging more doctrinal and thorough personal Bible study
among students. Guillebaud, a skilful and scholarly Bible translator who was later Archdeacon of Rwanda, was appointed
secretary of the new committee with an honorarium of £200 per
annum.[26] Alan M. Stibbs had served in West China with the China
Inland Mission from 1928 to 1935 and was now Vice-Principal of
Oak Hill Theological College. Not as formidable a character as
Manley, he was somewhat shy and self-effacing. He was a sharp
thinker and superb speaker, whose addresses at student conferences (especially at communion services) were memorable and
moving.[27] J. W. Wenham and Douglas Johnson were the other
founding members of the committee. (Norval Geldenhuys
had returned home to South Africa.) In October, a statement of
aims was approved. Their first concern was with 'the promotion

---

24. Wenham, *Facing Hell*, 77.
25. See Bebbington, *Evangelicalism*, 217f., for the reasons for this division.
26. This seems a high figure, but is clearly stated in the minutes; as Johnson
    later conjectured in his 1961 memorandum, it appears to have been pro-
    vided by Manley, presumably to make this a full-time post with the IVF.
    Guillebaud's book on the atonement, *Why the Cross?*, had been published
    by the Inter-Varsity Fellowship in 1937.
27. Some comments on Manley, Guillebaud and Stibbs are based on a letter
    from Oliver Barclay of 8 February 1996, in which he described Manley as
    'shrewd and visionary'.

of constructive and original research, and the production of
up-to-date conservative literature, with special reference to a
better understanding of Holy Scripture.'[28]

A panel of reference was appointed, including Dr D. Martyn
Lloyd-Jones, the minister of Westminster Chapel; Dr W. J. Martin,
Rankin Lecturer in Hebrew at the University of Liverpool; the
Revd W. Dodgson Sykes, Principal of the Bible Churchmen's
College in Bristol; Professor Daniel Lamont of New College,
Edinburgh; and Professor Donald Maclean, Principal of the Free
Church of Scotland College in Edinburgh.[29] Various suggestions
had been collected from the referees for a meeting of the committee on 8 December, including W. J. Martin's vision of founding
a school with six or seven young men starting research under his
guidance. The committee also took note of Mr F. F. Bruce, lecturer in Greek at the University of Leeds: 'This gentleman's name
should be kept on the list of those in whom the committee is
definitely interested.'[30] By May 1939 they were discussing his offer
to write a commentary on the Greek text of Acts.

The meeting of 8 September 1939 was cancelled because of the
declaration of war. By April 1940 H. E. Guillebaud had left for
Rwanda and John Wenham was appointed secretary.[31] In December,

---

28. Douglas Johnson, 'The Origin and History of Tyndale House', unpub-
    lished paper, 1980, 4. A copy is lodged at Tyndale House. Johnson seems
    to be quoting another (later) draft of the paper than that included with the
    minutes of the BRC for 27 October 1938. The minutes also state that
    'the General Secretary' (Johnson himself), not 'the secretary' (Guillebaud)
    drew up the draft of the aims.
29. For both Lamont and Maclean, see the *Dictionary of Scottish Church History
    and Theology* (Edinburgh: T. & T. Clark, 1993).
30. Minutes of the Biblical Research Committee, 8 December 1938.
    F. F. Bruce quotes the minutes, including the succeeding words,
    'but that for the present no action should be taken on the
    suggestion to invite him', with evident amusement in his memoirs,
    In Retrospect: Remembrance of Things Past (Glasgow: Pickering &
    Inglis, 1980), 122f.
31. This was not a full-time appointment, but an honorary position.

a report was received from G. W. Bromiley[32] of a conference for theological students held in Edinburgh by T. F. Torrance, and Torrance was invited (unsuccessfully) to join the committee.[33] But this led A. M. Stibbs to suggest a planning conference, which he offered to host at Kingham Hill School in the Cotswolds near Oxford, the wartime residence of Oak Hill College.

The Kingham Hill conference

The conference, which met from 7 to 10 July 1941, was to be a seminal one. Douglas Johnson lists fifteen participants.[34] In addition to the four members of the Biblical Research Committee (G. T. Manley, A. M. Stibbs, Douglas Johnson and John Wenham), there were three members of the panel of reference, D. Martyn Lloyd-Jones, W. J. Martin and Prof. D. Maclean. Dr Martin was not at first expected, since he was busy on his farm at Boar's Hill near Oxford at weekends, travelling down overnight from Liverpool on Thursdays and back overnight on Mondays to lecture! He was also being used by the wartime Ministry of Information for Arabic broadcasts. In the end he came, with significant consequences. The list of those present also includes F. F. Bruce; J. Stafford Wright (later principal of Tyndale Hall, Bristol); the Revd J. C. Connell (a Baptist minister who later lectured at London Bible College); the Revd A. T. Houghton of the Bible Churchmen's Missionary Society; the Revd L. McCaw (a lecturer at All Nations Bible College); and three postgraduate students, D. Broughton Knox from Australia,

32. Geoffrey W. Bromiley had been a student at Emmanuel College, Cambridge (1933–36), then a contemporary of John Wenham and Leo Stephens-Hodge at Ridley Hall (1936–37) and of Stuart Barton Babbage at Clifton College (1937–38). He went to New College, Edinburgh to begin research in 1941.

33. T. F. Torrance's first publication was *The Modern Theological Debate: Notes of Three Addresses delivered at the T.S.P.U. Conference, Bewdley, Dec.30–Jan.2, 1941*, issued for private circulation by the TSPU of the IVF.

34. Johnson, 'History', 7. See also Johnson, *Contending*, 210f., and Fielder, *Lord of the Years*, 83. Professor Maclean's daughter, Mrs Una Mcleod, was also present.

S. Barton Babbage from New Zealand, and G. W. Bromiley. Among those unable to attend were G. R. Beasley-Murray (the IVF theological students' representative), H. G. G. Hooper and L. E. H. Stephens-Hodge.[35] The interdenominational character of the group is seen in that among those actually present there were eight Anglicans, two Baptists, two members of the Christian Brethren, one Presbyterian, and one Welsh Calvinistic Methodist who was now minister of a Congregationalist chapel.

The conference was entitled 'Revival of Biblical Theology'.[36] G. T. Manley gave the opening paper on 'The Evangelical Aim' when the conference met on the evening of Monday, 7 July. He argued that Evangelicals had to be united on the degree of latitude which could be permitted on the inspiration and authority of holy Scripture.[37] But the two most formative and significant contributions were made by Martyn Lloyd-Jones and W. J. Martin, representing two viewpoints which were to remain in dialogue within the Tyndale Fellowship over the succeeding decades.

The Doctor (as Lloyd-Jones was popularly known) presented his diagnosis of the state of the Evangelical cause, 'The Causes of Present Weakness', on the following morning. The general cause of the weakness of Biblical Theology among Evangelicals was that 'experience and subjectivity (in various forms) have been substituted in the pulpit for truly effective exposition of scripture'. This was worse in England than in the rest of the United Kingdom. The Evangelical forefathers, such as the Wesleys and Charles Simeon, carefully expounded Scripture. He went on to three particular causes of the weakness of scholarship amongst

---

35. BRC minutes, 25 March 1941. For W. J. Martin's busy life, see D. Johnson's reply to Broughton Knox's second letter of 7 October 1980 appended to his 'History'.

36. Johnson, 'History', 6. His notes of the conference are entitled 'The Revival of Evangelical Theology', but the two were no doubt regarded as synonymous!

37. For Manley's views, see his essay 'The Inspiration and Authority of the Bible', in *Evangelicalism*, ed. J. Russell Howden (London: Thynne & Jarvis, 1925), 121–155.

Evangelicals. The first was the heightened expectation of the Second Advent dating from around 1830. If the Advent was imminent, then any pursuit of scholarship in depth was clearly superfluous. The second was the influence of D. L. Moody, who brought an emphasis on the simple gospel and on evangelistic methods. Those responsible for the great city and university missions at the time of Moody and Sankey were far too concerned with taking the gospel to the masses to be much interested in the backroom work of scholars. Also, they had unconsciously tended to glorify the evangelist to the detriment of the careful exegete and teacher. The third was the Higher Life Movement, particularly Keswick, which isolated 'holiness' in the way Moody isolated evangelism and also represented an anti-intellectual, anti-theological trend. While 'Moodyism' and the holiness movement had value in other ways, they had been detrimental to Evangelical scholarship. The Missionary Volunteer Movement had thus sent hundreds of graduates to the world's mission fields, but it had had little place for the scholar, except perhaps as a Bible translator.[38]

G. T. Manley's reaction was interesting. As the Doctor proceeded, he was observed to turn round gradually in his chair, until he was sitting almost with his back to the speaker! We may be sure that 'the Grand Old Man of Evangelical scholarship and missionary vision' was challenged and disturbed by the Doctor's diagnosis.[39] Had not Moody's Cambridge mission led to the 'Cambridge Seven' and the great surge of missionary zeal half a century before? Had not the Keswick Convention and the holiness movement in general shaped Evangelical piety and missionary commitment for more than half a century – including that of the original leaders of the Inter-Varsity Conference such as Godfrey Buxton and Norman Grubb? But there was no doubt that the same era had seen a drastic decline in Evangelical scholarship.

---

38. Johnson, 'History,' 7f. and notes of the conference.
39. See Fielder, *Lord of the Years*, 85ff., for this, including this designation of Manley. To one of the younger participants, Geoffrey W. Bromiley, Lloyd-Jones's explanation of the dearth of Evangelical scholarship seemed to be coloured too much by his pet aversions (Letter of 8 June 2004).

Professor Donald Maclean followed with the second paper of the morning, 'A Long Term Policy', which included some proposals for encouraging and safeguarding Evangelical postgraduate students. In the long and lively discussion which followed, the proposal for a new interdenominational theological college was raised. A. J. Vereker, the General Secretary of Crusaders,[40] had made this proposal and IVF had initiated the meetings of representative Evangelicals which were to lead to the founding of London Bible College.[41] Professor Maclean was emphatically opposed to this idea, but it gave W. J. Martin the opportunity to float a proposal which he had privately promoted for some four years: an Institute and Library for Biblical Research.

A Biblical Research Library

Martin had first put this proposal to Douglas Johnson in July 1937, during the International Conference of Evangelical Students held in Budapest. The same year he had also advocated the idea to others, including his friend the builder John W. Laing, who was chairman of the IVF Business Advisory Committee.[42] He pressed his idea even more vociferously on Douglas Johnson at an International Students Conference in Cambridge in July 1939.[43]

---

40. The Crusaders Union of Bible classes for boys.

41. Recently renamed the London School of Theology. Cf. Johnson, 'History', Addendum of October 1980 (written in reply to Broughton Knox's first letter of 16 September), and notes of the Kingham Hill conference, Section III. See also I. M. Randall, *Educating Evangelicalism: The Origins, Development and Impact of London Bible College* (Carlisle: Paternoster, 2000).

42. Both Martin and Laing were active in the Christian Brethren. It was to be pre-eminently Laing's investment in Tyndale House which was to make possible its role in the revival of Evangelical biblical scholarship. See R. Coad, *Laing: The Biography of Sir John W. Laing, CBE (1879–1978)* (London: Hodder & Stoughton, 1979).

43. See Johnson, *Contending*, pp. 184ff., for an account of this significant conference when almost 1,000 students from throughout Europe gathered in Cambridge on the brink of the Second World War.

But the Kingham Hill conference was the first occasion on which
he had advocated the idea at a meeting. A graduate of Trinity
College, Dublin, Martin had pursued postgraduate research at
Princeton and Leipzig, completing his doctoral work at Leipzig
under Benno Landsberger, one of the most brilliant Assyriologists
of the day.[44] Martin was concerned about the decline in standards
of Semitic scholarship in Britain and sought to impress upon the
conference the necessity for a much higher all-round technical
standard in scholarship. He outlined to the conference the long
and rigorous preparation he considered essential: a basic Arts
degree; a German (!) doctorate; a year in Rome at the Pontifical
Biblical Institute; and a year at the centre of Arabic culture in
Egypt.[45] He was later to write (in a statement of the aims of
Tyndale House):

> Our faith is inseparably linked with certain historical events recorded in
> an extensive corpus of written documents, hence its credentials are
> open to objective investigation. The need for the scholarly defence of
> the faith is as great today as ever. The qualifications required to
> participate in this defence can be obtained only by years of study and
> application.[46]

Martin was clearly interested in a form of apologetics, the
defence of the faith. But for him, this was not in conflict with
scholarly objectivity. The personal presuppositions of the
Christian scholar motivated his study, but 'objective investigation'
was nonetheless possible and indeed obligatory, and Martin was
convinced that such objective investigation would destroy

---

44. Letter of 3 July 2004 from Terence Mitchell. Martin's thesis, *Tribut und
    Tributleistungen bei den Assyrern*, was published in 1936. As a Jew,
    Landsberger left Germany in the 1930s and eventually taught at the
    University of Chicago.
45. Johnson, 'History', 9, and his notes of the Kingham Hill conference,
    Section III (iii) and Section IV, 8.
46. W. J. Martin, 'A Later Statement of the Aims of Tyndale House',
    Appendix II, on p. 27 of Johnson's 'History'.

'theories inimical to any view of the trustworthiness of the Biblical narratives'.[47]

As it happened, Martin had discussed his idea for a research institute overnight with one of the student members of the Kingham Hill conference, David Broughton Knox. Knox had come from Australia for postgraduate study in 1939 and had spent his first long vacation in 1940 at St Deiniol's, the Gladstone Memorial Library founded on Gladstone's own collection at Hawarden in Cheshire. This had given him the idea of a similar residential library for Evangelical scholars, and Martin incorporated this emphasis on the value of a residential library with his own idea of an institute promoting (as he always insisted) 'research at university standards'.

The idea met with wide support at the conference, and at lunch Alan Stibbs asked Canon Horsefield, headmaster of Kingham Hill School, about the neighbouring property of Daylesford, which was for sale. Martin wanted to view it immediately and after lunch, several members of the conference, led by Alan Stibbs, walked over to the property and around the locked house.[48] But despite

------

47. Geoffrey Bromiley's reaction to Martin ('an illustrious scholar') was that he 'seemed to be pressing us all into one mould' of defensive apologetics, whereas a more offensive strategy was called for (Letter of 8 June 2004). According to John Marsh ('Not Watching the Wind', *Christian Arena*, November 1994, 16), while emphasizing standards of scholarship, Martin had declared that a real scholar should be able to translate an OT passage from Hebrew into Greek and then back into Hebrew near its original form. F. F. Bruce challenged him to a competition which took place one day after lunch. The other scholars present decided that it was a dead heat, with Martin better on the Hebrew and Bruce on the Greek!

48. Douglas Johnson's reply to Broughton Knox's second letter of 7 October 1980, appended to his 'History'. Daylesford House, once the residence of Warren Hastings, the first Governor-General of India, had been the country house of the Victorian philanthropist Charles Baring-Young, who established Kingham Hill School in 1886 for poor boys from London, and whose town house in Southgate became through his bequest Oak Hill College. According to a letter from Broughton Knox to

Martin's enthusiasm, and the welcome given to the idea in principle, no-one at the conference regarded the idea as a practical
proposition in the immediate future, and it was not included therefore in the recommendations from the conference to the Biblical
Research Committee.

There was also a different perspective given by Martyn Lloyd-
Jones on the value of specialist research in the open discussion on
the Wednesday, the final day of the conference. Douglas Johnson
later recalled the substance of the Doctor's remarks:

> During the next day's discussions, following the papers, Dr Martyn Lloyd-
> Jones gave expression to one reservation which, in the light of church
> history, he had concerning the proposal to found a residential library
> devoted to biblical research. It was a reminder of the ever present danger
> in the Church that specialised scholarship can so easily become master
> rather than servant of the Gospel. It is one thing for linguistic and
> historical scholarship (i) to ensure the validity of the primary sources of
> our knowledge, (ii) to ensure the accuracy of the accepted texts and,
> then, (iii) to be concerned about the precision in the use made of such
> data in exegesis and translation. But it is quite another matter when the
> technical scholar – and he must remember that he is really a 'technician' –
> goes further and determines doctrine and its application. This is the
> sphere of the biblical theologian who must be equally careful to maintain
> a biblical perspective and to see things whole, when employing the
> findings of a scholar.

Lloyd-Jones compared the specialized biblical scholar to the
research worker in the basic sciences or the different specialist
branches of medicine:

> [T]he individual research worker becomes more and more limited to his
> narrow wave-band and remote from the real world of its application in

---

Bruce Winter of 3 July 1992, Broughton Knox was a cousin (presumably
once or twice removed) of Baring-Young, and he (Broughton Knox) had
suggested to Douglas Johnson that they should walk over to look
at Daylesford House.

40

treatment . . . The patient is then at risk [if] . . . a general consultant
physician or an experienced general practitioner (full of common sense)
is not available and does not remain in charge! For the ultra-specialist
may overlook the obvious if it does not belong to his own highly-
specialised little world.

He emphasized (still as reported by Douglas Johnson):

> that care must always be taken to ensure that, when ultra-analysis in
> research has finished its due task, there will follow an appropriate
> synthesis based on an equally accurate and reliable systematic Biblical
> Theology. Some of the most gifted linguistic and historical scholars had
> shown themselves to have been hopelessly short-sighted and unbalanced
> as theologians. Some have seemed to lack a true appreciation of the
> perspectives of Christian doctrine.[49]

These opposite but complementary emphases of W. J. Martin and
Martyn Lloyd-Jones on the need for detailed specialist scholarship
and the importance of a systematic doctrinal overview were to be in
dialogue in the Tyndale Fellowship over the succeeding decades.

The Kingham Hill recommendations

In the year following the conference several of its recommendations were taken up. First, on 15 August 1941, the BRC agreed to
publish a one-volume Bible dictionary (another of W. J. Martin's
suggestions).[50] Martin was to allocate and edit the Old Testament
articles and Bruce the New Testament articles. Lamont, Lloyd-
Jones and T. F. Torrance were all suggested as possible editors of
articles on 'Dogmatics'. Progress on this project was to be slow,
and when the *New Bible Dictionary* was eventually published over
twenty years later in 1962, F. F. Bruce was the only original nominee

---

49. Johnson, 'History', 8f. Geoffrey Bromiley's reaction to this was that
    Lloyd-Jones had a good point that scholarship has a servant role, 'but
    since all that we do is service, we should not regard scholarship as of
    lesser account, as the medical analogy seems to do' (letter of 8 June 2004).
50. BRC minutes, 15 August 1941; Johnson, 'History', 11f. and Appendix I.

listed among the editors. Secondly, a summer school was held in July 1942 at St Deiniol's Library, Hawarden. W. J. Martin and F. F. Bruce tutored a group of theology graduates to advance their skills in Hebrew and Greek. Some difficulty was found in arranging similar seminars in Dogmatics, but in the end A. M. Stibbs was present to lead these. Thirdly, the BRC accepted Professor Maclean's offer of the ownership of *The Evangelical Quarterly*. Maclean, the sole surviving founding editor, was about to retire. Despite the feeling that the journal should be independent of any particular denomination or organization, it was agreed that the IVF publications department should publish it during the war and its aftermath. Prof. J. H. S. Burleigh of New College, Edinburgh, became editor with F. F. Bruce as his assistant, succeeding him in 1950. In 1955, the *Quarterly* was transferred to Paternoster Press.

Three other recommendations about books were pursued: to collect copies of scholarly Evangelical classics (many of which, according to Douglas Johnson, were already being exported to America); to publish summaries of those classics now unobtainable (L. McCaw's summary of Zahn's *New Testament Introduction* was the only significant one completed); and to publish new books. A. M. Stibbs's *Plea for Theology* was one of these.[51] The seventh recommendation was that the BRC should encourage the formation of a 'Fellowship in Study', research study groups of suitably qualified scholars in the universities. These, together with the summer schools, may be seen as the forerunner of what was to become the Tyndale Fellowship.

The other major proposal being talked about – but not yet a firm recommendation – was the ambitious idea of a residential research library. This was not included in the discussions at the next meeting of the BRC in August 1941 and accordingly not included in the 'Report on the BRC projects arising out of the Kingham Hill Conference July 7th to 10th, 1941' which John Wenham, the secretary, was asked to draw up.[52] The IVF Business

51. Johnson, 'History', 13.
52. BRC minutes of 15 August 1941. The report appears as Appendix I in
     D. Johnson's unpublished history. Broughton Knox used this lack of

Advisory Committee was decidedly cautious about the idea, and
its chairman, John Laing, took the view that it was first necessary
to find a leading scholar to attract research students: 'First let us
find the one who is clearly the right man and then we can soon put
a roof over his head.'[53]

---

reference to the proposal in Wenham's report to argue in 1980 that the
residential research library had not been mentioned at the Kingham Hill
conference and, indeed, that W. J. Martin had not been there! It is clear
from D. Johnson's reply that the idea was presented by W. J. Martin and
discussed, but was not included among the practical propositions taken
up by the BRC at its next meeting. See Broughton Knox's letter of
7 October 1980 to D. Johnson and Johnson's reply in the appendices to
his history. See also Broughton Knox's letter to Bruce Winter of 3 July
1992 with an attached memorandum which still maintained his version of
events: that he had not discussed the idea with W. J. Martin until the
following September. But G. W. Bromiley's recollections of Martin's presence at the Kingham Hill conference and the story of the translation
competition between Bruce and Martin both confirm the accuracy of
Douglas Johnson's account that Martin was present at Kingham Hill and
presented the idea of a residential research library. F. F. Bruce, in an article
of 1947, 'The Tyndale Fellowship for Biblical Research', *Evangelical
Quarterly*, 19 (1947), 52–61, refers to three 'decisions' reached at Kingham
Hill, including 'to secure a residential centre and library for biblical
research' as the third, but the word 'decision' must be understood very
loosely!

53. Quoted by Johnson, 'History', 13. He gives an extended version of the
quotation on p. 4 of his reply to Broughton Knox's second letter.

2. FOUNDATIONS

F. F. Bruce in the chair, 1942–51

Following the Kingham Hill conference, F. F. Bruce was invited to join the Biblical Research Committee, and during 1942 he was asked to succeed G. T. Manley in the chair. At a conference of the committee held at 37 Trinity Street, Cambridge, during the IVF Leaders' Conference from 7 to 10 September 1942, Manley 'called vigorously for young men to *act*'.[1] Bruce became chairman and Stuart Barton Babbage, now an RAF chaplain with the rank of squadron leader, succeeded John Wenham as secretary. Of all the business transacted at this significant meeting, none was of greater significance for the future than W. J. Martin's presentation of a report written by Broughton Knox (also now on the committee, but abroad for two years) to advocate their joint proposal for a residential research library.[2]

---

1. Johnson's 1961 memo, prepared for the day conference of the BRC at Waverley Hotel (see below, Chapter 4, pages 111–115).
2. Johnson, reply to B. Knox's second letter of 7 October 1980, 6.

Major proposals

The Martin–Knox proposal

Douglas Johnson gives this account of the salient points of the proposal put forward by Martin and Broughton Knox:

1. That a large house should be taken for the purposes of a library in which sufficient accommodation for resident scholars and small conferences was available. It would provide a headquarters for the co-ordination, and direction, of Conservative Evangelical biblical scholarship.
2. That the biblical library should be stocked with the emphasis on quality rather than quantity, and with a view to the technical needs of workers in biblical research rather than in general theology.
3. That the library should be open to both men and women engaged in Biblical Studies (but not for any prolonged period of residence) who might not be engaged in, or qualified to carry out, original research.
4. That two Wardens should be appointed, one an expert on the Old Testament, and the other in the New Testament. They should be those capable of acting as directors of study and of editing, from this centre, a scholarly journal.
5. That summer schools should be held there and possibly also winter courses, and other types of study course for theologians and teachers in the vacations when research scholars would be away.

The remaining salient points included recommendations that the house should be near a university library and that full bibliographical details of works in Biblical Studies and Christian Doctrine should be kept. But it was reiterated:

That the primary object should be constantly emphasized and preserved, that is, to make the library a research centre, and that it should maintain a high standard in all publications which may be issued from it and in any study courses which should be organised. All other functions should be strictly subservient to this primary aim.[3]

---

3. D. Johnson, 'The Origin and History of Tyndale House', 14f.

This paper from Martin and Knox was endorsed unanimously by the BRC, and the secretary was asked to request the Business Advisory Committee of the IVF to search for property without delay. Daylesford, or any other property in the country, was now thought unsuitable. The library should be in a university city, ideally Cambridge with its tradition of New Testament exegesis. The period of hesitation and reflection following the first presentation of the idea at Kingham Hill was at an end and the establishing of a residential research library was firmly on the agenda.

The Bromiley proposal

At the same meeting it was decided to ask Geoffrey Bromiley to present his proposal for 'study circles' in Old and New Testament and in Dogmatics, an idea which foreshadowed the eventual shape of what was to be the Tyndale Fellowship. He had suggested a list of established and younger scholars who might participate in each. In Old Testament his list included Allis, Aalders, Ridderbos and E. J. Young, along with Donald Coggan, Stafford Wright, Derek Kidner and Donald Wiseman. In New Testament he listed twenty-three, including among the younger men Broughton Knox, Leo Stephens-Hodge, J. Connell, George Beasley-Murray and Marcus Loane. Among his twenty-one 'Dogmaticians' he included G. T. Thomson, Daniel Lamont, Francis Davidson, Martyn Lloyd-Jones, T. C. Hammond, A. M. Stibbs, O. Hallesby, Auguste Lecerf and T. F. Torrance.[4] Manley and Martin also continued to press for a one-volume 'Concise Bible Dictionary', and three full lists of

---

4. BRC minutes, 7–10 September 1942. G. T. Thomson was Professor of Christian Dogmatics and Daniel Lamont Professor of Practical Theology at New College, Edinburgh. Francis Davidson was Principal of the Bible Training Institute, Glasgow and Professor of Old Testament and New Testament Languages in the Original Secession Church of Scotland. Professor O. Hallesby was a Swedish Lutheran and Auguste Lecerf in the Reformed Church of France. T. F. Torrance was at this point a parish minister, but serving as an army chaplain. Cf. Alister E. McGrath, *T. F. Torrance: An Intellectual Biography* (Edinburgh: T. & T. Clark, 1999), 59–78.

Old Testament, New Testament and theological contributors were drawn up for this.[5]

'Tyndale' Lectures

It was also agreed to launch a lecture series, possibly to be named after Bishop H. C. G. Moule. Moule had been the most prominent English Evangelical academic of the previous generation, chairman of the Keswick Convention and also in succession Principal of Ridley Hall, Norrisian Professor of Divinity at Cambridge and Bishop of Durham. Like G. T. Manley, he had given his strong support to CICCU when it seceded from the SCM in 1910. F. F. Bruce and W. J. Martin were invited to give the inaugural lectures in New Testament and Old Testament respectively. Bruce delivered his lecture on 'The Speeches in the Acts of the Apostles' at a conference from 17 to 19 December 1942 for theological students and graduates in Wadham College, Oxford. The BRC met during the conference, by which time it had been agreed that the lectures should be named after William Tyndale. W. J. Martin had by this time been appointed to the wartime Ministry of Information and was leaving for Jerusalem. There was some hope that his lecture would be read for him and be published along with F. F. Bruce's, but in the event it was not delivered until 1949.[6] At the committee

---

5. This is according to Johnson's 1961 memo for the day conference held at the Waverley Hotel (see below Chapter 4, 'The Waverley Hotel conference').

6. Johnson implies on p. 14 of his history that Martin delivered this lecture at the 1942 conference, and F. F. Bruce states that he did so in his article 'The Tyndale Fellowship for Biblical Research', *EQ*, 19 (1947), 52–61. *Theological Notes* for May 1944, edited by A. M. Stibbs, reported that Professor Edward Robinson had delivered 'the second Tyndale Old Testament Lecture' in January 1944. (Despite the date, this counted as the 1943 lecture.) Yet Johnson maintained in his reply to D. B. Knox's second letter of 7 October 1980, 5 f., that Martin's lecture (supposed to be the 'first') was not delivered and he did not list it in his Appendix III, his List of Tyndale Lectures, till 1949. Martin's lecture, 'Stylistic Criteria and the Analysis of the Pentateuch', was published as a Tyndale Monograph in

meeting during the conference in December 1942 it was agreed to ask Martyn Lloyd-Jones to join the committee. He and Basil Atkinson, under-librarian at Cambridge University Library and a mentor of CICCU, attended their first meeting on 13 April 1943.[7]

Tyndale House and Fellowship

The choice of William Tyndale's name for the lecture series by the end of 1942 emphasized the long tradition of Evangelical scholarship which aimed to make the Scriptures available even to 'a boy that driveth the plough'. F. F. Bruce commented a few years later:

> The name of William Tyndale is one in which no one party or section of English-speaking Christendom has a special interest; he and his work are our common heritage. And – rather strangely – Tyndale's name had not been already appropriated by a learned foundation, as those of Wycliffe, Ridley, and others had been.[8]

Edward Robertson, Professor of Semitic Languages and Literature at Manchester, delivered what now became the first Old Testament Tyndale Lecture, 'Samuel and Saul', at the Theological Students' Conference in Cambridge in January 1944. Basil Atkinson delivered the second New Testament lecture, 'The Theology of

1953. J. P. U. Lilley's recollection of being present at the lecture (in notes sent to the author in November 2004) gives further confirmation that it was given in 1949.

7. On Basil Atkinson, see Oliver R. Barclay and Robert M. Horn, *From Cambridge to the World* (Leicester: IVP, 2002), 115; Geraint Fielder, *Lord of the Years* (Leicester: IVP, 1988), 67–68; and Timothy Dudley-Smith, *John Stott: The Making of a Leader* (Leicester: IVP, 1999), 184–185. See also Basil F. C. Atkinson, *Life and Immortality* (Taunton: Phoenix Press, n.d.), a meticulous Biblical word-study rejecting the 'natural immortality' of the soul and advocating as biblical a doctrine of the annihilation of the wicked.

8. Bruce, 'The Tyndale Fellowship', 1947.

Prepositions', at the same conference.[9] The summer school in 1944
was from 31 August to 14 September, again at Wadham College,
Oxford (as in 1943). Prof. G. T. Thomson of New College,
Edinburgh, F. F. Bruce, L. E. H. Stephens-Hodge and A. M. Stibbs
provided tuition, and Geoffrey Bromiley ran seminars in German
for theological students.[10]

Selwyn Gardens

By that time property had been secured for a residential research
library. The Business Advisory Committee of the IVF had met on
28 January 1943 and had accepted W. J. Martin's proposal, remitted
to them by the BRC the previous September. Although wartime
conditions were difficult, property prices were at their lowest and
would probably rise steeply after the war. It was decided to set up a
charitable trust to keep the finances of the Tyndale Lectures and
the proposed property separate from the IVF's general finances,
but it was then felt that the IVF itself needed such an arrangement
for property and that one trust rather than two should be set up.

While these legal arrangements were under way, Basil Atkinson
offered to sell IVF the lease of his own home, College House in
Grange Road, Cambridge. But just at this time Oliver Barclay,
then a Cambridge science student and chairman of the IVF
Universities Executive Committee, visited relatives at 16 Selwyn
Gardens, Cambridge (later renumbered 36) and discovered that
they were planning to sell the property.[11] The house stood in an

---

9. These seem to have been regarded as the 1943 Lectures. Cf. Johnson,
   'History', Appendix III. Robertson's lecture was published in *The Bulletin
   of the John Rylands Library*, 28 (1944), 175–206.
10. These were advertised in *Theological Notes*, ed. Alan M. Stibbs, of January
    and May 1944, published by IVF.
11. A descendant of the leading Quaker Robert Barclay, whose family gave
    their name to Barclays Bank, Oliver Barclay was related to Godfrey
    Buxton, one of the initiators of the Inter-Varsity Conference in 1919
    (see Chapter 1, 'Evangelical students', pages 23f.). Cf. 'Barclay,
    Oliver Rainsford' in the *Biographical Dictionary of Evangelicals* (Leicester:
    IVP, 2003) and Oliver Barclay's own article on his ancestor in the

acre and a quarter of land in a small island of freehold property surrounded by leaseholds dependent on the Ecclesiastical Commissioners, the Charity Commissioners and university colleges. It was within easy walking distance of the University Library, and the owners, hearing of the use intended, were willing to accept the very reasonable price of £4,500. John Laing, the chairman of the Business Advisory Committee, offered to contribute £1 for every £2 which could be raised. The required £3,000 was soon subscribed by former Christian Union members and the property purchased on 18 February 1944. The Memorandum and Articles for the new IVF Trust had just been agreed in January, so that the property was held by the lawyers until 14 April, when the Trust was registered with the Register of Companies and the Charity Commissioners and so was able to take possession.[12]

Plans and policies

The BRC met on 20 April 1944 and appointed a sub-committee of three: F. F. Bruce, Douglas Johnson and Leo Stephens-Hodge. Stephens-Hodge was welcomed to this meeting (along with Geoffrey Bromiley *in absentia*) and was appointed secretary in succession to Barton Babbage, who had been posted overseas.[13] The sub-committee was to search for a librarian and prepare plans for the use of the research centre during the next two or three years.

In their report, dated 5 May 1944, Bruce, Johnson and Stephens-Hodge presented plans for both short-term and long-term policy.[14] The short-term priority was to collect materials and 'tools' for research and to catalogue the books already acquired.[15]

Dictionary of Scottish Church History and Theology (Edinburgh: T. & T. Clark, 1993).

12. Johnson, 'History', 16f.

13. BRC minutes, 20 April 1944.

14. The full text of this sub-committee report of 5 May appears as Appendix IV in Johnson's 'History'.

15. See Johnson, 'History', 12, for his story about his fortuitous purchase of Prof. G. A. Cooke's library on Semitic Studies at Thornton's in

They recommended that the BRC's next annual conference, in January 1945, should take place in the newly acquired property if adequate furniture and domestic help were available. Some of the interested graduates could be accommodated in the annexe at 9 Madingley Road, which had been taken on a very reasonable short-term lease. A 'House Committee' should be formed, adding Basil Atkinson and Oliver Barclay to the sub-committee, since they were resident in Cambridge and could be consulted by the resident Librarian on urgent and local decisions. The name 'Tyndale House' was already favoured by the BRC and should be formally ratified. ('Simeon' as well as 'Moule' had also been suggested, but these luminaries were identified more with one tradition within Evangelicalism.)[16] The name should be adopted quietly and unobtrusively, and a private meeting for prayer should be held at the opening for members of the BRC and the Trust.

In their plan for long-term policy, the sub-committee recommended an examination of the constitution of Pusey House, which held a relationship to Oxford University analogous to that which they would like the new research centre to have with Cambridge. They believed that the success of the new House would turn upon finding a 'Principal' with the necessary qualifications: one who was 'scholar, saint and business man'. They proposed guidelines for policy in finance and the running of the library. They also recommended:

> the organizing of a 'TYNDALE SOCIETY' or the 'TYNDALE FELLOWSHIP', so that the research workers and members of the Biblical Research Committee Conference can feel they belong to an entity (cf. the references on the part of the Founders of the Royal Society to 'The Invisible College').

Oxford. (A. R. Millard points out that it was not Prof. S. A. Cook, as Johnson erroneously states.)

16. Both Broughton Knox and Douglas Johnson each thought that he had been first to suggest the name of Tyndale; see the extract from Knox's letter of 7 October 1980 and Johnson's reply.

But of equal importance was a paragraph in the report of Bruce, Johnson and Stephens-Hodge entitled 'General Principles Governing the Research Activity':

> Academic activity of any kind must be FREE if it is to be effective. In all other branches of learning this is generally recognised, and it is equally true of biblical and historical research. Freedom of teaching and learning, thoroughness of research and investigation with a fearless and unequivocal statement of the resultant findings, must therefore be explicitly and unambiguously safeguarded in the inauguration and prosecution of such an enterprise as we envisage.

After comparing unfavourably the stultifying effect of external interference on free inquiry, whether political as in Nazi Germany or religious as in the Church of Rome, they continued:

> The genius of Evangelical Protestantism, on the other hand, had always been averse from such stultifying policies. Evangelical scholars have not found the results of their unfettered studies and research to be inimical to the historic Christian faith. Error is manifold, but Truth is one, and those who, in dependence upon God Whose Word is Truth, set out to discover fresh Truth therefrom, are well assured that Truth can never be self-contradictory, but must invariably promote the glory of Him who says, 'I am the Truth'.[17]

---

17. In an edition of *Theological Notes* published in the same month as this report, Bruce reviewed the second volume of Dr Edward J. Kissane's *The Book of Isaiah*, under the heading 'The Second Isaiah', and deplored the part allotted to the Papal Biblical Commission, which, in practice, prescribed the conclusion which Roman Catholic biblical scholars must reach. He continued: 'The Reformed Churches have wisely never seen fit to make authoritative utterances about the higher and lower criticism of the books of the Bible, so that even those who adhere most closely to the Reformed doctrine of Scripture are not thereby impeded in the free scientific study of the canonical books.' See also Bruce's clear assertion of liberty of opinion in such matters as Pentateuchal criticism, the date of Daniel and the authorship of Isaiah in 'The Tyndale Fellowship', *EQ*,

It followed that the direction of research should be in the uncontrolled discretion of the 'Principal' and the academic council who would assist him. It was then emphasized in capital letters: 'He will of course, be formally and sincerely committed to the historic Christian faith as set out in the doctrinal basis of the IVF.'

Those who used the centre were also to be 'Christian men who were judged likely to advance the cause of the Christian faith by their further studies'. This report of Bruce, Johnson and Stephens-Hodge, dated May 1944, is an important statement of their conviction that biblical criticism was compatible with belief in the authority of Scripture and loyalty to the historic Christian faith.

Believing criticism

That same summer, F. F. Bruce published a significant article in *Theological Notes*, an IVF periodical edited by Alan Stibbs and soon to be renamed *The Tyndale Bulletin*. In the combined issues for July and October 1944 (which he wrote almost entirely), F. F. Bruce wrote an article entitled 'True and False Criticism':

> It is clear that even at this late date there are still some Evangelical circles where the use of the word 'criticism' in connection with biblical study causes fear and misgivings. Still more is this said to be the case when to the substantive 'criticism' there is prefaced the adjective 'higher'.

After an explanation of 'lower' and 'higher' criticism, he continues:

> In fact, both these designations are largely obsolete to-day; we talk almost always of 'textual' and not of 'lower' criticism, and it is preferable to divide the 'higher' criticism into literary and historical criticism. Indeed the terms 'higher criticism' and 'higher critic' survive nowadays

---

19 (1947), 52–61. In the same issue of *Theological Notes* a report is given of an address by Mr E. M. Blaicklock MA, Senior Lecturer in Classics in Auckland University College, University of New Zealand, on 'Scholarship and Evangelism', advocating a revival of scholarship among Evangelicals. He deplored Evangelical obscurantism and advocated a long-term strategy to win back the colleges to Evangelical theology.

mainly in a few conservative backwaters as terms of reproach, as though
all who had ever investigated the date and authorship and other
circumstances of the composition of the Biblical books were
unbelieving rationalists!

He insists that 'in the true sense of the term, many devout and
loyal Evangelical Christians have been "higher critics" as much as
Wellhausen'. After arguing that 'Higher Criticism' is not part of
'some innate perversity of the German make-up' (no doubt the
kind of comment which might be made during the war), he wrote:
'At the moment, however, what we are emphasizing is that there is
a true, constructive, biblical criticism as well as a false destructive
brand.'

For support, he quotes extensively from Sir Robert Anderson,
'a doughty opponent of Wellhausenism', and concludes:

> There is still ample scope for the exercise of real biblical criticism, as
> more and more is discovered of the original context of thought and
> action amid which the self-revelation of God in history was manifested.
> For a true conservatism is not unprogressive; while it conserves all of
> truth and value that has been handed down from the past, it is equally
> ready to discard lumber and to welcome all the new light that can be
> thrown upon the biblical record.[18]

At the meeting of the full Biblical Research Committee on
1 September 1944, a house sub-committee was appointed to
take care of day-to-day management: F. F. Bruce, O. R. Barclay,

---

18. *Theological Notes*, July and October 1944, 5–7. In the same issue, Bruce
    reviewed Edward Robertson's articles in the *Bulletin of the John Rylands
    Library*, where he argued that the whole Pentateuch was fashioned at the
    instigation and under the supervision of Samuel, and an earlier work by
    Dr F. Cawley (by then a member of the BRC), *The Transcendence of Jesus
    Christ: A Study of the Unique Features of His Person, with Special Reference to the
    Fourth Gospel*. He considered the latter much superior to Loraine
    Boettner's *The Person of Christ*, which was orthodox but of little use to the
    theologian and gave the impression of 'scrappiness'.

B. F. C. Atkinson and L. E. H. Stephens-Hodge. Stephens-Hodge was appointed resident Librarian. A. M. Stibbs was added to the committee soon afterwards. This meeting also finally determined that the name 'Tyndale House' would be adopted and agreed that Martyn Lloyd-Jones would be asked to preside at the official opening on 3 January 1945. Despite the misgivings he had expressed at Kingham Hill, Lloyd-Jones graciously agreed.[19] He clearly supported biblical research as such and was concerned only that technical research should not be isolated from the broad sweep of a biblical theology.

The dedication of Tyndale House
The Tyndale Bulletin, as the privately circulated *Theological Notes* now became, reported in its edition of January 1945:

> Tyndale House has been established by the Inter-Varsity Fellowship
> Trust as a Residential Library and Research Centre devoted to the
> highest and most permanent interests of biblical scholarship. The
> control of the centre is in the hands of the Biblical Research Committee,
> which was inaugurated in 1938 for the promotion of such scholarship in
> a spirit of loyalty to the historic Christian faith . . .
> Situated in beautiful grounds quite close to the 'Backs', Tyndale House
> is within easy reach of the Colleges and the University Library. It already
> contains the nucleus of a Research Library in Theology and this is
> steadily growing. Residential facilities in the House are offered at a
> weekly fee of £2 10s., reduced to £2 5s. for members of the Tyndale
> Fellowship, a society open to those who have at heart the accurate study
> of the Old and New Testaments and a revival of Biblical Theology.

The *Bulletin* also reported on the first conference at the new Tyndale House, from 2 to 5 January 1945, on 'The Interpretation of Scripture', with contributions by the Revd R. F. Hettlinger, the

---

19. BRC minutes of 1 September 1944. The House Committee minutes of
    13 September indicate that F. F. Bruce was to chair and Douglas Johnson
    states that Martyn Lloyd-Jones dedicated the House to the extension of
    the kingdom of God ('History', 17).

Revd J. Stafford Wright and Professor G. T. Thomson. Other papers were read by the Revd D. R. Davies and the Revd Gilbert W. Kirby. Prof. N. W. Porteous (of New College, Edinburgh) had given the Tyndale Old Testament Lecture on 'The Church in the Old Testament', and Mr E. K. Simpson, an Oxford graduate and Independent layman, had given the Tyndale New Testament Lecture on 'Words Worth Weighing in the Greek New Testament'.[20] The report concluded with the official opening of the House on Wednesday, 3 January 1945:

> The House was dedicated to the service of God by the Rev. Dr D. Martyn Lloyd-Jones. The Revs. G. T. Manley and Prof. G. T. Thomson took part in the service, and a brief account of the purpose of the House was given by the Chairman of the Biblical Research Committee.

When the BRC met on the day after the opening, the report of the Tyndale House Committee was accepted, including qualifications for residence, library rules, a budget and a prospectus. Leo Stephens-Hodge was to be resident Librarian for six months, after which the appointment could be renewed. The existing members of the BRC circle were to be regarded as the foundation members of the Tyndale Fellowship and admission would now be by nomination. The work of the Fellowship would find literary expression in *The Tyndale Bulletin*, a continuation and expansion of the existing *Theological Notes* for which F. F. Bruce and A. M. Stibbs would continue to share responsibility.

At this first meeting in Tyndale House, the BRC considered a letter from Broughton Knox proposing the separation of the BRC conference from the conference of the Theological Students' Prayer Union, but F. F. Bruce considered that the time had not yet come for that. When the meeting resumed after dinner in Dr Barclay's rooms in Trinity College, the publishing projects were reviewed. Bruce's commentary on Acts was now

---

20. On Simpson, see F. F. Bruce, *In Retrospect: Remembrance of Things Past* (Glasgow: Pickering & Inglis, 1980), 124f. This lecture was published as a Tyndale Monograph in 1946.

ready for publication, but the one-volume Bible dictionary was at a standstill, since W. J. Martin was abroad. Geoffrey Bromiley was trying to persuade Karl Barth and Émil Brunner to allow their two pamphlets on Natural Theology to be published in English in one volume. Prof. Francis Davidson had agreed to edit a one-volume Bible commentary with three collaborators.[21]

When they met again on 18 April 1945, Bruce announced that he had submitted his resignation to the General Secretary to facilitate the reorganization connected with the formation of the Tyndale Fellowship, but neither Douglas Johnson nor the IVF Executive nor the BRC would accept it. It appears that up to this point there had been no formally defined constitutional link between the BRC and the IVF, but now the BRC was to become the council of the Tyndale Fellowship and was to be responsible to the IVF Executive Committee. It was to be relieved of administrative business, now to be entrusted to the Tyndale House Committee, which was to be responsible directly to the IVF Trust.[22]

The constitution of the Tyndale Fellowship

At the same meeting a constitution was approved for 'The Tyndale Fellowship for Biblical Research'. It was declared to be 'affiliated to the Inter-Varsity Fellowship of Evangelical Unions' and its theological outlook was to be that of the IVF Doctrinal Basis. The object of the Fellowship was:

> to maintain and promote Biblical Studies and research in a spirit of loyalty to the Christian Faith as enshrined in the consensus of the Historic Creeds and the Confessions of the Reformation, and to

---

21. BRC minutes, 4 January 1945.
22. This Tyndale House Committee replaced the sub-committee appointed the previous year (see page 49), and the local Cambridge members were to oversee the daily running of the House. Until 1957 (see page 100) the local members were to include J. W. Buckton, who had a printing business, as chairman and treasurer; Dr Donald Denman, a Reader in Estate Management at Cambridge; Dr A. Hanton, a Cambridge doctor; Basil Atkinson; Dr A. P. Waterson; and Malcolm Jeeves.

re-establish the authority of Evangelical scholarship in the field of Biblical and Theological Studies.

The Fellowship was to endeavour:

(a) to encourage younger scholars to engage in biblical research, along linguistic, historical, archaeological or theological lines, bearing upon the right understanding of the Bible;

(b) to call attention to and to examine contemporary research bearing upon a right understanding of the Bible;

(c) to urge the claim of Biblical Studies to a permanent and influential place in the national system of education;

(d) to create opportunities for intercourse and co-operation between those who have at heart the objects which the Fellowship desires to promote, and to co-operate with similar bodies among the English-speaking nations and on the European continent and elsewhere.

A President, Vice-President and Annual General Meeting were all envisaged. An entry fee of five shillings was set, along with an annual subscription of seven shillings and sixpence, which included a subscription to *The Tyndale Bulletin*, or a life membership fee of four pounds. By the meeting of the BRC on 8 September 1945 there were thirty-five members, including thirteen who had taken membership for life.[23]

The first Warden: J. N. D. Anderson

The Revd and Mrs Leo Stephens-Hodge were first to take up residence in Tyndale House, in the summer of 1944.[24] His appointment

---

23. BRC minutes, 18 April and 8 September 1945.

24. Johnson states ('History', 18) that the Stephens-Hodges took up residence in the summer of 1945 and left late in 1946 for Hatch Beauchamp. But in his list of Librarians (23), he gives the dates 1944–45 for Stephens-Hodge.
According to the minutes, Stephens-Hodge was appointed resident Librarian on 1 September 1944, and appointed again in January 1945 for six months.

as Librarian was apparently seen as a temporary arrangement, however, and he was soon invited to become chaplain of Trinity College. He remained resident in Tyndale House until he became rector of Hatch Beauchamp with Beercrocombe in Somerset in the summer of 1945. That summer, the summer school was held in Tyndale House for the first time. Twenty-four attended from 27 August to 8 September, twenty sleeping in the House.[25] F. F. Bruce led sessions on the Gospel of John during the first week and A. M. Stibbs on 'The Biblical Doctrine of the Church' during the second.[26]

Following the Stephens-Hodges, the house was then occupied temporarily by the Revd Henry Chadwick, later to be a distinguished Regius Professor of Divinity at both Oxford and Cambridge. As the Chaplain of Queens' College wishing to marry, he had to find some place to live out of college, and although he was not a member of the Tyndale Fellowship, this was a mutually convenient arrangement. Working on his doctoral thesis on Origen, Henry Chadwick enthusiastically collected books on the first Christian century for the new library. The other property at 9 Madingley Road had been occupied by the Revd A. T. Houghton (one of the participants in the Kingham Hill conference). He should have been consecrated Bishop of Rangoon, but had been unable to return to Burma during the Japanese occupation, and was acting as a travelling secretary for IVF.[27] At the end of the war he became General Secretary of the BCMS, and when the expected influx of postgraduate students to Tyndale House did not materialize, 9 Madingley Road was sold.

A nomination from W. J. Martin
By September 1945, W. J. Martin was able to come to the BRC with a nomination for Warden. While in Egypt, he had talked with a Colonel Norman Anderson, who had been President of CICCU

25. Hopefully not in class!
26. *The Tyndale Bulletin*, June 1945, and the BRC minutes, 8 September 1945.
27. See Douglas Johnson, *Contending for the Faith: A History of the Evangelical Movement in the Universities and Colleges* (Leicester: IVP, 1979), 203f.

in 1930–31. After graduating in Classics and Law, he had become a missionary with the Egypt General Mission, had volunteered for national service during the war, and was now second-in-command of civil affairs in Cyrenaica. He was a fluent Arabic scholar concerned with a literary approach to Muslim intellectuals. In W. J. Martin's opinion, he would have no difficulty in equipping himself as a Hebrew scholar and theologian. He was a man of private means who would be free in a few months and might be willing to take charge of Tyndale House for a period.[28]

G. T. Manley asked for other names, and those of T. C. Hammond, F. F. Bruce and W. J. Martin himself were put forward as possible wardens. T. H. L. Parker, J. W. Wenham and F. D. Kidner were suggested as possible librarians. But it was agreed that, for Warden, an approach should be made to J. N. D. Anderson and that references should be sought.[29] At the same meeting, J. Stafford Wright succeeded Leo Stephens-Hodge as secretary of the BRC and the Tyndale Fellowship. A letter was also received from J. H. Hubbard of CSSM expressing anxiety lest summer schools in August should take students away from beach missions. It was agreed that July was better for summer schools.

By January 1946 it was agreed that J. N. D. Anderson was suitable, but it was May before the nomination was placed before the Trust. In the meantime, Henry Chadwick received guests, organized the library, purchased works in church history, particularly patristics, and 'showed great keenness in arranging the books'. It was decided, however, that it would not be wise to have two families in the house by acceding to the Chadwicks' request to remain in the top floor of the house once the new Warden moved in.

Reconsideration

Douglas Johnson encouraged the BRC to set objectives for the Tyndale Fellowship and F. F. Bruce agreed to produce a draft

---

28. See J. N. D. Anderson, *An Adopted Son: The Story of My Life* (Leicester: IVP, 1985); and D. J. Goodhew's article in *Biographical Dictionary of Evangelicals* (Leicester: IVP, 2003).

29. BRC minutes, 5 April 1946.

brochure with the Fellowship's aims. By January 1946 there were nineteen life members and thirty-six annual members. In a committee discussion on the Tyndale Lectures, it was felt better to confine invitations to 'loyal men', those who were wholly in accord with the aims of the Fellowship, and to maintain a balance between well-established and younger men.[30] Two proposals were not pursued: the first was to invite Sir Frederick Kenyon to become President of the Fellowship; the second was to found another research centre in Jerusalem! The latter was proposed in a letter from Palestine, then still under the British mandate, from the indefatigable John Wenham, who was serving there as an RAF chaplain.[31] When Colonel Anderson visited Tyndale House while on 'release leave' and joined the committee in July 1946, he commented that a live and sane Research Institute would be of great value in Jerusalem since the city was 'full of cranks'! But the proposal seemed to be far beyond the resources of the IVF, and indeed questions were soon to arise about the viability of Tyndale House itself.

After serving on the staff of the British Foreign Secretary, Ernest Bevin, at a conference in Paris of the Big Four (Britain, France, America and Russia) on settling the Balkans, J. N. D. Anderson moved into Tyndale House with his wife and two little daughters in September, 1946. Two maids and a part-time gardener completed the establishment. The new Warden had high ideals of Christian hospitality and worked hard to establish links with CICCU, feeling that they needed to be reassured about this research centre. But by January 1947 the domestic arrangements had to be reviewed. Many visitors had been entertained, including CICCU speakers, and Mrs Anderson was tired. G. T. Manley was not sure of the wisdom of all this. Also, by the summer of 1947 there were still no resident students, and by the end of the year, at

---

30. BRC minutes, 1 January 1946. One may speculate that some members of the committee were not sure about the position of some of the eminent professors who had been invited to deliver Tyndale Lectures.

31. BRC minutes, 5 April 1946, and John Wenham, *Facing Hell: An Autobiography 1913–1996* (Carlisle: Paternoster, 1998), Chapter 14.

the December committee meeting, it seemed as if Tyndale House, with a paid Warden, was not an economic proposition. The House had cost the IVF £460 in that financial year, not including any salary for the Warden. It seemed as if the BRC had been too optimistic about an influx of postgraduate students at the end of the war. A rethinking of the project was necessary, especially since the Warden had now been invited to become a Lecturer on Muslim Law at the University of London and would probably leave before the start of the next academic year. He had started classes in Hebrew, wondering if he could make himself into a professional biblical scholar at the age of thirty-eight. But almost at once he had been asked to give university lectures on Islam, which had been requested by the Foreign Office. This soon led to the invitation to the School of Oriental and African Studies in the University of London.[32]

Stibbs and Manley were asked to draw up a memo on the whole problem. At the same time J. Stafford Wright wished to resign as secretary, and, in March 1948, Oliver Barclay also resigned from the committee. Donald J. Wiseman, present *ex officio* as chairman of the IVF Executive, was made a full member of the committee at the December 1947 meeting, and in March 1948 succeeded Stafford Wright as secretary.[33] By March it had become clear that the Warden was able to extend his service till 1949, thus completing three years, and a memo from Manley, Wright and Johnson was adopted, recommending that thereafter Tyndale House should be run by a woman hostess, a single Librarian (who would be paid less than a married and more senior Warden) and domestic help.

By December 1948 the full memorandum was adopted. The compilers began by expressing their anxiety that nothing in the report should reflect on their efficient Warden, 'who was beloved

32. This paragraph includes information from the BRC minutes of 1 January, 3 May, 12 July and 19 December 1947 and from a letter of 12 December 1993 from Sir Norman Anderson. A little social history is evident in the difference between the minutes, which refer to 'maids', and the later letter, which refers to 'Scandinavian au pair girls'.

33. BRC minutes, 19 December 1947 and 25 March 1948.

by all'. They reviewed the original aim: to encourage biblical research among Evangelical Christians, to encourage young workers to take higher degrees, and to organize summer schools and reading parties. The actual attainments were, however, that very little biblical research had been done at the House and no higher degrees had been gained. Four summer schools and several reading parties had been held, as well as two theological conferences for women. The hindrances to progress were noted: military service, the lack of first-rank scholars, the lack of money and the fact that the House was not large enough to be economic. Their recommendation was that, while priority should be given to TF members and to those engaged in biblical research, in order to make the house viable it should be open to undergraduate students in Biblical Studies and to research students in other fields.[34] Before the summer conferences of 1949, the Anderson family (including now their baby son, Hugh) left for London. The Warden was not replaced, and for two years Miss Atkinson (Basil Atkinson's sister) served as acting Librarian.[35]

Conferences, summer schools and study groups

The one bright spot was the continuing growth of the Tyndale Fellowship and the success of the summer schools and conferences. By the end of 1947, the Fellowship had 129 members, thirty-six of these being life members and the other ninety-three paying annual subscriptions.[36] By then, there had been seven residential conferences at Tyndale House and a northern conference, which twenty-nine had

34. BRC minutes, 17 December 1948.
35. I owe the confirmation that Miss Atkinson was Basil Atkinson's sister to a telephone conversation with Prof. Andrew Walls and to a letter from Bishop J. B. Taylor of 6 September 1999. Not even Douglas Johnson, who compiled a list of Librarians for his history of the House, appeared to know whether this venerable lady had a Christian name (at least he did not give it), but according to John Taylor, Basil called her Eileen. Andrew Walls also recalled constant tension arising from Basil Atkinson's objection to certain 'poisonous books'!
36. BRC minutes, 19 December 1947.

attended, held at Hey's Farm at Clitheroe, Lancashire, in 1946. But a second northern conference in April 1947 on 'Principles and Methods of Biblical Interpretation' had to be cancelled.[37] In March of that same year, IVF published *The New Bible Handbook*, edited by G. T. Manley with the assistance of G. C. Robinson of the Baptist Missionary Society and A. M. Stibbs.[38] During that same spring, F. F. Bruce left his post as Lecturer in Greek at Leeds to become Senior Lecturer in charge of a new department of Biblical History and Literature at the University of Sheffield. 1947 also saw the publication of Bruce's article on the Tyndale Fellowship in the *Evangelical Quarterly*, an issue which also included papers on Scripture by Basil Atkinson, Stafford Wright, A. M. Renwick, G. W. Bromiley and G. T. Manley.[39] That same year a debate was planned at Tyndale House on the historicity of the resurrection of Jesus, in which J. N. D. Anderson would state the case for the Resurrection against P. Gardiner Smith, a Cambridge don.[40] But this was cancelled when Basil Atkinson objected to giving a platform to a modernist. The 1948 Tyndale Lectures were given by Prof. G. C. Aalders of the Free University of Amsterdam on 'The Problem of the Book of Jonah', and by Dr Donald Coggan, Principal of the London College of Divinity, on 'The New Testament Basis of Moral Theology.'[41] From

---

37. *The Tyndale Bulletin*, October 1946, and BRC minutes, 3 May 1947.

38. Eleven of the twenty-three other contributors listed in the *Handbook* feature in the BRC minutes; although no membership list exists, it is a reasonable surmise that most of them (if not all) were TF members.

39. F. F. Bruce, 'The Tyndale Fellowship for Biblical Research', *Evangelical Quarterly*, 19 (1947), 52–61. The article by G. T. Manley, 'Co-operation in Biblical Research' (296–299), recounts a visit to the University of Lausanne in June 1946 to meet Prof. Jean de Saussure, one of the corresponding editors of the *Quarterly*, and promote cooperation with Evangelical scholars.

40. John Taylor recalls Gardiner Smith (his director of studies) as an austere-looking New Testament scholar who was Dean of Jesus College and lived to a great age.

41. *The Tyndale Bulletin*, January 1948; Johnson, 'History', 28 (Appendix III). Dr Coggan, later Archbishop of Canterbury, was editor of the

now on the lectures were to given at the Tyndale Conferences in the summer instead of at the TSF conferences in December–January.

In July 1949 a significant decision was taken to follow Geoffrey Bromiley's suggestion that different leaders could organize specialist reading parties. After a few years 'study groups' rather than general conferences and summer schools became the main annual activity of the Tyndale Fellowship. It was suggested that James Packer might organize a study group on the Puritans, Donald Wiseman an Old Testament study group, Glyn Owen or T. H. L. Parker one on Calvin, J. P. U. Lilley a group on the intertestamental period, and Leo Stephens-Hodge (with 'A. N. Other') a New Testament study group. It was also agreed to add a third annual Tyndale Lecture, on Biblical Theology. Memos were to be prepared on the conduct and aims of reading parties and on the purpose of the Tyndale Lectures.

At the same meeting plans were laid for a summer school in 1950 on 'Modern Trends in Theology in the Light of Holy Scripture'. Cornelius Van Til of Westminster Theological Seminary, Philadelphia, and G. C. Berkouwer were to be invited, as was T. F. Torrance with any colleague of his choice, to state his position on 'Barthianism'.[42] The sessions were to be chaired by Martyn Lloyd-Jones. Van Til was also to be asked to give the first Tyndale Lecture

---

Intervarsity Magazine in the early 1930s and editor of an early history of IVF, *Christ and the Colleges* (IVF, 1934). Cf. Johnson, *Contending for the Faith*, 161; Barclay and Horn, *From Cambridge*, 116; and Fielder, *Lord of the Years*, 62.

42. Van Til had published an attack on Barth entitled *The New Modernism: An Appraisal of the Theology of Barth and Brunner* (Presbyterian & Reformed, 1946). Geoffrey Bromiley reflected over fifty years later (letter to the author of 8 June 2004): 'Why did I want a discussion of Barth? I did not want us to become Barthians (something Barth himself disliked!). But Barth, for all our disagreements on some of his reconstructions, would be a valuable ally. For he had a fair grasp of the Trinity, the Incarnation, the virgin birth, the atonement, the resurrection, the authority and power of scripture, and the church's primary mission. Did we really do any good by treating him as a foe, as Van Til had done?'

in Biblical Theology. At the November meeting, it was reported that Van Til and Berkouwer had provisionally accepted the invitation. But by the meeting in January 1950 all three protagonists had reluctantly declined. The committee decided to keep the topic and to set up preparatory study groups in several colleges.

By the BRC meeting of July 1950, F. F. Bruce was expressing the desire to relinquish the chair after eight years to 'someone more in touch with the centre'. Plans were laid for the 1951 summer school on 'Justification by Faith' to be chaired once again by Martyn Lloyd-Jones, and four members of the committee were appointed to run the specialist study groups. Donald Wiseman was to lead the Old Testament group, F. F. Bruce the New Testament group, A. M. Stibbs the Biblical Theology group, and James Packer a group to study the Puritans. By the time the BRC met on 9 July for the 1951 summer school, Martyn Lloyd-Jones had indicated his willingness to become chairman of the committee, and F. F. Bruce vacated it after welcoming E. F. Kevan and James Packer as new members.

Formative years

Bruce's eight years were formative for the whole later development of both Tyndale House and the Tyndale Fellowship. During his time as chairman of the Biblical Research Committee, the decision had been taken to buy property, Tyndale House had been established, and the Tyndale Fellowship formed. The guidelines for a research centre fulfilling W. J. Martin's dream had been laid down, guidelines which combined commitment to the historic Christian faith with genuinely free and open inquiry. At a time when commitment and objectivity were often assumed to be incompatible, this was a considerable venture of faith for the young IVF, not only financially but also intellectually. It was inspired by the belief in the validity and value of 'believing criticism', that Christian faith and biblical criticism were not incompatible, but that the exercise of reason under the authority of the inspired Scriptures could only enrich faith. As Bruce, Johnson and Stephens-Hodge declared in their 1944 report:

> Error is manifold, but Truth is one, and those who, in dependence upon God whose Word is Truth, set out to discover fresh Truth therefrom, are

well assured that Truth can never be self-contradictory, but must invariably promote the glory of Him who says, 'I am the Truth'.

The same year in which he resigned the chairmanship, F. F. Bruce's first commentary was published: *Acts of the Apostles: The Greek Text with Introduction and Commentary*. There had been negotiations with the publisher James Clarke,[43] but in the end this was IVF's first major academic publication and the first major publication in which they used the imprint 'Tyndale Press'. Mark Noll comments:

> This book marked a major breakthrough. Bruce was then head of the Biblical Department at Sheffield University, and before this time he had divided his writing between essays for scholarly journals and more popular books for the Inter-Varsity Press. In 1951 the two parts of his work came together as an evangelical press issued this major and well-received reassessment of the text of Acts and its interpretation.[44]

Noll quotes Howard Marshall's judgment that the appearance of this book marked 'the decisive date in the revival of evangelical scholarship and in its recognition by other scholars'.[45]

---

43. BRC minutes, 5 April 1946.
44. Mark A. Noll, *Between Faith and Criticism: Evangelicals, Scholarship, and the Bible* (Leicester: Apollos, 1986), 102f.
45. I. Howard Marshall, 'F. F. Bruce as a Biblical Scholar', *Journal of the Christian Brethren Research Fellowship*, 22 (1971), 6. The topic of this issue of the *JCBRF* was 'The Contribution of Frederick Fyvie Bruce'.

3. DEBATES

D. Martyn Lloyd-Jones in the chair, 1951–57

The change of chairman was significant for the direction of Tyndale House and the Tyndale Fellowship. Lloyd-Jones may justifiably be seen as the intellectual leader of the Inter-Varsity Fellowship, and indeed of conservative British Evangelicalism, at the midpoint of the twentieth century, and Bruce was soon to be widely recognized as its most prominent biblical scholar. Neither was the product of a theological education. F. F. Bruce was a classicist, a graduate of Aberdeen and Cambridge. While a lecturer in Greek at the University of Leeds, he had developed a professional interest in Biblical Studies, claiming to approach the biblical literature with the same historian's objectivity as he employed in approaching any other ancient literature. In 1947, he transferred to the University of Sheffield as head of the new department of Biblical Studies, being appointed Professor of Biblical Studies in 1955.[1] But he made no claim to be a theologian, even doubting

1. For Bruce delightful reminiscences of Aberdeen and Cambridge (both of academics and of Christian Unions), see the early chapters of *In Retrospect*:

whether a unified dogmatic scheme could be derived from holy Scripture. This stance united the historiography then dominant among classicists and historians with Bruce's approach to Scripture as a member of the Christian Brethren.[2] The Brethren eschew not only a professional clergy but also the emphasis upon systematic theology which is historically part of the education of clergy, at least in the Reformed tradition. Under Bruce, therefore, Tyndale House had been founded to fulfil the dreams of W. J. Martin, also in the Brethren tradition, for untrammelled scholarly study of Scripture. For both of them, the authority of Scripture was exercised in the church through careful scholarship and exegesis, not by reference to any ecclesiastical tradition of creeds or systematic theology.[3]

Remembrance of Things Past (Glasgow: Pickering & Inglis, 1980). For his development as a biblical scholar, cf. 109f.; for his move to Sheffield, cf. 138ff.; and for his appointment as a professor, 142.

2. The Christian Brethren referred to are those sometimes known (particularly in North America) as the 'Plymouth Brethren' in order to distinguish them from Mennonite and other 'Brethren'. For a history, cf. F. Roy Coad, *A History of the Brethren Movement* (Exeter: Paternoster, 1968) and, a more recent work, Roger N. Shuff, *Searching for the True Church: Brethren and Evangelicals in Mid-twentieth-century England* (Carlisle: Paternoster, 2005). Cf. Bruce's comments in Chapter 34 of *In Retrospect*.

3. The writer was present on two occasions when F. F. Bruce denied that he was a theologian. The first was in 1975, when Bruce gave the address (on 'The Catholicity of the Canon') as honorary President of the Edinburgh Theological Society at New College. There, in answer to a question, he said that, while Edinburgh might not be the best place to state it (!), he did not think it was possible to construct a comprehensive Dogmatics based on Scripture. The second occasion was his address to the Manson Society at Manchester University on his retirement in 1978, when in answer to a persistent questioner who wished to know whence he derived his theology, the Professor insisted that he was not a theologian, but simply a scholar, an historian and exegete, who explained the meaning of ancient authors in their historical context!

Theological debate

The influence of Martyn Lloyd-Jones

Martyn Lloyd-Jones belonged to the different Evangelical tradition of Welsh Calvinistic Methodism, and his different perspective had already been evident at the Kingham Hill conference. Experiencing evangelical conversion while Chief Clinical Assistant at Bart's to the Harley Street physician Sir Thomas Horder, he had abandoned a potentially brilliant medical career in 1926, to become pastor of a mission hall in a working-class area of Port Talbot.[4] Such was his impact throughout Wales and beyond, that when he felt his ministry in Port Talbot was complete, he was invited by Dr Campbell Morgan to share the ministry at Westminster Chapel in London's west end, one of the leading Congregational churches in the country. Like the rest of his generation of Evangelical leaders in England, Campbell Morgan, who had re-established Westminster Chapel as one of the capital's leading pulpits, did not share Lloyd-Jones's Calvinism, but he recognized the spiritual and intellectual impact of his preaching.

Lloyd-Jones had been initially cool to an interdenominational body such as Inter-Varsity Fellowship, finding much English Evangelicalism shallow and subjectivist, and mistrusting the predominance of Anglicans. But he had been persuaded by Douglas Johnson to speak at the IVF Annual Conference at Swanwick in 1935.[5] DJ persuaded him that the Anglican Evangelicals were actually moderate Calvinists in the tradition of Charles Simeon. Thereafter the Doctor had been President of IVF for three consecutive years during the war (1939–42), and in 1947 had become first chairman of the executive committee, and then first President of the IFES, the International Fellowship of Evangelical Students. He had given the addresses at the conference of delegates which met to set up the IFES in Harvard in 1947. He was again President

---

4. Iain H. Murray, *D. Martyn Lloyd-Jones: The First Forty Years 1899–1939* (Edinburgh: Banner of Truth, 1982). For Lloyd-Jones's conversion, cf. 57–65; for his early association with IVF, cf. 292–298, and 366f.

5. Murray, *Lloyd-Jones*, 294ff.

of the British IVF in 1951–52.[6] His seniority had been recognized
in the invitation to dedicate Tyndale House in January 1945. By the
time he succeeded F. F. Bruce, eleven years his junior, as chairman
of the BRC and thus of the Tyndale Fellowship, he had already
been established for over a decade as one of the outstanding
British preachers of the day and a leading senior figure in IVF.

Like F. F. Bruce, Martyn Lloyd-Jones had undertaken no
formal study of theology, but neither had he any formal
qualifications or academic standing as a biblical scholar. Noted
for his prodigious memory and his keen analytical and diagnostic
gifts as a physician, his ability to expound the biblical text and
apply it to the human condition was second to none. But unlike
Bruce, he had never wrestled at first hand in an academic context
with the problems raised by biblical criticism. Like an intellectual
but deeply conservative Christian layman, he had tended to be
rather suspicious of 'Higher Criticism'. Theologically, his intellectual grasp of the faith had begun with his acceptance of the
Calvinist view of predestination at the age of 17.[7] His own conversion came later through a deepened awareness of sin both in
the lives of patients, poor and rich, and in himself,[8] and his early
preaching was predominantly evangelistic, focusing on sin and
conversion.

Accepting the critique of a fellow minister early in his ministry
that he talked of God's sovereignty like a Calvinist and of spiritual
experience like a Quaker, but had little to say about the cross and
the work of Christ, Lloyd-Jones read Forsyth, Dale and Denney
diligently to correct this deficiency.[9] But it was in 1932, in the
library of Knox College, Toronto, that he discovered the collected
works of the theologian with whom he was to identify most, B. B.
Warfield of Princeton. He was later to describe Warfield, who had

6. Johnson, *Contending for the Faith: A History of the Evangelical Movement in the
    Universities and Colleges* (Leicester: IVP, 1979), 200f., 351 and 271. Cf. also
    John Peters, *Martyn Lloyd-Jones Preacher* (Exeter: Paternoster, 1986), 72.

7. Murray, *Lloyd-Jones*, 60.

8. Murray, *Lloyd-Jones*, 61ff.

9. Murray, *Lloyd-Jones*, 190f. On Lloyd-Jones's early preaching, see 146–151.

died in 1921, as 'undoubtedly the greatest theologian of the past
seventy years in the English-speaking world'.[10] Owing primarily to
the Doctor's influence, this representative of the old Princeton
school, hitherto of little significance for British Evangelicals, was
to have considerable influence on their theology.

It was partly Douglas Johnson's profession of moderate sympathy with the theology of Charles Hodge and B. B. Warfield which
had persuaded Lloyd-Jones to preach initially at the IVF Conference
of 1935.[11] His critique of Evangelicalism at the Kingham Hill conference of 1941 had largely been aimed at what he saw as its
superficiality, activism and lack of sound theology. Now his
influence was to lead to a revival among Evangelicals not just of
theology, and of the old Puritan tradition of expository preaching,
but of Calvinist theology in particular.

The summer conferences

The new interest in theology in the Tyndale Fellowship was evident
in the series of summer conferences at Tyndale House in the early
1950s. As we have seen, it had been hoped that the 1950 summer
conference at Tyndale House would examine 'Barthianism'. Barth
was at the height of his influence, and there was a sympathetic
interest in his theology within Evangelical and IVF circles, mainly
on the part of those with Edinburgh connections. G. T. Thomson,
Professor of Christian Dogmatics at Edinburgh, who had participated in the dedication of Tyndale House, had translated the first
half-volume of Barth's *Church Dogmatics*. Geoffrey Bromiley, who
became rector of St Thomas's Episcopal Church, Corstorphine, in
Edinburgh in 1951 and was a member of the BRC, had promoted
the publication of the Barth–Brunner debate on Natural Theology.
With T. F. Torrance, it was more than sympathetic interest. He had
completed his doctorate under Barth at Basel, and was becoming
his main advocate in the English-speaking world. Torrance was
appointed Professor of Church History at Edinburgh in 1950 and
two years later succeeded G. T. Thomson as Professor of Christian

10. Murray, *Lloyd-Jones*, 285f.
11. Murray, *Lloyd-Jones*, 295.

Dogmatics.[12] Torrance and Bromiley were to be the joint editors of
the English edition of the *Church Dogmatics*.[13] But in fact (as we
have already seen) the lively debate planned for the 1950 conference never took place.

In 1951, the summer conference was on 'Justification by Faith'.
The sessions were held in the lounge at Tyndale House, and papers
were given by Leon Morris, R. V. G. Tasker, Broughton Knox,
Geoffrey Bromiley, T. H. L. Parker, James Packer, G. Bolster,
Philip E. Hughes and Alan Stibbs.[14] Discussion was chaired by the
Doctor.[15] Some significant new names were appearing on the programme for the first time. R. V. G. Tasker was already a senior
scholar as Professor of New Testament at King's College London
and so a considerable addition to the ranks. He had been deeply
influenced by listening to Martyn Lloyd-Jones at a CU mission in
King's College in 1944.[16] Leon Morris had come to Britain from

---

12. See Alister McGrath, *T. F. Torrance: An Intellectual Biography* (Edinburgh:
    T. & T. Clark, 1999).
13. Further evidence that there was a certain sympathy with so-called
    'Barthianism' within the IVF circle was the hesitation expressed in the
    BRC (by Oliver Barclay) about publishing anti-Barthian books (particu-
    larly Stonehouse, *The Infallible Word*) which 'would offend some of our
    constituency' (BRC minutes, 5 April 1946). But Douglas Johnson had
    been warning about 'the pitfalls of Barthianism' at a Scottish IVF confer-
    ence early in the war (cf. Geraint Fielder, *Lord of the Years*, Leicester: IVP,
    1999, 125). Reviews in *The Tyndale Bulletin* had also criticized 'Barthian'
    views of Scripture. Cf. the comments on Alan Richardson's *Preface to Bible
    Study*, SCM, 1943, in October 1945, under the heading 'What is the Word
    of God?', and the review of *The Infallible Word* in July 1946, which warmly
    welcomed Stonehouse's critique of Barthianism, while noting the general
    welcome given to dialectical theology by Donald Maclean, Auguste Lecerf
    and Daniel Lamont.
14. These papers were published in *The Evangelical Quarterly*, 24 (1952).
15. This was as planned at the last meeting of the BRC chaired by F. F. Bruce
    (BRC minutes, 13 December 1950). See above, 55–56.
16. See Oliver Barclay, *Evangelicalism in Britain, 1935–1995* (Leicester: IVP, 1997),
    72. Timothy Dudley-Smith quotes evidence from Leith Samuel and

Australia for postgraduate study and was to receive a Tyndale research grant towards his Cambridge doctoral studies in the doctrine of the atonement.[17] T. H. L. Parker was to become a significant Calvin scholar.[18] James Packer had been converted to Christ as an undergraduate in an OICCU meeting in 1944, and had been influenced by the writings of the great John Owen when he was given charge of a collection of Puritan works in the OICCU library. After graduating, he was tutor in Latin and Greek at Oak Hill College for a year (1948–49), and after studying theology at Wycliffe Hall, back in Oxford, he had won an award in 1950 to undertake doctoral studies.[19]

Four members of the committee chaired four study groups: D. J. Wiseman the Old Testament group; F. F. Bruce the New Testament group; Alan Stibbs a study group on Biblical Theology; and J. I. Packer, a study group on the Puritans. Packer, whose doctoral research was on Richard Baxter, had joined the committee along with E. F. Kevan on 9 July 1951, the same meeting at which Bruce handed on the chairmanship to Lloyd-Jones.

The theme of the summer conference of 1952 was 'Principles of Biblical Interpretation'. There were contributions by Stafford Wright, Martyn Lloyd-Jones, H. L. Ellison (of London Bible College), A. M. Stibbs, E. F. Kevan (Principal of London Bible College), Basil Atkinson, John Stott and E. J. Young of Westminster Theological Seminary.[20] Martin Lloyd-Jones took the chair at the third Tyndale Biblical Theology Lecture, given by A. M. Stibbs (and published as a Tyndale Monograph), on 'The Finished Work of

Oliver Barclay that Tasker was virtually ostracized by his colleagues when he took a conservative position (Timothy Dudley-Smith, *John Stott: A Global Ministry*, Leicester: IVP, 2001, 130f.).

17. Published by IVF as Leon Morris, *The Apostolic Preaching of the Cross* (London: Tyndale Press, 1952).
18. Following a book on Calvin's preaching, he published his first book on Calvin's theology: T. H. L. Parker, *The Doctrine of the Knowledge of God: A Study in the Theology of John Calvin* (Edinburgh: Oliver & Boyd, 1952).
19. Cf. Alister McGrath, *J. I. Packer: A Biography* (Grand Rapids: Baker, 1997).
20. BRC minutes, 9 July 1951 and 7 July 1952.

Christ'.[21] F. F. Bruce chaired John R. W. Stott's New Testament Lecture on 'The Biblical View of the Kingdom of God', and the Old Testament Lecture, 'The Building of the Second Temple', was given by J. Stafford Wright.[22] Later that same year, John Stott, a Cambridge graduate who had been rector of All Souls, Langham Place, for a year, was to lead a notable CICCU mission to the university. This was the first of his many university missions and introduced a new style of thoughtful evangelism. Crowds attended, many professed faith, and Stott's addresses were to form the basis of his widely selling book *Basic Christianity*.[23]

The conference of 1953 more directly reflected the new interest in Calvinism. One title proposed was 'The Elements of the Reformed Faith in the Light of Holy Scripture', but the alternative title 'The Plan of Salvation' was preferred. In fact the conference was an examination of the five points of Calvinism as defined by the 1618 Synod of Dort. John Murray, a Scot who was Professor of Systematic Theology at Westminster Theological Seminary, Philadelphia, gave the Tyndale Biblical Theology Lecture on the evening of Monday, 6 July, on 'The Covenants'. As a public Tyndale Lecture, this was given in the hall of Selwyn College. The next morning, with about fifty members of the Fellowship gathered in the lounge at Tyndale House,[24] J. I. Packer introduced the

21. For the Tyndale Monographs, see Appendix E.
22. BRC minutes, 7 July 1952, and Tyndale Fellowship Committee minutes of 15 December 1952. (This was the same committee with a change of name.) Cf. also Johnson, 'History', 28f.
23. Cf. Oliver R. Barclay and Robert M. Horn, *From Cambridge to the World* (Leicester: IVP, 2002), 138f.; and Timothy Dudley-Smith, *John Stott: The Making of a Leader – a Biography: The Early Years* (Leicester: IVP, 1999). John Stott, *Basic Christianity* (London: IVP, first ed. 1958). Barclay and Horn note that it sold well over a quarter of a million copies in English and has been translated into fifty-two languages (*From Cambridge*, 236).
24. Andrew Walls, the new secretary at Tyndale House (see p. 81), listed forty-nine expected participants to be resident in Tyndale House or Selwyn College. These included F. F. Bruce (who arrived halfway through the conference); the Revd Morgan Derham (who became a member of

theme of the conference. W. G. M. Martin had been invited to give
the first paper, on 'Total Inability', but had withdrawn after an
attack of jaundice,[25] his place being taken by E. E. King.[26] In the
late afternoon, J. B. Torrance (younger brother of T. F. Torrance)
spoke on 'Unconditional Election', and the next morning, John
Murray on 'Limited Atonement', followed by O. J. Thomas of
LBC on 'Irresistible Grace'.[27] John Wenham gave the Tyndale New
Testament Lecture on 'Christ's View of the Old Testament' that
evening. On the final day, J. G. S. S. Thomson spoke on 'Final
Perseverance'. A paper on the Holy Spirit by Gwyn Walters was
added, and the closing discussion followed. Martyn Lloyd-Jones
chaired the conference.

There were members of the BRC who wished to make it clear
that neither the committee, nor indeed the Tyndale Fellowship as a
whole, was committed to the five-point Calvinism of Dort. It was

---

the Tyndale Fellowship that year); the Revd Dr William Fitch from
Glasgow with his brother and two friends; the Revd Philip E. Hughes
(then secretary of the Church Society); Iain Murray from Durham
with three fellow students; and Norah Nixon from the IVF office.
But there must have been a number of local participants, bringing the
number above fifty. The file of correspondence with the participants
survives.

25. W. G. M. Martin was minister of First Presbyterian Church, Carrickfergus
in Country Antrim, and contributed the commentary on Ephesians to
The New Bible Commentary.

26. The Revd Edwin E. King had just resigned from the Baptist Church in
Dorking, Surrey, and was hoping to settle in the Free Church of
Scotland.

27. J. H. Stringer of LBC had been invited first to present the paper on
'Irresistible Grace'. In his reply to the invitation he identified himself as
an Arminian Evangelical taking the view of the Dutch Remonstrants and
of the Wesleys. He thought he could give an objective account of the
Calvinist doctrine, but he preferred that someone else be invited. Andrew
Walls (a Methodist) encouraged him to come to the conference to engage
in the discussion, but he was in poor health and withdrew from the conference altogether at the last moment.

agreed that the programme would have the following preamble,
written by John Wenham:

> One of the most famous formulations of Protestant soteriology was
> made by the Synod of Dort when it adopted the so-called 'Five Points
> of Calvinism' . . . Some Evangelicals today believe these Five Points to
> be entirely valid and to be fundamental to any true and systematic
> statement of Biblical doctrine; others are quite unconvinced. The aim of
> the summer school is to obtain a careful exposition of these classical
> doctrines, and then to submit them to the most searching examination in
> the light of Holy Scripture.

James Packer's opening paper argued that the 'Five Points'
formed the most logically consistent system of biblical doctrine.
To accept one implied accepting all. But a split in the conference
emerged with James Torrance's paper on 'Unconditional Election'.
Torrance had been reading Calvin extensively at Basel (under
Barth) and Oxford, and argued that Calvin never allowed his doctrine of election to lead to a doctrine of limited atonement. He
was immediately challenged by John Murray, who asserted that
Calvin did teach that Christ died only for the elect. But since he
could not quote Calvin to that effect, Murray retreated to the
ground that the doctrine was implicit in Calvin's thought. James
Torrance quoted Calvin's sermon on 1 Timothy 2:4: 'How sad it is
that souls should perish which had been purchased by the blood of
Christ', and referred to the 'all' passages of the New Testament
and 2 Peter 2:1, referring to those who go to destruction, 'denying
the Lord who bought them'. James Packer then took up the
cudgels, asking whether Christ made our salvation actual or possible. When Torrance said 'actual' he then pressed upon him the
logical alternatives of universalism or limited atonement.[28] The
arguments from history and exegesis having made no headway,
recourse was made to logic.

Lloyd-Jones, often seated on a table, chaired the discussion sessions, giving very crisp – not to say cutting – comments. There

---

28. Letter from Prof. J. B. Torrance, 17 August 1998.

was a memorable confrontation between him and his good friend Alan Stibbs, who had argued that one became regenerate by receiving Christ as Saviour. The Doctor retorted that the one who receives Christ as Saviour does so because he has already been regenerated by the Holy Spirit. He held Stibbs on 1 Corinthians 2:14: 'The natural man receiveth not the things of the Spirit of God,' and the argument went round and round. Eventually, Stibbs was stirred to give a five-minute discourse on mission, but the Doctor's response was dismissive: 'Well, that's your opinion!'[29] Lloyd-Jones did, however, try to encourage the young James Torrance, who had felt the reaction to his paper to be rather aggressive.[30] Lloyd-Jones himself, though a Calvinist, was not yet persuaded about the doctrine of limited atonement, and on that point he was at one with the majority at the conference. While held by some, this view of the atonement had long since been rejected by the consensus of Evangelical opinion, expressed for example in the IVF's 1937 publication by H. E. Guillebaud, *Why the Cross?* That same year (1953) saw an estrangement between the Torrance brothers and IVF when the Edinburgh Christian Union, led by students who had studied under Prof. T. F. Torrance, wanted to co-operate with the SCM despite differences over the

---

29. Based on the recollections (written on 11 December 1998) of Canon Peter Cook, who was one of the Durham students taken to the conference by Iain Murray. He recalled the Doctor sitting on the table with his boots dangling (he despised new-fangled shoes!) and shooting down all opposition with the Lloyd-Jones 'leer' on his face. Canon Cook remembered the exchange with Stibbs as more good-humoured than the confrontation between J. B. Torrance and John Murray, but Professor Torrance recalled that Stibbs was moved to tears by the resuscitation of the doctrine of limited atonement. Cf. Dr Gaius Davies's reflections on the personality of Dr Lloyd-Jones in *Genius, Grief and Grace* (Fearn: Christian Focus Publications, 2001), Chapter 11 (331–377).

30. James Torrance, letter to the writer, 17 August 1998. He had run the youth group at Westminster Chapel during 1943–44, when he was stationed in London with the RAF and spent a number of weekends in the Lloyd-Jones's home.

Doctrinal Basis. This led to a confrontation between T. F. Torrance and Douglas Johnson and the disaffiliation of Edinburgh CU by the IVF.[31]

Having taken the lead in reviving the five-point Calvinism of Dort, James Packer proceeded two years later to attack another element of the pre-war Evangelical consensus with his critique of the Keswick movement. While there had always been a body of opinion which preferred Bishop J. C. Ryle's interpretation of Christian holiness to that of Bishop Handley Moule, it was the latter's Keswick position which was dominant.[32] At the Kingham Hill conference, Lloyd-Jones had criticized its influence, but Packer's open attack in the *Evangelical Quarterly* led to the dominance of his Puritan approach and the eclipse of the Keswick tradition in the next generation.[33]

---

31. Geoffrey Bromiley recalled being present at the confrontation between Johnson and Torrance in his letter of 8 June 2004. The students who wished to remain affiliated with the IVF formed the 'Evangelical Union', which changed its name to the 'Christian Union' when the breakaway group faded away. The following year (1954), F. F. Bruce published in *The Evangelical Quarterly* an article by H. L. Ellison which led to Ellison's resignation from LBC because it was held to be too 'Barthian'. See Shuff, *Searching for the True Church*, 90ff.

32. Cf. Handley G. C. Moule *et al.*, *Holiness by Faith: A Manual of Keswick Teaching* (London, 1904); and J. C. Ryle, *Holiness* (London, 1877). For the dominance of the 'holiness movement' in early twentieth-century Evangelicalism, cf. D. W. Bebbington, *Evangelicalism in Modern Britain: A History from the 1730s to the 1980s* (London: Unwin Hyman, 1989), esp. Chapter 5, 'Holiness unto the Lord,' 151–180.

33. J. I. Packer, '"Keswick" and the Reformed Doctrine of Sanctification', *EQ*, 27 (1955), 153–167. Cf. Alister McGrath's discussion of this in *J. I. Packer: A Biography* (Grand Rapids: Baker, 1997), 76ff. This issue of the *EQ* in July 1955 was devoted to the doctrine of sanctification. It included articles by Pierre Marcel, 'The Relation between Justification and Sanctification in Calvin's Thought' (132–145); by R. B. Larter, 'The Doctrine of Sanctification' (146–152); a review of Walter Marshall, *The Gospel Mystery of Sanctification*, by O. R. Johnston; and a review of

Biblical research

The future of the House and Fellowship
While these conferences of the early 1950s were shaping the theological direction of IVF and Conservative Evangelicalism, the
Biblical Research Committee was wrestling with the future shape
of Tyndale House and of the Tyndale Fellowship. At the first
meeting of the BRC after F. F. Bruce's resignation as chairman, on
17 December 1951 (when Bruce himself was absent), a review of
policy led to the following conclusions. First, the original aim of
stimulating only first-class biblical research had perhaps been too
ambitious. Secondly, however, potential biblical research scholars
were being encouraged through the newly established study
groups, and, thirdly, the secondary aim of encouraging ministers
and others interested in the results of research was being met by
the annual summer school. Fourthly, it was considered important
that 'senior men' should encourage younger Evangelicals in sound
biblical interpretation; and, finally, it was agreed that in view of the
post-war development of the Graduates' Fellowship by IVF,
membership of the Tyndale Fellowship should be limited in future
to members of the GF. To improve liaison, Freddy Crittenden, the
Graduates' Fellowship Secretary, had joined the committee three
years earlier.[34]

The immediate problem, however, was the financial viability of
Tyndale House. The BRC endorsed a report from the Tyndale
House sub-committee:

> It will be possible for Tyndale House to fulfil its functions, and even be
> maintained, only if there is an endowment or other annual income
> covering its overheads, and a series of bursaries to attract research
> students.

George Allen Turner, *The More Excellent Way* (one of the early works in a
scholarly revival of interest in Wesley's doctrine of sanctification), by
A. Skevington Wood.

34. On the Graduates' Fellowship, cf. Johnson, *Contending*, 213f, 236ff. and
294ff. Crittenden joined the BRC at their meeting on 17 December 1948.

The sub-committee felt that if, in the end, IVF could not maintain Tyndale House, 'it would be preferable to transfer it to some other trust or society rather than to sell the house'.

The BRC forwarded this to the IVF Business Advisory Committee with the recommendation that Tyndale House be retained for an experimental period of five years if a Warden could be found, and £1,000 per annum could cover salary and overheads. But Alan Stibbs's suggestion that the BRC should concentrate on training ordinands and ordained men to expound the Scriptures, rather than on technical research, caused considerable discussion. The whole original strategy of re-establishing Evangelical biblical scholarship was being questioned in the light of hard economic facts.[35]

This was unwelcome news to the small community of residents living and working at the House. John B. Taylor, who as a young graduate was one of the first residents from 1950 to 1952, recalls would-be purchasers going round the property deciding what they might do with each room while the residents 'were praying like steam that no sale would go through'. He comments: 'Mercifully better counsels prevailed and the house was saved.'[36] John Lilley recalls that the Domestic Bursar, Mrs Lilian MacLean, known to all as 'Mrs Mac', was effectively house mother while there was no Warden: 'Her kindness and gentle but firm discipline nurtured a very happy community.' Full board was provided, so that the residents were a community sharing family meals together, as well as such country-house pursuits as the croquet lawn. H. W. Oldham, who was resident at the House for some time from 1950 while working on the editing of the one-volume Bible commentary, made himself responsible for keeping 'Billy', the kitchen boiler, well-fed and in a good temper, and John Lilley remembers helping Mrs Mac to gather fruit from the fruit garden. The library was crammed into one room in the south-west corner of the House, with one old round table and book stacks so close that it was difficult to move.[37]

---

35. BRC minutes, 17 December 1951.
36. Letter to the author, 6 September 1999.
37. Notes of 1 November 2004 from J. P. U. Lilley.

By the next meeting of the BRC, however, on 7 July 1952, there were more hopeful developments. First of all, it was reported that A. F. Walls, an Oxford classics graduate and a Methodist, had accepted an invitation to be an IVF travelling secretary based at Tyndale House and to act as honorary assistant secretary. Andrew and Doreen Walls were soon resident in the House as a newly married couple, and the community there was also joined by two cats acquired by Mrs Mac, whom the residents named Gunkel and Mowinckel.[38]

Secondly, finances improved. An appeal for funds through the newly formed 'Friends of Tyndale House' was thought likely to produce the set minimum of £400 per annum, and the IVF Business Advisory Committee had approved the continuance of Tyndale House subject to progress towards financial self-support.

Thirdly, John Wenham presented a seven-point memorandum to the committee. His analysis was that, in spite of tactical successes, Evangelicals were still losing the strategic battle in biblical scholarship. He posed the question whether they should be interested in the whole field of biblical scholarship, or only in exegesis, leaving aside questions of higher criticism. For him the answer was obvious: Evangelicals had to engage in the whole field of biblical scholarship, since exegesis and criticism were so inextricably interwoven. Given that, it was necessary to contrive machinery for continuous long-term advance. He felt that fifteen years of continually changing leadership had resulted in the dissipation of effort. There needed to be consistent generalship. This required some measure of independence from IVF, so that the axe did not fall every time IVF had a lean year. The BRC therefore had to break out of a vicious circle: that money could not be raised without an imaginative plan, but that no plan could succeed without money. The key was to find a man who would give himself full-time to money-raising and the fostering of biblical scholarship. A bold strategic plan was therefore needed, covering the whole field of the library, the annual Tyndale Lectures, the theological students of

38. Gunkel, a ginger cat, was owned by the Walls, and Mowinckel, who was black, by Mrs Mac.

TSF, publications, research bursaries, the building of a house for the Warden in the grounds of Tyndale House, and so on.[39]

Wenham may have been a little pessimistic in saying that little had been achieved in the fifteen years since the Biblical Research Committee had been formed.[40] In fact, under F. F. Bruce, the foundations had been laid for later significant development. But in 1952, that foundation seemed financially shaky, there was no Warden, there were no funds to support a Warden, and it was not at all certain that anything lasting was being achieved. John Wenham was convinced (as John Laing had been before Tyndale House was established) that the key was to find a suitable academic and man of business to spearhead the whole project. But what really mattered at this point was Wenham's positive thinking about the future at a time when it was quite possible to be discouraged. There was also encouragement for the committee in the news from Australia of the intention to form a Tyndale Fellowship there.

Following discussion, it was agreed to alter the committee's structure, renaming the whole committee the 'Tyndale Fellowship Committee', and creating a smaller sub-committee to be called the 'Biblical Research Committee'. The Tyndale Fellowship Committee, chaired by Martyn Lloyd-Jones, was to be responsible for the wider activities, including the summer school, which attracted those who were not technically qualified for research, but were interested in exegesis. The smaller sub-committee, now to bear the older name as the BRC, would be chaired by John Wenham and would include W. J. Martin, J. Stafford Wright, F. F. Bruce, J. I. Packer, D. J. Wiseman, and Andrew F. Walls as secretary. D. J. Wiseman was to remain secretary of the wider Tyndale Fellowship Committee.

Refocusing on research

At the first meeting of the new, more specialist, BRC on 15 December 1952, held after the whole TF committee had met, Wenham, Walls and Wiseman were present, together with the General Secretary, Douglas Johnson. They defined their task as

---

39. BRC minutes, 7 July 1952.
40. It was actually fourteen.

promoting biblical research at the most advanced level, keeping this goal constantly before the wider Tyndale Fellowship Committee, devising a general strategy (a good Wenham word!) and seeking out and encouraging individual Evangelical research students. They began by compiling lists of 'experts', 'journeymen' and 'novices', including in the first category Dr W. J. Martin, the Revd J. G. S. S. Thomson, the Revd F. D. Kidner, the Revd J. Stafford Wright, the Revd A. M. Stibbs, Prof. R. V. G. Tasker, Principal P. W. Miller of the Free Church of Scotland College in Edinburgh, and Messrs F. F. Bruce, H. L. Ellison and D. J. Wiseman. They then discussed research priorities for Evangelicals and methods of promoting research. John Wenham was to prepare a draft on the inspiration of the Bible.[41]

On 1 January 1953, Andrew Walls sent out a circular letter from the Tyndale House Committee, Basil Atkinson (chairman), J. W. Buckton (Hon. Treasurer), Mary Neill, and himself as secretary. He enclosed a leaflet describing the House as 'the Inter-Varsity Fellowship's centre for Biblical study and research', and appealed for supporters to join 'The Friends of Tyndale House, a body of those who have the aims of the House at heart and who are pre-pared to give an annual subscription, preferably covenanted, towards their accomplishment.'[42]

Six months later, on 6 July 1953, when the Tyndale Fellowship Committee met at Tyndale House,[43] Andrew Walls reported an improvement in the finances of Tyndale House, thanks to the Friends. Residence facilities were now being used by research workers, ministers, theological students and scholars and students from overseas. He had begun a register, which listed twenty-eight resident and twenty-four non-resident readers from September

---

41. BRC minutes, 15 December 1952.
42. Giving which was 'covenanted' benefited from tax refunds.
43. Martyn Lloyd-Jones (chairman), Philip E. Hughes, Douglas Johnson, E. F. Kevan, G. T. Manley, J. I. Packer, A. M. Stibbs, J. W. Wenham, D. J. Wiseman and A. F. Walls. Apologies were received from J. N. D. Anderson, F. F. Bruce, Ronald Inchley (the IVF Publications Secretary), David Broughton Knox and J. Stafford Wright.

1952 to August 1953.[44] It looked as if Tyndale House had reached a turning point, and that after some lean years the vision of the founders was just beginning to materialize. The library sub-committee (Bruce, Kevan, Wiseman and Walls) presented a statement of purpose which was amended to read:

---

44. The register also lists (in Section B) fourteen visitors during this period, from Japan, the Netherlands, North Africa (a bishop, the Rt Revd G. F. B. Morris), South Africa, Finland and the USA (Prof. and Mrs E. Cailliet from Princeton, and two ladies from Bethel and Hesston Colleges in Kansas), and alludes to 'students and others from Finland, Germany, South Africa, Sweden, the Netherlands and Australia'. Section A lists the studies pursued by residents at Tyndale House before September 1952: the Revd H. Chadwick, Origen's *Contra Celsum*; the Revd L. L. Morris, expiation and propitiation in the doctrine of the atonement; the Revd Dr D. M. L. Urie, commerce in the Old Testament; Pastor J. Crumvellier, the doctrine of eternal punishment; the Revd E. Evans, eschatology in the Pauline Epistles; the Revd Canon M. L. Loane, Cambridge and the Evangelical succession; the Revd J. R. W. Stott, the biblical view of the kingdom of God; the Revd D. W. B. Robinson, Josiah's reforms; the Revd H. W. Oldham, editorial work for the IVF one-volume commentary; the Revd L. E. H. Stephens-Hodge, Habbakkuk for the IVF one-volume commentary; the Revd L. L. Morris, The Johannine Epistles for the IVF one-volume commentary; A. F. Walls, Old Testament bibliography; the Revd G. T. Manley, Deuteronomy; the Revd D. B. Reed, 'Son of Man' in St John's Gospel; J. N. D. Anderson, Arabic studies and the evidence for the resurrection; and J. P. U. Lilley, Syriac studies.

The same register, in Section C, 'Activities Based on Tyndale House', lists the following for the academic year 1952–53:

- Talks to theological students (seven by the Revd A. M. Stibbs, one by A. F. Walls)
- Theological Colleges Study Circle – three sessions: 4 February 1953, 'The Biblical Doctrine of Resurrection' (the Revd B. D. Reed); 3 March, 'The Vocabulary of Redemption-Faith' (J. W. L. Head); 7 May, 'Kenosis and Scripture' (S. C. Clark)

The purpose of the library is to equip scholars to assert, maintain and
defend the evangelical faith. It is the wish of the committee that books
be selected with this end in view.

Thanks were expressed to Miss Atkinson for her service as
acting Librarian. Andrew Walls was now Librarian and secretary,
and, in the absence of a Warden, effectively in charge of the day-
to-day running of Tyndale House. A move was made towards
restricting attendance at the summer schools to those engaged in
academic work. It was agreed:

That the standing committee consider the desirability of restricting
attendance at the summer school from 1954 onwards with a view to
maintaining a high standard of study and discussion and of a

- Course in Old Testament Language (Dr W. J. Martin), 22–27 June
  1953
- Old Testament Study Group, 3–6 July 1953: main theme 'The Exile
  and After'; main contributors D. J. Wiseman, H. R. Minn,
  H. L. Ellison, the Revd Dr J. G. S. S. Thomson, Dr R. E. D. Clark;
  communications from H. L. Ellison, Dr R. E. D. Clark, the Revd
  G. T. Manley, K. A. Kitchen, J. P. U. Lilley, the Revd W. Kelly, the
  Revd B. D. Reed
- Tyndale Summer School, 6–10 July 1953: theme 'The Plan of
  Salvation'; host Dr D. M. Lloyd-Jones; main contributors Prof.
  J. Murray, the Revd J. W. Wenham, the Revd J. I. Packer, the Revd
  E. E. King, the Revd O. J. Thomas, the Revd Dr J. G. S. S. Thomson,
  the Revd J. B. Torrance, the Revd Dr G. Walters
- New Testament Study Group, 10–13 July 1953: main contributors
  F. F. Bruce, D. Guthrie, S. C. Clark, the Revd B. D. Reed, the Revd
  J. I. Packer
- Vacation Bible Study Course, CICCU: the Revd A. M. Stibbs and
  Dr B. F. C. Atkinson, with Dr D. R. Denman, Dr C. M. Dixon,
  Dr D. M. Mackay, J. N. D. Anderson, F. H. Crittenden, Maj. W. F. Batt.

Accommodation was lent to CICCU; The Graduates' Fellowship; The
Cranmer Society; and CSSM (local groups).

theological conference for ministers being held at another time and place.[45]

When the TF committee met again on 14 December 1953 in the IVF offices at 39 Bedford Square, the same policy of developing a more specialized group of scholars committed to academic research was pursued. The smaller BRC – Wenham, Johnson and Walls – met first and proposed a restriction in the membership of the Tyndale Fellowship:

> That membership of the Fellowship should be for those who desire to advance the evangelical Christian faith by research, advanced study or writing in the field of Biblical Studies or in other fields of study that will contribute to the evangelical Christian faith.[46]

When the full Tyndale Fellowship Committee met at 4.00 pm, A. M. Stibbs took the chair in the absence of Martyn Lloyd-Jones,[47] and, on the recommendation of the BRC, the plans for the summer of 1954 were altered to cater more specifically for those engaged in academic research. A Biblical Theology Study Group, restricted to Tyndale Fellowship members and others who could make a useful academic contribution, would now meet from 5 to 9 July, on the dates previously assigned to the summer school, and a conference of a less specialized nature would be arranged in the following summer to meet the needs of ministers, avoiding the dates of the new Biblical Theology Group.

Also, from this point onwards, applications for membership of the Tyndale Fellowship would be considered and approved by the whole committee. Intending members would have to be members of the Graduates' Fellowship and must be nominated by someone

---

45. TFC minutes, 6 July 1953.
46. BRC minutes, 14 December 1953.
47. Congratulations were also expressed at this meeting to J. N. D. Anderson
    on his appointment to the Chair of Oriental Laws at the University of
    London and to D. Broughton Knox on his DPhil and his appointment as
    Vice-Principal of Moore College, Sydney.

already a member of the TF. No present members would be removed, but new members would be expected to be engaged in academic work.[48] It was reported that twenty-two TF members were preparing theses or engaged in similar study, and it was agreed that a list of members' publications should be circulated. Members should be encouraged to submit articles to the *Evangelical Quarterly*.

On the matter of publications, Douglas Johnson reported that Inter-Varsity Fellowship was considering publishing a series of commentaries as 'Tyndale Press' publications. These would be of the size and type of Moule's *Romans* in the Cambridge Bible series, and R. V. G. Tasker was to be asked to be general New Testament editor.[49] No doubt a new confidence in such an undertaking was engendered when *The New Bible Commentary* was published during that same month, December 1953. Edited by Francis Davidson,[50] assisted by Alan M. Stibbs and Ernest F. Kevan (and in the early stages by the Revd H. W. Oldham, a retired Church of Scotland minister living in London), *The New Bible Commentary* rapidly became a best-seller, a far bigger undertaking than anything the IVF publications department had tackled. Of the first printing of 30,000, 22,000 had been ordered from the USA by Eerdmans and the Inter-Varsity Christian Fellowship.[51] The contributors were by and large members of the Tyndale Fellowship.

---

48. The new procedure was put into effect immediately, and five new members were accepted to the Fellowship: H. D. McDonald, F. H. Palmer, G. H. W. Parker, Dr M. Patterson and D. F. Payne.
49. TFC minutes, 14 December 1953.
50. The Revd Francis Davidson, MA, DD, was Principal of the Bible Training Institute in Glasgow (founded after D. L. Moody's Scottish campaigns). He was also Professor of Old Testament and New Testament Language and Literature in the United Original Secession Church of Scotland, a small denomination of seceders who had refused to join in the unions which eventually led to the reunited Church of Scotland in 1929. Cf. the *Dictionary of Scottish Church History and Theology* (Edinburgh: T. & T. Clark, 1993), 235.
51. Cf. Ronald Inchley's account in Johnson, *Contending*, 323.

By 1954, the original aim of promoting serious academic research had been re-established, and at its July meeting the Tyndale Fellowship Committee decided that it was no longer necessary to maintain the distinction between the TFC and the BRC. They would revert back to one committee, which would meet twice a year and be known by its original name, the Biblical Research Committee. It would of course continue to be the committee of the Tyndale Fellowship. But a 'Board of Studies' would be formed to encourage advanced students. It was also now felt that the proposed conference for ministers, previously proposed for the summer of 1955, was outside the province of the Tyndale Fellowship.[52] The original vision, that Tyndale House and Fellowship were not in existence to be a theological society, but to promote Evangelical research, had been reasserted.

The new library at Tyndale House

By this time, the prospects for Tyndale House had been transformed to such an extent that the proposal to build an extension to house the library was noted at the same July meeting, and supported.[53] From September 1953 to August 1954 there had been a similar number of residents as in the previous year. These had included Professor Hooykaas, pursuing research on 'The Reformation and Scientific Progress'; the Revd A. W. H. Moule, working on the life of Bishop Handley Moule; G. T. Manley, continuing his studies in Deuteronomy; and younger researchers such as E. E. Ellis.[54]

The structure of committees was clarified again at the BRC meeting on 20 December 1954. The Studies Committee was to report to the Biblical Research Committee, and the Awards

---

52. BRC minutes, 8 July 1954.

53. Although the BRC minutes are not explicit on this, the decision was presumably taken by, or with the approval of, the Business Advisory Committee chaired by John Laing, and his company presumably supplied the plans and built the new library.

54. These are listed in Andrew Walls's register of residents.

Committee (including a member of the BAC) was to be a sub-committee of the Studies Committee and would recommend research students for Tyndale House grants. The Tyndale House Committee, which administered the House and supervised the residential facilities, would also report to the BRC, but major matters of property or appointments were to be referred to the IVF Business Advisory Committee.

The same meeting on 20 December also heard a proposal for a new annual Tyndale Lecture in Church History and Historical Theology, and agreed that the Puritan study group, which catered for a wider group than those engaged in academic research, could continue its affiliation to the Tyndale Fellowship meantime.[55] At the next meeting, on 4 July 1955, the BRC agreed to establish a Tyndale Lecture in Historical Theology, beginning in 1956, and to consider the possibility of publishing a Tyndale Fellowship journal. The original *Theological Notes*, edited by A. M. Stibbs and F. F. Bruce, had become *The Tyndale Bulletin* in January 1945, but after the issue of January 1948 had been merged into *The Christian Graduate*, the quarterly magazine of the Graduates' Fellowship. Also on 4 July, the Tyndale House Committee reported that the extension to the library would be ready by January 1956, and that the official opening would take place in April.[56] While the Old Testament study group was at the House, a stone was laid on the outside wall with the inscription 'The fear of the Lord is the beginning of wisdom.'[57]

By the end of 1955, the plans for the new bulletin were advancing. It would be published twice a year and would report on work done in Tyndale House and in the study groups. Tyndale Fellowship news, notes on criticism and exegesis and recent work in theology would be included, and the bulletin would be free to all members of TF. There was also a proposal from John Balchin, presented to the committee on 19 December, to begin a study group in Scotland. He

---

55. BRC minutes, 20 December 1954.
56. BRC minutes, 4 July 1955. The first Tyndale Historical Theology Lecture was not given till 1957.
57. Notes from J. P. U. Lilley, 1 November 2004.

was advised to consult Prof. R. A. Finlayson of the Free Church College, Dr J. G. S. S. Thomson of the Church of Scotland, and Dr Arthur Skevington Wood of the Methodist Central Hall in Paisley.[58]

At the same meeting of the Biblical Research Committee on 19 December 1955, the committee structure was clarified yet again, and Terms of Reference presented. The Studies Committee was to consist of specialist members of the BRC, who would act as an advisory and consultative body on academic matters, particularly seeking out and encouraging new and potential scholars, recommending them to the Awards Sub-committee for Tyndale research grants and maintaining contact with all who were receiving grants.[59] They were also to keep research in biblical and theological fields under review, looking for needs to which Evangelical scholars should direct their attention. They were to recommend to the IVF Literature Committee Tyndale Lectures or other productions which should be published or republished, and were also to recommend additional works for the library to the Library Committee. The Studies Committee would report to the BRC, but its Awards Sub-committee would have a representative from the IVF Business Advisory Committee. The Tyndale House Committee, however, was no longer to be responsible to the BRC, as had been stated a year earlier. Now this committee was to be 'directly responsible to the Business Advisory Committee of the

---

58. BRC minutes, 19 December, 1955. Arthur Skevington Wood had completed his PhD at New College, Edinburgh, under the supervision of J. H. S. Burleigh. Cf. Paul Taylor and Howard Mellor, *Travelling Man: A Tribute to the Life and Ministry of Arthur Skevington Wood* (Calver: Cliff College Publishing and the Wesley Fellowship, 1994).

59. Five months earlier, on 10 May, Andrew Walls had written to Douglas Johnson with some observations on grants in connection with 'the first batch of applicants'. He thought it would be valuable 'if our people . . . could be encouraged to take up other scholarships and grants'. They gave 'a certain standing' which would be valuable in view of 'the incredible prejudice there is against the IVF and the rising cold war against "fundamentalism"'.

IVF', yet it was desirable that it maintain a close liaison with the BRC.[60]

It cannot be denied that the committee structure seemed to be subject to something like 'permanent revolution'! Was this a sign of flexibility, of adapting structure to function? But then surely the 'function' – or, to use other terminology, the 'mission' of Inter-Varsity Fellowship – was not constantly changing? Perhaps it was because the work of the student Christian Unions and the work of research did not fit easily together into the same structure. Or did the continual changes reflect the different agendas of some of the key people involved? This may be part of the explanation, at least in the 1950s, when the chairman of the BRC may possibly not have been entirely enthusiastic about the place of biblical research. And yet it has to be said that the seemingly endless 'musical chairs' of committees continued for decades afterwards.

The Tyndale House Bulletin

The first issue of *The Tyndale House Bulletin* (later to become *The Tyndale Bulletin*) appeared, marked 'No. 1, Summer, 1956'. Under the title it was declared: 'Issued by the Tyndale Fellowship for Biblical Research, Tyndale House, Selwyn Gardens, Cambridge (Price to non-members: 1/3)'. No indication was given as to the editor, but it was Andrew Walls, the indefatigable secretary and Librarian, who produced it. There were articles by J. A. Motyer on Jeremiah 7:22; by E. A. Judge[61] on 'The Penetration of Graeco-Roman Society by Christianity'; by A. M. Stibbs on 'Modern Christological Trends';

---

60. By the beginning of 1956, the Tyndale House Committee had eleven members, but only the Cambridge members attended regularly. At the meeting on 2 February 1956, for example, there were five members present: Mr J. W. Buckton (chairman), Dr D. R. Denman, Dr A. Hanton, Mr M. A. Jeeves and the secretary, Andrew Walls. Apologies for absence were received on that occasion from Prof. J. N. D. Anderson, Dr Basil Atkinson, the General Secretary (Douglas Johnson), Mr J. W. Laing, Dr Waterson and Mr D. J. Wiseman (Tyndale House Committee minutes, 2 February 1956).

61. Judge's name actually appeared as 'E. A. Jude'.

and by J. Dale on 'Unpublished Hymns by Charles Wesley'. The 'Notes and News' began with a report on the opening of 'The New Wing at Tyndale House':

> The opening by Mr J. W. Laing of the new wing at Tyndale House, containing the new library and improved residential facilities, on April 21st, is a new landmark in the Fellowship's history for which it is fitting that we render thanks to God. More than 150 guests witnessed the unveiling of a plaque marking the dedication of the building to the glory of God alone and for the furtherance of Christian scholarship. Two stout friends of the Fellowship since its inception, the Revd A. M. Stibbs and the Revd J. Stafford Wright, spoke at the meeting, and Professor Norman Anderson, a former Warden of Tyndale House, presided. After tea, Mr D. J. Wiseman gave a public lecture on the Babylonian texts illustrating Nebuchadrezzar's capture of Jerusalem, for the interpretation of which he has been largely responsible.

The *Bulletin* did not, however, give the inscription on the plaque which John Laing unveiled:[62]

SOLI DEO GLORIA
BIBLIOTHECAM TYNDALIANAM
STVDIA SACRA FOVENDI CAVSA
DICAVIT
IOHANNES W. LAING
A:D XI KAL: MAI
ANNO SALUTIS MCMLVI

This first issue of *The Tyndale House Bulletin* also included notices inviting enquiries about the Church History study group and announcing a meeting of the Puritan studies group under the chairmanship of Dr Martyn Lloyd-Jones at Westminster Chapel

---

62. 'To the glory of God alone John W. Laing dedicated the Tyndale Library, founded to further sacred study, eleven days before the calends of May in the year of salvation 1956.'

on 18 and 19 December. Speakers would include the Revd
J. Gwyn-Thomas, Mr O. R. Johnston, the Revd E. F. Kevan and
the Revd Dr J. I. Packer.

Joy was expressed in the *Bulletin* at the re-formation of the
Australian Tyndale Fellowship, with Dean Barton Babbage as chairman and Dr Leon Morris as secretary. Fraternal greetings had been
received from the Evangelical Theological Society of the USA, and
these were reciprocated. It was reported that ten new members had
been welcomed to the Fellowship: Mr J. A. Balchin, the Revd
Principal R. N. Caswell of Belfast Bible College, the Revd P. H.
Hacking, the Revd G. J. C. Marchant, Mr R. J. McKelvey, Mr R. E.
Nixon, the Revd G. V. Prosser, Mr M. A. Saward, Mr S. S. Smalley
and the Revd Dr A. Skevington Wood. Twelve recent appoint-
ments were noted, including the Revd Dr G. C. B. Davies to the
Chair of Ecclesiastical History at Trinity College, Dublin, the
Revd D. A. Hubbard (later President of Fuller Theological
Seminary)[63] as a temporary Lecturer in Hebrew at the University of
St Andrews, Mr M. A. Jeeves as Lecturer in Psychology in Leeds,
Mr E. A. Judge as Lecturer in Ancient History in Sydney, the Revd
Dr G. R. Beasley-Murray to be Professor of New Testament at the
International Baptist Seminary in Switzerland, Mr D. F. Payne as
Research Fellow in the Hebrew University of Jerusalem, and Mr S.
S. Smalley to Eden Theological Seminary, Missouri. Publications
were listed for twenty-nine TF members. There were signs that
Evangelical scholarship was beginning to revive in the academic
world.[64]

In the year following the opening of the new library wing and
the publication of the first edition of *The Tyndale House Bulletin* in
1956, the House Committee had to deal with the usual practicalities. An old garage had to be removed and a new bicycle shed had
to be constructed. The old fence in front of the new wing had to

63. Hubbard came into contact with the Tyndale Fellowship through George
    Beasley-Murray and Donald Wiseman. Cf. David A. Hubbard,
    'Evangelicals and Biblical Scholarship, 1945–1992: An Anecdotal
    Commentary', *Bulletin for Biblical Research*, 3 (1993).
64. *The Tyndale House Bulletin*, 1 (1956), 2ff.

be dismantled, turf to be laid and trees planted.[65] The Chief Constable's suggestion that this space should be used as a car park was not accepted, and volunteers from among the residents, notably Mr N. A. Richards and Mr R. N. Glen, carried out the clearance, drainage and relaying of the frontage.[66] Messrs Richards and Glen had their residence fees waived for one week.[67] An extra grant of £1,000 from IVF cleared the deficit, so that money from the Tyndale House Appeal would be used to pay off the capital loan. The accounts from May to October 1956 indicate that £1,056 11s 9d was collected from residents in those six months, that the Librarian was paid £63 4s 5d, the Bursar £150, the Daily and Gardener £170 0s 6d, and that £156 14s 11d was spent on books. It was agreed upon the recommendation of the IVF Business Advisory Committee that the Treasurer of IVF, Mr B. M. Harris, should become a member of the Tyndale House Committee. The linoleum in the library was unsatisfactory and had to be replaced, and the central heating and domestic water circuits were affecting each other and had to be isolated. The central heating in the old house was not working. Names of businessmen were considered for inclusion on the Appeals Committee, including, for example, Mr John Catherwood and Mr Carr of Carr's Biscuits. It was decided that it was impracticable to accept a married couple with a child as residents, and that Dr W. F. Arndt of the Lutheran Missouri Synod could not give tuition in Tyndale House to students from Luther House (since that would be a

---

65. John Lilley recalls that the 'old fence' was round the fruit garden where he had helped Mrs Mac with the harvest. He notes (1 November 2004): 'A pitiful remnant of the red currants survived by the side entrance to the grounds until this year: still tasty.'

66. Prof. Andrew Walls recalled (in a telephone conversation) that Norman Richards was President of CICCU and later worked for a time for CSSM, and that Bob Glen was a New Zealander who later taught in Tanzania and eventually returned home to become Vice-Principal of the Bible College of New Zealand.

67. The House Committee minutes of 5 April 1957 actually record that the fees were to be 'waved' for one week!

denominational activity) but could be resident in order to work on a New Testament commentary and translate Chemnitz.[68] Altogether nineteen scholars, including D. Millard,[69] T. C. Mitchell and R. T. Beckwith, are listed in the register as having been resident in the newly extended Tyndale House for all or part of the academic year 1956–57.

The Old Testament and New Testament study groups, chaired by D. J. Wiseman and F. F. Bruce, were now regular summer events. G. T. Manley was the doyen of the Old Testament group. Age was beginning to tell, and he was rather unsteady on his feet, but he still took a useful part in the discussion and published his book on Deuteronomy in 1957.[70] He remained critical of 'higher critics' who were prone to 'speculate freely'. W. J. Martin seldom read a paper, but made valuable contributions to discussion from his expert command of the Semitic languages. On some visits to Tyndale House he would bring a bright young assistant from Liverpool, Kenneth Kitchen, to help him to teach a crash course in Hebrew lasting two days! John Lilley recalls Kenneth Kitchen giving a paper in 1953 on 'Egyptian Sidelights on Jericho'.[71] John Wenham, Derek Kidner, Arthur Cundall and Terence Mitchell were also among those who attended the group, the visitors sharing a dormitory in what had been the servants' quarters. Terence Mitchell was a resident from 1956 to 1958. Among his recollections are Bill Martin's introduction of himself as a 'Landsberger baby' and Donald Wiseman's active encouragement of the younger members of the group.[72] No

---

68. These details are from the minutes of the Tyndale House Committee for meetings on 6 June, 25 July and 10 October 1956, and 5 March, 5 April and 5 June 1957.

69. Presumably this should read 'A. R. Millard'.

70. G. T. Manley, *The Book of the Law: Studies in the Date of Deuteronomy* (London: Tyndale Press, 1957).

71. Notes of 1 November 2004.

72. Letter of 3 July 2004 from T. C. Mitchell. He also recalls great amusement at the New Testament group when F. F. Bruce was asked for an opinion on a text and replied that he would have to look that up in his commentary!

doubt the Old Testament group felt a special interest in the two resident cats, Gunkel and Mowinckel. John Lilley recalls: 'I was introduced to M (black) in the kitchen, but he appeared conscious of his superior status as a scholar and didn't really want to know me.'

During the year from the summer of 1956 to the summer of 1957, the Biblical Research Committee reviewed the effectiveness of the annual study groups. At their meeting on 2 July they noted the formation of a study group in Scotland, recommended to the IVF Literature Committee that a working party in Philosophy and Apologetics be formed with a view to a publication, and took in new members, including a Mr I. H. Marshall. The Standing Committee (Johnson, Wiseman, Walls and Crittenden, with Stibbs in the chair) met on 29 November and their recommendations were considered by the Studies Committee on 17 December, before the meeting of the full BRC. The assessment of the Studies Committee was that the Old Testament Study Group was the most advanced of the groups, but lacked younger scholars,[73] and that the New Testament group was improving with Professor Bruce as its focus and a core of young Cambridge graduates. The Church History group was making progress, but there were too many contributions from the less advanced. There were two constant needs: a constant accession of new members, and a good all-round standard where men of university lecturer calibre could find profit, stimulus and fellowship. The restricting of membership to those engaged in academic research had been satisfactory, but it had meant excluding ministers, teachers and others and might frighten away potential research students. The Studies Committee therefore accepted the proposal from the Standing Committee that there should be three levels of activity: the study groups for specialists and research workers; a summer school with lecturers from the Fellowship for ministers, teachers, students and any who might benefit; and linguistic courses. The Studies Committee also agreed to recommend the production of a Bible dictionary or

73. A strange comment in view of the younger members T. C. Mitchell recalls.

encyclopaedia. All of these recommendations were then accepted in full by the full BRC.[74]

The Tyndale House Bulletin No. 3 appeared in the summer of 1957. The 'Notes and News' recorded two lectures which had been held under the auspices of the Friends of Tyndale House. One was by G. E. Ladd of Fuller Theological Seminary, on 'The Place of Apocalyptic in Biblical Religion', and the other by Dr W. F. Arndt. Dr Arndt, who had been Professor of New Testament Interpretation at Concordia Theological Seminary in St Louis, lectured on the *Arndt-Gingrich Lexicon of the Greek New Testament*, his translation along with Dr Gingrich of the famous lexicon of Walter Bauer, on the day of its publication by Cambridge University Press.[75] Terence Mitchell remembered Arndt as a pleasant, courtly man in his seventies, telling the other residents how some of the proof sheets of the new German edition of Bauer being sent for translation had been lost in the Atlantic. The ship, the *Flying Enterprise*, had got into difficulties and the captain had ordered the crew to abandon ship while he remained on board alone. Dr Arndt had listened for several days to reports on the radio until the ship finally sank. Sadly, Arndt died in February 1957, while staying at Tyndale House.

At the annual meeting of the Friends on 29 June, Dr D. R. Denham had presented a report on the Tyndale House Development Fund, established to clear the deficit on the new building and provide grants for postgraduate research. In that same summer of 1957, Andrew Walls resigned as secretary and Librarian to accept an appointment to the staff of Fourah Bay College in Sierra Leone.[76] In October, the Standing Committee (Stibbs, Crittenden, Johnson, G. H. W. Parker and Wiseman) discussed the composition of the BRC in the light of Lloyd-Jones's wish to stand down. Wiseman recommended Stibbs to succeed

---

74. BRC minutes of 2 July 1956 and 17 December 1957; minutes of the Standing Committee, 29 November 1956; Agenda and Minutes of the Studies Committee, 17 December 1957.

75. Letter from T. C. Mitchell of 3 July 2004.

76. Minutes of the Tyndale House Committee, 5 June 1957.

him and Stibbs recommended Wiseman! They were asked to decide between them. But it was felt that the BRC should be reconstituted as a working group, meeting at least four times a year and including the secretaries of the study groups. At the end of that year, Douglas Johnson reported to the BRC that Martyn Lloyd-Jones wished to relinquish the chair and D. J. Wiseman was elected to succeed him.

Had the Doctor lost interest? The earlier years of his chairmanship had seen the theological debates at the summer conferences in Tyndale House and a revival of interest in Calvinist theology led by himself and James Packer. But these years had also seen the lowest years of Tyndale House as a centre for biblical research. With the work of Andrew Walls, however, and the renewed focus on the strategy of research, it is possible that his old hesitations, expressed at the Kingham Hill conference, began to reassert themselves. His priority was in preaching what he believed to be a 'biblical' theology, rather than in specialist research. But with the new library extension and the reappearance of an annual bulletin, Tyndale House and Fellowship were now taking some significant steps towards the revival of Evangelical biblical scholarship.

4. RESTART

Wiseman, Bridger and Morris, 1957–64

D. J. Wiseman, who was elected chairman of the Biblical Research Committee in succession to Martyn Lloyd-Jones at the end of 1957, was to be appointed as Professor of Assyriology at the University of London four years later. Beginning his student career in Classics at King's College, London in 1937, he had been encouraged by W. J. Martin, a friend of his father, to switch to Semitic Languages. Dr Martin had put it to him while out on long walks that, in the face of attacks on the reliability and relevance of the Bible, he should devote himself to Semitic languages. This would open the door to more new discoveries and unresearched documents than was ever likely in classical Greek and Roman studies. His father, P. J. Wiseman, who was an RAF officer, had engaged in archaeological work in Iraq and had published *New Discoveries in Babylonia about Genesis* in 1936. During the war Donald Wiseman also served in the RAF as an intelligence officer. As Personal Assistant to Air Vice-Marshal Park during the Battle of Britain he had to answer calls from 10 Downing Street to report on the battle, the phone at No. 10 being sometimes grabbed by Churchill himself. Later, as one of the limited few who were

trusted with information from the ultra-secret source known as
Enigma, Wing Commander Wiseman served as Senior Intelligence
Officer with the Mediterranean Allied Tactical Air Force during
the invasion of Sicily and the Italian campaign. He was awarded
the OBE (Mil) and the USA Bronze Star and was mentioned in
dispatches. After the war he had returned to postgraduate study at
Wadham College, Oxford, where he was President of OICCU in
1947–48, and was appointed to the British Museum in 1948.[1] The
BRC had asked him to chair the Old Testament group in 1949 and
he had given the Tyndale Old Testament Lecture in 1950.

The election of D. J. Wiseman as chairman of the Biblical
Research Committee was accompanied by another bout of committee reorganization. The Studies and Standing Sub-committees
were suspended and it was agreed that the Biblical Research
Committee as a whole (which was also the committee of the
Tyndale Fellowship) would meet four times a year. The chairman,
vice-chairman (Alan Stibbs), the secretary (G. H. W. Parker *pro tem*)
and John Wenham would have interim powers. But the Awards
Sub-committee, which was responsible for Tyndale research
grants, continued to meet from time to time under the chairmanship of Martyn Lloyd-Jones. It is clear therefore that the Doctor
still had an interest in the financing of research by Evangelical
postgraduates.

Changes also took place in the organization of Tyndale House.
The members of the Tyndale House Committee who were
Cambridge residents (J. W. Buckton, Basil Atkinson, Dr D. R.
Denman and Dr A. Hanton) agreed to resign in October 1957 to
facilitate a reorganization of the administration proposed by the
IVF Business Advisory Committee, and the status of the Tyndale
House Committee was clarified. It was to be regarded as a sub-
committee of the BAC, which represented the legal *owner* of the
House, the IVF Trust, and was in effect the 'host' of the *user* of the
House, the Tyndale Fellowship with its research students, summer

---

1. See Donald J. Wiseman, *Life Above and Below*, memoirs published privately
   in 2003. Later memories include archaeological expeditions in Iraq with
   Sir Max Mallowan and his wife, the novelist Agatha Christie.

schools and reading parties. The functions of the Tyndale House Committee were first, to attend to day-to-day finances and amenities through the officers of the House; secondly, to select residents and supervise discipline and the spiritual and moral leadership of the officers; and thirdly, to promote major financial development and public relations. Some younger graduates (Dr A. P. Waterson, Martin Rudwick, the Revd Mark Ruston) met the following month with the Domestic Bursar, Miss E. M. Ware, as the new committee.[2] The former local committee members (Atkinson, Buckton, Denman and Hanton) were to become 'Referees' or 'Associates', as senior advisers to whom the officers could turn. Ellen Ware, formerly of Homerton College, married Tony Waterson (who became a university lecturer in medicine) the next year, and was succeeded as Domestic Bursar by Miss Pamela Allen.[3]

The priority of biblical scholarship

Behind the institution of quarterly meetings of the Biblical Research Committee there lay something of a change of direction. Lloyd-Jones had been interested in what he called 'biblical theology', not meaning by this the same as the contemporary 'biblical theology movement'. That movement attempted, in the tradition of J. P. Gabler, to lay aside systematic theology, and to delineate in an 'objective' or descriptive kind of way the theology of the biblical writers themselves, using essentially their own categories. But when Lloyd-Jones spoke of 'biblical theology', he meant Reformed theology! And he had no doubt that Reformed theology was in fact the theology of the Bible. As he had declared so strongly at the Kingham Hill conference, specialists were of use only if their work, concentrated in a narrow field of study, were taken up and

---

2. The replacement of the old committee seems to have followed a difference of view between Dr Denman and Douglas Johnson.
3. Telephone conversation with A. F. Walls. Alan Millard remembers that Pam Allen used to hold regular tea parties and Bible studies at the House on Sundays for overseas au pair girls and others.

used by 'an experienced general practitioner (full of common
sense)', who must 'remain in charge'. He presumably had in mind
here essentially the 'Reformed pastor', who expounded the Bible
week by week in the context of the gathered church, and – far from
being a remote specialist – counselled his flock in the practical business of Christian living. When the 'ultra-analysis' of research had
finished its task, there had to be 'an appropriate synthesis based on
an equally accurate and reliable systematic Biblical Theology'.[4]

The conferences of his early years as chairman may be seen as
an attempt to explore this 'accurate and reliable systematic Biblical
Theology', which was to be the basis of the synthesis. In accordance with this approach, attendance at conferences had continued
to be wide enough to include those in pastoral ministry and not
just those in research. Alan Stibbs too, when the future of Tyndale
House was in doubt in 1951, had advocated that the BRC should
concentrate on training ordinands and ordained men to expound
the Scriptures rather than on technical research. The renaming of
the committee as the 'Tyndale Fellowship Committee', with the
'Biblical Research Committee' as a sub-committee concerned with
research, seems to have reflected the same priorities.[5] But John
Wenham and the members of the sub-committee had continued
to press the case for research. The work of Andrew Walls, the
launching of *The Tyndale House Bulletin*, the opening of the new
library wing at Tyndale House and the growth of the Old and New
Testament study groups led by Wiseman and Bruce all meant that
the cause of research, so badly in the doldrums in 1951, was once
again the focus of Tyndale House and Fellowship. Now, as Lloyd-
Jones resigned as chairman, the ending of the two-tier committee
structure and the focus on research by the whole BRC, meeting
quarterly, reflected the return to the original priorities of Martin
and Bruce. At the first meeting of the BRC chaired by Donald
Wiseman, on 16 December 1957, John Wenham proposed a one-
day conference to discuss 'strategy' for the Tyndale Fellowship.

---

4. For Lloyd-Jones's remarks on this at the Kingham Hill conference see
   above, Chapter 1, 'A Biblical Research Library', pages 39f.
5. Above, pages 82–83.

Bridger, Douglas and Duffield

By April 1958, the growth in the use of Tyndale House was such that it had become possible after almost a decade to appoint a Warden and Librarian once more, and it was announced that J. R. Bridger would take up his duties as Warden in September. Bridger had been converted as a schoolboy through a Scripture Union house party run by the Revd E. J. H. Nash and had started a Christian Union at his school, Rugby, to which he invited his fellow pupil John Stott.[6] He had been a member of CICCU and he and Stott had been fellow students at Ridley Hall. J. D. Douglas was to be Librarian and organizing editor of the one-volume Bible dictionary first proposed at the Kingham Hill conference.[7] F. F. Bruce, R. V. G. Tasker, J. I. Packer and D. J. Wiseman were to be the consulting editors.

A graduate of St Andrews, who had worked briefly for the *British Weekly*, James Douglas set out for Cambridge from Glasgow on a 'Dandy' scooter. In Lincolnshire he traded it for another scooter when the big end gave up! He started work at Tyndale House on 1 April 1958, asking himself, 'Now, what exactly is a Bible dictionary?'[8] He discovered that there had not been a one-volume Bible dictionary 'from the Evangelical stables' for about eighty years, but learned that Wilbur Smith of Fuller Theological Seminary had made a special study of the genre. With

6. Always known as 'Bash', this Scripture Union evangelist was the means of the conversion of a number of Christian leaders, including John Stott, John Eddison, Dick Lucas, Michael Green and John Pollock. See *Bash: A Study in Spiritual Power*, ed. John Eddison (Basingstoke: Marshall, 1983). On Bridger's association with John Stott, see Timothy Dudley-Smith, *John Stott: The Making of a Leader – a Biography: The Early Years* (Leicester: IVP, 1999), 90f., 101f., 112 and 196.

7. See above, page 40. *The New Bible Dictionary* (London: Inter-Varsity Fellowship, 1962) was reprinted thirteen times before a revised edition was published in 1982. James Douglas also recatalogued the library in 1958.

8. Details in this paragraph are drawn from Douglas's unpublished and colourful memoirs, 'The Half that Can Be Told'.

advice from Smith and helpful notes from Andrew Walls,[9] he set about his task. He discovered gaps in previous Bible dictionaries (for example, that no previous Bible dictionary had ever dealt with biblical references to parts of the body or diseases) and, having drawn up the list of articles, he had to allocate lengths to each entry. 'My total word-allowance was 1.3 million. Within that limitation, how many words should be given to Jezebel, Revelation, Hazor, Pseudepigrapha or Leprosy?' He amused himself by matching names: 'For Spitting I wrote to Denis Tongue, for Baking to Ken Kitchen, for Foundation to A. F. Walls. Most of those chosen entered into the spirit of the game.' He had to conduct the enormous correspondence without clerical assistance, and hung the long scrolls of galley proofs round his room (Howard Marshall remembers) 'like so many rolls of toilet paper'.[10] 'Jimmy' Douglas did not always find his relationships with IVF staff easy: 'In some quarters I acquired the reputation of being "difficult".'

That same month he began work, James Douglas reported to the TF committee the success of the first Scottish Tyndale Fellowship Conference. Thirty had participated and a Scottish committee had been elected, including R. A. Finlayson and W. J. Cameron, professors at the Free Church College, John Balchin (the IVF travelling secretary), James Taylor (a Baptist) and Geoffrey Grogan (also a Baptist and a lecturer at Glasgow's Bible Training Institute), Douglas himself as secretary, and G. S. M. Walker. Walker was a Church of Scotland minister, a 'brilliant scholar, and convert at the Billy Graham Crusade',[11] but the idea that he should succeed James Douglas as secretary when Douglas moved to Cambridge was ended by Walker's appointment as Lecturer in Church History at Leeds.[12] At the same April meeting

9. 'Husband of Doreen, who made the best jam I have ever tasted.'
10. Howard Marshall remembers him as 'certainly the most colourful member of staff' (e-mail of 4 October 2004).
11. BRC minutes, 14 April 1957. The crusade mentioned was the All-Scotland Crusade of 1955 at the Kelvin Hall in Glasgow.
12. BRC minutes, July 1958.

of the BRC, D. J. Wiseman reported that a small study group in Biblical Archaeology had met for the first time at Tyndale House.

At the meeting in July 1958, Ronald Inchley, the IVF Publications Secretary, suggested that a booklet on the Reformers' view of Scripture was needed 'in the light of the Barthian teaching'. This led to a discussion about the place of Church History in the Fellowship. It 'did not fall properly within the limits of biblical research, but it was finally agreed that it should be developed in relation to the original aim of the BRC since Church History gave essential depth and strength for biblical understanding'.

Curiously, in the light of that discussion, it was an historical theologian present in the committee, James Packer, who published that same year a trenchant defence of the Evangelical position on the authority of the Bible. Packer was replying to an attack on 'Fundamentalism' by the Bishop of Durham (A. M. Ramsey), Gabriel Hebert, and others, provoked by the Billy Graham 'crusades' at Harringay in 1954 and the Glasgow Kelvin Hall in 1955. The growth of the Inter-Varsity Fellowship in the universities and the national visibility of the Graham crusades alarmed both High Church Anglo-Catholics and those who classed themselves as 'Liberals'. They saw in all this a revival of obscurantist 'Fundamentalism', particularly perhaps because of the American revivalism of the Graham crusades. Even more scandalous to them was the CICCU mission to Cambridge University in 1955, when Billy Graham was missioner, following in the steps of D. L. Moody seventy-three years before.[13] In reply to Hebert's *Fundamentalism and the Church of God*,[14] IVF published James Packer's *'Fundamentalism' and the Word of God*. The quotation marks

---

13. See Barclay and Horn, *From Cambridge*, 141 and 148ff.; Douglas Johnson, *Contending for the Faith: A History of the Evangelical Movement in the Universities and Colleges* (Leicester: IVP, 1979), 246ff. Billy Graham's own account is in his autobiography, *Just as I Am* (New York: HarperCollins, 1997), 255ff. Cf. also Timothy Dudley-Smith, *John Stott: The Making of a Leader*, 344–365.

14. Gabriel Hebert, *Fundamentalism and the Church of God* (London: SCM, 1957).

in the title were significant. 'Fundamentalism' was an American term which he did not own, but what was being attacked under this term of abuse was in fact the Evangelical faith of the Reformation.[15] He identified three possible authorities in matters of faith. For all who took a 'Catholic' position, tradition was in effect the final authority; for 'Liberals' it was either the 'reason' or the 'experience' of the individual (hence it was 'subjectivist'); but for Evangelicals it was the revelation of God in holy Scripture. This robust defence of the historicity and cogency of the Evangelical position was widely influential. At the same time, it was influenced more by the approach of the American B. B. Warfield of the 'Old Princeton school' than by the earlier British treatments of James Orr or G. T. Manley.[16]

By the end of 1958, Gervase Duffield, a former secretary of the TSF at Oxford, had been elected a member of the Tyndale

---

15. American Fundamentalism was characterized not only by a literalism in its interpretation of Scripture, but also by opposition to Darwin's theory of evolution, which developed into so-called 'Creationism', and usually by a dispensationalist eschatology. It is quite clear that neither James Packer nor any other leader of British Evangelicalism at this period was a 'Fundamentalist', and Billy Graham (whose crusades provoked these attacks) had quite clearly separated himself from the Fundamentalists in the United States led by Carl McIntyre. But the word was already a convenient term of abuse. Cf. D. W. Bebbington, *Evangelicalism in Modern Britain: A History from the 1730s to the 1980s* (London: Unwin Hyman, 1989), 217ff. and 275f., on British attitudes to Fundamentalism. For the American history, see G. M. Marsden, *Fundamentalism and American Culture: The Shaping of American Evangelicalism, 1870–1925* (New York: OUP, 1980) and *Reforming Fundamentalism: Fuller Seminary and the New Evangelicalism* (Grand Rapids: Eerdmans, 1987).

16. James Orr, *Revelation and Inspiration* (London: Duckworth, 1910); G. T. Manley, 'The Inspiration and Authority of the Bible', *Evangelicalism*, ed. J. Russell Howden (London: Thynne & Jarvis, 1925), 121–155. Cf. also David F. Wright, 'Soundings in the Doctrine of Scripture in British Evangelicalism in the First Half of the Twentieth Century', *Tyndale Bulletin*, 31 (1980), 87–106.

Fellowship and appointed secretary of the BRC. It was reported
that recataloguing was in progress in the library and there was a
concentration on Biblical Studies in the accessions. There were
fifteen residents of Tyndale House, but of the eleven graduates
only five were doing research in theological areas. A small house
for the Warden was to be constructed in the grounds. In the study
groups planned for 1959, Church History would meet in January,
Old Testament on 2–6 July, Biblical Theology from 6 to 9 July on
'The Biblical Doctrine of Man in Society', and New Testament on
9–11 July on Hebrews. There were to be two Tyndale New
Testament Lectures: R. P. Martin would present a lecture on
Philippians 2:5–11,[17] and E. M. Blaiklock, a classics scholar from
New Zealand, would give an additional lecture on 'Rome in the
New Testament'.[18]

Tyndale research grants

The Awards Sub-committee met in May 1959. Chaired by Martyn
Lloyd-Jones, the committee included the Warden (John Bridger),
the chairman of the BRC (Donald Wiseman), the General
Secretary (Douglas Johnson) and John Wenham (who sent apologies). They received short written reports from five research
students who had received earlier grants, including Leon Morris
and Andrew Walls. Several grants were now available, including
two of £300 each from 'an individual', one of £330 from the IVF
Literature Committee, and a bursary which Dr D. R. Denman was
raising. There were applications from Australia, Canada and India
and from a research chemist who wanted to write on the theology
of evangelism. The Warden outlined his future policy. In order 'to
lodge sound biblical theology in the minds of students', it was
necessary 'to train men for the occupation of theological posts
and the writing of Biblical and Theological books'. Therefore,
they must 'look for men with a first class degree'. He was going to

---

17. Later published as *An Early Christian Confession: Philippians II, 5–11 in
    Recent Interpretation* (London: Tyndale Press, 1960).
18. J. P. U. Lilley notes that this was published in November 1959 by IVF but
    not identified as a Tyndale Lecture.

'search amongst second and third year men in Unions such as
CICCU and OICCU'. Members of the committee added the comments that '2nd class honours (part 1) men are often better than
"firsts" for good solid work'; that 'we must hammer away at the
gaps and subjects where Evangelicals are weak'; and that 'we must
not stray more than we can help into Church History and other
subjects, but adhere to Biblical Linguistics and Biblical Theology
where the whole country is weak at the present time'. The committee were agreed that they were looking for 'men' of any
denomination with genius and ability 'allied to a warm Evangelical
heart'.

The building of the Warden's house facing across the garden to
the south side of the Tyndale House did not start till September
1959. It obliterated a small lawn with rose-beds, where (as John
Lilley recalls) Stafford Wright used to pitch his tent in preference
to taking a room in the house.[19] The new house was to serve as the
Warden's Lodge until it was adapted for the families of postgraduate students in the 1990s.

Also in 1959, Bridger proposed the merging of *The Tyndale
House Bulletin* and the TSF members' letter to make a journal to be
published twice annually, but instead it was decided after consultation to leave the TSF letter and to publish an expanded *Bulletin*
twice a year. The idea of an associate membership was considered, but was thought premature. By March 1960, a new draft
constitution for the Tyndale Fellowship was presented by a sub-
committee, with the proposal to change the title from 'The
Tyndale Fellowship for Biblical Studies and Research' to 'The
Tyndale Fellowship for Biblical and Theological Studies and
Research'. Some of the senior members of the committee – Basil
Atkinson, F. F. Bruce, G. T. Manley, Martyn Lloyd-Jones and
J. Stafford Wright – were to be asked whether they could attend

---

19. Dorothy Barter-Snow, the Principal of St Michael's House, also preferred
    to camp in the garden (notes of 1 November 2004 from J. P. U. Lilley).
    John Lilley recalls some of the residents going out in heavy rain to see if
    the campers would like to come into the House, but they preferred to
    stay put!

more frequently. In fact, Manley's last recorded attendance was in June of the previous year.

The Warden also had a further proposal, which he presented in a two-and-a-half-page report: that 'greater coherence would be given to the work of the Fellowship if the present committee would . . . produce for each of its groups an accurate statement of the projects that needed tackling'. He had discussed with the secretary the idea that, after consultation with the study groups, this might lead to symposia. Such clear goals would retain younger scholars in TF ranks. But while Bridger was giving evidence of some strategic thinking about the work of the Tyndale Fellowship, domestic affairs were not good at the House. There had been disagreement between members of the domestic staff, and the Warden was reputed to be absent too often. Douglas Johnson wrote in confidence to the Revd Noel Pollard, who had been appointed 'senior resident' to fulfil a chaplaincy role at the House while working on his thesis, and a man he felt he could trust, to give him a discreet and balanced assessment. At the next committee meeting on 12 July 1960, he reported that the Warden had had a breakdown and had resigned on grounds of health.

Discussion followed on the process of appointing a successor. The IVF Council had appointed a sub-committee for nominations, and Johnson explained in answer to questions that the appointment of a Warden was not in the competence of the Biblical Research Committee. Tyndale House was owned by the IVF Trust, and so the making of the appointment (as with all IVF appointments) was in the hands of the IVF Council. The BRC was of course welcome to refer to it any nominations if it so desired. The committee felt that the discussion made clear the need to clarify once again the respective spheres of the House and Fellowship. Clearly there was some expectation, at least perhaps among the newer members of the BRC, that they would appoint the new Warden, or at least have some say in the matter. Historically, it was certainly true that the first Warden, now Prof. J. N. D. Anderson, had been appointed by the BRC following a nomination by W. J. Martin. But that was fourteen years earlier. Only three years before, Bridger's appointment had been announced *to* the BRC. In the meantime, Noel Pollard was appointed acting secretary, and ran the affairs of the House in very close communication with the General Secretary for almost a year.[20]

At the same committee meeting (July 1960), J. D. Douglas could report a steady expansion of the library and progress on the Bible dictionary, and Gervase Duffield reported on the study group conferences, which had just finished. The Old Testament Study Group was growing despite the 'difficulties of the preceding few months' (a reference presumably to the Warden's difficulties). It was strong in archaeology and philology but weak in Old Testament theology. The Biblical Theology group had had one of its most encouraging years, but it faced particular problems 'since the courses offered by English universities were not geared to producing students trained in Biblical and Systematic Theology'. The New Testament group had suffered most from the Warden's breakdown in health, but it was hoped that Professor Tasker would lead it next year when Professor Bruce was abroad. It was said to be a question of controlling difficult members, a permanent problem, but one best tackled by strong chairmanship and restricted attendance.

At the meeting of the BRC in December 1960, it was reported that the Church History group was larger than ever, and that G. S. M. Walker's help was invaluable. The Puritan and Reformed Studies conference held at Westminster Chapel now attracted more than 200, two-thirds of whom were ministers and theology students. The question was raised whether this Westminster conference should cease to be a Tyndale Fellowship study group, but James Packer requested that this question be deferred to the one-day conference which had been proposed.

Before the day conference met, the Australian Dr Leon Morris had been appointed as Warden of Tyndale House. He took up his duties in May 1961. *The Tyndale House Bulletin* gave a resumé of his career: a BSc from Sydney, a London BD and MTh, postgraduate studies in Cambridge (when he had been a resident of Tyndale

---

20. Noel Pollard's file of correspondence with Johnson survives, demonstrating the latter's 'hands-on' supervision during this difficult year. Pollard, like Andrew Walls, was in fact acting Warden.

House) and appointment as Vice-Principal of Ridley College, Melbourne.[21] Leon Morris's research had concentrated on the doctrine of the atonement. His Cambridge thesis had been the second major work published by IVF under the 'Tyndale Press' imprint, and he had also published a series of articles defending the biblical basis of the concept of 'propitiation'.[22] This was a hot issue for Evangelicals, since the Revised Standard Version, published in 1952, had followed C. H. Dodd's rejection of 'propitiation', substituting instead the translation 'expiation' in several key biblical passages.

The Waverley Hotel conference

The strategy conference proposed by John Wenham[23] met at the Waverley Hotel in Southampton Row, London SW1, on 29 May 1961. D. J. Wiseman was in the chair and the participants included Oliver Barclay, F. F. Bruce, H. M. Carson, Ronald Inchley, W. J. Martin, Leon Morris, J. I. Packer, Noel Pollard, A. M. Stibbs, J. B. Taylor, John Wenham and Douglas Johnson.[24] In the absence of Gervase Duffield, who was completing work, Johnson was currently acting as secretary. Apologies were received from Basil Atkinson, John Balchin, J. D. Douglas, Philip Hughes and Martyn Lloyd-Jones.

Dr Leon Morris was welcomed as the new Warden of Tyndale House, and the chairman outlined the reasons for the day

---

21. *The Tyndale House Bulletin*, Nos 7–8 (1961).
22. In addition to his published thesis, *The Apostolic Preaching of the Cross* (London: Tyndale Press, 1952), Dr Morris had published a series of articles on the atonement, including one which refuted C. H. Dodd's rejection of the translation 'propitiation' in Rom. 3:23: 'The Meaning of ἱλαστηριον etc. in Romans 3:25', *New Testament Studies*, 2 (1955), 33–43. For the first 'Tyndale Press' publication, F. F. Bruce's commentary on Acts, see above, page 66.
23. See above, page 102.
24. The minutes record that Bruce, Carson and Martin were present only for part of the time, and that Noel Pollard (senior resident at Tyndale House) was present 'by invitation'.

conference. First, with the changes in personnel, it was an appropriate time for long-term planning for the next phase of development.
Secondly, there was a divergence of opinion about the development
of the Fellowship, particularly with how far the term 'Biblical
Research' could be applied to other activities (profitable in themselves though they might be) such as (i) Expository Preaching, (ii)
Historical Theology, (iii) Church History and (iv) a Puritan Studies
conference. Thirdly, the need remained for first-class scholars to
work on the basic documents of the Christian faith: Evangelicals
were still without sufficient Old and New Testament scholars of the
first rank. Fourthly, there was a need to concentrate on the job in
hand – biblical research and scholarship – in distinction from a
more general fellowship. Douglas Johnson then added a memo on
the original aim of the Biblical Research Committee.

James Packer immediately entered a plea that in concentrating
on the original aim other necessary areas such as theology and
church history should not be neglected, but the tide was against
him. The discussion centred around the small success up to this
point. They had a few of the better minds, they had issued a few
Tyndale monographs and books, notably F. F. Bruce's commentary
and Leon Morris's thesis, but the 'reigning monarchs of scholarship' had taken scarcely any notice. On the other side, Evangelical
attitudes to biblical scholarship still had to be changed. The lack of
Hebrew scholars provided an opportunity and the vocation of
biblical scholarship should be presented to sixth-formers. James
Packer pled for the unity of theological studies as an organic
whole, but against this the committee was reminded that the original aim of developing Evangelical scholarship in biblical studies
had scarcely been started.

The tentative finding of the first session was that the Biblical
Research Committee should revert to its original aim in close
association with the Old Testament, New Testament, Biblical
Theology and Biblical Archaeology study groups and Tyndale
House. But the Tyndale Fellowship, with a distinct Tyndale
Fellowship committee, should make provision for other scholarly
interests such as Historical Theology and Church History.

At the second session the issue of research was tackled. There
was discussion of the difference between linguistic and textual

biblical research and other derivative theological studies. The crucial question was defined: 'Are people side-tracked from the linguistic and other essentially basic biblical research by theological and historical studies, which in any case were often at lower standards of scholarship and (sometimes at least) came to be regarded as soft option?' W. J. Martin, supported by F. F. Bruce, emphasized the difference between the task of the true scholar, working on primary sources and dealing objectively with what he finds, and others working on secondary sources and admitting judgments of value. Frequently, he opined, the latter were only comparing and contrasting the value judgments of other minds. But the first principle of true scholarship was to confine itself to the primary sources and to exclude, as far as the mind would allow, judgments of value. The findings must be integrated by the backroom workers, who should present what they have found as objectively as possible for the judgment of their peers.

A. M. Stibbs offered his support: far more people were working and were prepared to work on various peripheral studies than on these harder, seemingly barren, fields of necessary technical scholarship. The consensus was that there was a need to narrow the aim and that a boundary was required to conserve resources and create a team spirit giving priority to the 'foundation' studies. Fighting a losing battle, James Packer again put the view that provision must be made for research in the theological fields of study other than the strictly biblical. But the division of labour suggested at the first session was confirmed. The focus would be on Biblical Studies: the Biblical Research Committee and Tyndale House were to concentrate on the original aim, but the 'Tyndale Fellowship for Biblical and Theological Research' could make provision for other studies in its study groups.

The agenda proper was then begun! A review of the membership of the Tyndale Fellowship showed that of the 346 members, 299 were in the British Isles.[25] There were twenty-two in the

---

25. These numbers seem high compared with those reported previously and later, but if the numbers given in the minutes in several categories are added up (and if it is assumed that the last category, women, does not

universities, fourteen in theology and eight in other disciplines. Twenty-three taught in theological colleges and fifteen in Bible colleges, and there were ten postgraduate students. But the largest group (133) were ministers, with seventy-three laymen. The total number of women was twenty-three.

In the third and final session, the membership of the present Biblical Research Committee was reviewed. Among the present membership, D. J. Wiseman, J. B. Taylor and W. J. Martin represented Old Testament studies. New Testament specialists included A. M. Stibbs, J. W. Wenham and F. F. Bruce (also Basil Atkinson, but he had not been attending). H. M. Carson, Philip Hughes and James Packer were listed under Biblical Theology (but Martin Lloyd-Jones had not been attending). The *ex officio* members included John Balchin for Scotland, James Douglas as Librarian, Ronald Inchley representing the IVF publications department, Oliver Barclay representing the Graduates' Fellowship and Douglas Johnson as the General Secretary. Since Atkinson had offered his resignation and Lloyd-Jones was known to be willing to retire, it was agreed to invite D. F. Payne (Old Testament), Michael Green (New Testament) and Howard Marshall (to represent Biblical Theology) to join the committee. The new Warden would be a member *ex officio*.[26] This committee was now to be renamed the 'Tyndale Fellowship Committee' and was to be responsible to a new 'Biblical Research Committee' of senior academics.

After some further matters, the one-day conference adjourned. The priorities had been firmly established. Theology and historical studies had been put firmly in their place within the wider concerns of the Tyndale Fellowship. The focus of the Biblical Research Committee and of Tyndale House was the priority of

---

overlap with any of the others) the total comes to 299, suggesting that these figures are an analysis of the 299 in the British Isles. It is unfortunate that apparently no annual register of members has been kept.

26. G. T. Manley is not mentioned in this list of the committee and no reference is made to his death early in 1961. Cf. Ronald Inchley's tribute to his chairmanship of the IVF Literature Committee in Johnson, *Contending for the Faith*, 324 and 329.

the 'foundation' studies – first-class, front-line, objective, technical and linguistic biblical research. It was imperative that Evangelicals should excel there.

Reorganizing to refocus

The day conference at the Waverley Hotel was a significant land-mark. Coming just four years after D. J. Wiseman had become chairman of the Biblical Research Committee, it refocused the academic leadership of British Evangelicalism in biblical and theological studies on the business of research. The Tyndale Fellowship was not to become merely a theological debating society, and the practical demands of operating an institution like Tyndale House were not to divert time and energy from that original and primary objective of the Biblical Research Committee. Now the delegation of the study groups and lectures to the Tyndale Fellowship Committee would leave the senior academics to focus on the heart of the BRC's mission.

The Tyndale Fellowship for Biblical and Theological Research
When the newly constituted 'Committee of the Tyndale Fellowship for Biblical and Theological Research'[27] met in December 1961 (still chaired by D. J. Wiseman),[28] three new members were welcomed: E. M. B. Green, I. H. Marshall and D. F. Payne. While the Fellowship had a wider remit than the BRC, extending to History and Theology, the focus on narrowing the aim to scholarly research continued. Those participating in study groups were to be suitably qualified and Dr Packer (who was absent) was to be asked to ensure that this applied also to the Biblical Theology group which he chaired. It was recognized that this was difficult, but it was essential

---

27. This fuller title, proposed in March 1960, first appears in the minutes of this meeting and presumably reflects the wider remit the committee had in comparison with the newly reconstituted Biblical Research Committee.

28. Donald Wiseman became Professor of Assyriology at the University of London that year and gave his inaugural lecture in February, 1962.

if significant research was to be done. Out of 383 members of the Fellowship, 200 had replied to a questionnaire. Of these, ninety-three were qualified to do genuine research, twelve were 'border-line', eighty-six were really 'Friends' of Tyndale House, and six were no longer available. The problem was that too little research was being done. Nothing could be achieved unless a more integrated working fellowship were established for technically equipped workers. It was agreed that there was also a need to encourage deeper theological studies among those who were interested in the results gained by the research team. A proposal was made to transfer such people to a separate 'Fellowship for Theological and Church Historical Studies', which would be a section of the Graduates' Fellowship. But despite the consensus that these studies were not first-rank technical research, and that it was 'clear to all' that they really belonged in the Graduates' Fellowship, it was agreed in the end to let the Church History group stay in the Tyndale Fellowship. Joyce Baldwin (teaching Old Testament at Dalton House, Bristol) and Geoffrey Grogan were among those accepted into membership.

Promoting and financing research
The next month, January 1962, the Awards Sub-committee met at 39 Bedford Square.[29] Professor Wiseman chaired the meeting in the absence of Dr Lloyd-Jones, and F. F. Bruce, W. J. Martin and Douglas Johnson were present. Apologies were received from Prof. J. N. D. Anderson, W. Kirby Laing, B. M. Harris (the Treasurer), and the Warden, who had been invited to attend, in addition to the chairman. The successful completion of research by Andrew Walls, Leon Morris, James Dale (DLitt, Cantab.) and Noel Pollard (PhD, Cantab.) was noted along with the appointments of several grantees (Terence Mitchell, Alan Millard and Richard Hosking) to the British Museum. James Douglas's successful three-year completion of *The New Bible Dictionary* was also noted. But two notable

---

29. The minutes indicate that it was now a sub-committee of the IVF Business Advisory Committee, no longer the Biblical Research Committee.

disappointments among the research students who had received help led to discussion. It was agreed that future awards would be restricted to work of fundamental biblical research, 'by which is meant original work based on primary sources'. This committee of senior academics also reviewed the work of the Tyndale Fellowship, noting its four study groups – for Old Testament, New Testament, Biblical Theology and Biblical Archaeology. They agreed that the Historical Theology group should be left where it was for three years to see if it worked within strict limits with a sufficient bearing on the Bible, but that the Reformed Puritan group, the General Church History group and General Theological activities were best left to the Graduates' Fellowship.

An application from the USA for a Tyndale grant received by the Warden was considered, but it was agreed that the awards were primarily for graduates of British universities. There was considerable discussion of the desirability of finding the right 'men'.

Two days later, exactly the same people – Professors Wiseman and Bruce, and Doctors Martin and Johnson – with the addition of Leon Morris as Warden, met at 39 Bedford Square this time as the reconstituted Biblical Research Committee! According to the new structure outlined at the Waverley Hotel conference, their remit was directly promoting research (as opposed to running the Tyndale Fellowship). They noted their reconstitution:

> AGREED to reconstitute the Biblical Research Committee on its original aims and for its original purpose, viz. to endeavour to find and to aid in the training of linguistically and academically equipped Biblical Scholars, who would be able to produce the technically accurate monographs and books needed by Evangelicalism in the Old and New Testament fields.

It was agreed to invite Prof. R. V. G. Tasker to join the committee (and, should he decline, another Anglican), together with a Presbyterian and a Methodist of suitably senior academic status. They then turned to 'the Needs of the Evangelical World', and drew up a list of five:

• Up-to-date Aramaic studies relating to the intertestamental period

- Work on the Old Testament texts (cf. Strack-Billerbeck)
- Rabbinics (a translation and key to important section)
- Old Testament commentaries on the Hebrew text
- New Testament commentaries on the Greek text.

They reviewed suitable young scholars who might undertake these tasks. The Warden then presented a more detailed outline of the scholarly needs of Evangelicals. This included a work on the Pentateuch, given current uncertainty about JEDP; a work on the Psalms dealing with sacral kingship; a book on Old Testament Theology; any number of solid commentaries (there was a big lack here); a book on the Wisdom literature; and something on the message of the prophets. Less was being heard about the prophets than in the days when they were regarded as the real founders of ethical monotheism. In New Testament studies a work on history and the Gospels was needed, together with works on the Fourth Gospel and recent criticism, on Lukan problems, on the Pauline corpus 'including the authenticity of Ephesians', and on apocalyptic. 'Solid' commentaries were needed on the Greek text, along with something to replace Edersheim's *Life and Times*. In Biblical Theology, something was needed on 'demythologization' together with monographs on a wide variety of topics – the Trinity, the church, eschatology, man, unity and the ecumenical movement, and the sacraments. In short, the committee saw that there was an enormous amount of work to be done! Thought was given to the recruiting of young scholars.

Douglas Johnson made it clear that he was continuing as acting secretary of the BRC and Tyndale Fellowship only *faut de mieux*. D. J. Wiseman thought it would be better to have someone else chair the Tyndale Fellowship Committee so that he could be freer to speak there on Old Testament subjects, and it was agreed to nominate the Warden, Leon Morris, to the TF committee.

Leon Morris as chairman of the TFC
When the Tyndale Fellowship Committee next met in April 1962, Wiseman was absent but he sent word of his wish to resign as chairman of the TFC and his nomination of the Warden of Tyndale House, Dr Leon Morris, to succeed him. The committee

agreed. They then adjourned to meet Professor Tasker, and to present copies of *The New Bible Dictionary* to him and to Dr Packer and Professor Wiseman. The fourth consulting editor, Professor Bruce, could not be present. Douglas Johnson proposed a vote of thanks on behalf of the IVF Council, and A. M. Stibbs led in prayer.

The organizing editor, James D. Douglas, had already left for Washington, DC, to take a job offered to him by Carl Henry, the editor of *Christianity Today*. He had not felt in fact that his contribution to the dictionary had been fully appreciated at the IVF offices and had felt that he had been somewhat unfairly treated. At one point his study-bedroom at Tyndale House had been divided to make room for another resident, who had been understandably upset by the editor's typewriter tapping away far into the night! He had had to threaten to resign to have the necessary facilities restored. Of even greater concern to him was that his Herculean labours were not to be recognized on the title page of the dictionary, on the grounds that the editors employed by IVF were always anonymous. He enlisted the support of his fellow Scot F. F. Bruce, who insisted that as the organizing editor with nine years of university and seminary education, and not simply a subeditor, James Douglas had to be named.[30] When the dictionary appeared in May, the four consulting editors, Bruce, Packer, Tasker and Wiseman, noted in the Preface that it was 'the latest and thus far the major, product of the Tyndale Fellowship for Biblical Research' and gave full credit to Jim Douglas:

> Our special thanks are due to the Organizing Editor, Dr J. D. Douglas, formerly Librarian of Tyndale House, Cambridge. For more than three years he has devoted the greater part of his time to the preparation of this volume, planning the form which the contents should take and generally co-ordinating the work of the many contributors.

The dictionary, like *The New Bible Commentary*, was an outstanding success in both British and American markets, and had sold over

---

30. From the unpublished memoirs of the late James D. Douglas, 'The Half that Can Be Told'.

130,000 copies by 1979.[31] It was to be the first of a whole series of 'New' dictionaries published by what was to become Inter-Varsity Press.[32]

At that same meeting of the Tyndale Fellowship Committee in April 1962, the resignation of John Wenham owing to health and workload was received, and it was agreed to ask three others to join the committee: David Gooding, Kenneth Kitchen and Alec Motyer. David F. Wright and two others were accepted into membership.

Leon Morris chaired the November meeting of the TFC, when it was announced that Dr Packer wished to resign, but he was asked to stay. A theological studies group had been set up by the Graduates' Fellowship with Kenneth Prior in the chair and Robert Horn as secretary. J. B. Taylor was nominated as secretary of the committee. Morris again chaired the meeting in April 1963, when the study group officers were listed. The Old Testament group was chaired by D. J. Wiseman with Alan Millard as secretary; Wiseman also chaired the Biblical Archaeology group with Terence Mitchell as secretary. Bruce was chairman of the New Testament group (Morris being his deputy) and I. H. Marshall was secretary. J. I. Packer chaired the Biblical Theology group with Morris as acting secretary; and Arthur Skevington Wood chaired the Church History group. J. B. Taylor, now in parish work, declined appointment as secretary of the Tyndale Fellowship Committee, and Douglas Johnson agreed to continue meantime as acting secretary. But the secretary, it was felt, ought to be someone who was engaged in research.

Reorganization of the reorganized committees

By the beginning of 1964, significant changes were heralded. The Biblical Research Committee met on 1 January 1964 with only Wiseman, Bruce and Johnson in attendance. They expressed their

---

31. This is the figure given for sales by Douglas Johnson (*Contending*, 325).
32. The literature department of the IVF, which begun publishing in 1928, became the Inter-Varsity Press in 1968. Cf. *The First Fifty Years* (Leicester: IVP, 1986). For a list of the 'New' dictionaries, see p. 269, n. 31.

regret that Leon Morris had resigned as Warden of Tyndale House. He returned to Australia that month to become Principal of Ridley College, Melbourne. Douglas Johnson, who had been secretary of the Inter-Varsity Conference from 1924, and General Secretary of the IVF since it was founded in 1928, reported that he was retiring and that his successor, Dr Oliver Barclay, would take office on 1 January 1965. He would continue as secretary of the IVF Trust with particular responsibilities for Tyndale House and the Christian Medical Fellowship. The committee then endorsed some suggestions that W. J. Martin had added to his written apologies for absence (presumably after discussion with Douglas Johnson!) and forwarded them to the Trust Committee. Martin's recommendation was that with the loss of the Warden and the imminent retiral of the General Secretary, the Biblical Research Committee should reassume responsibility for the administration of Tyndale House and all the associated research projects. It was proposed that the newly constituted BRC should include academic members (Bruce, Martin, Stibbs, Wiseman and the new Warden) and administrative members. For the latter they proposed Prof. J. N. D. Anderson representing the IVF Council, Dr Oliver Barclay *ex officio* as the new General Secretary, B. M. Harris as chairman of the Trust and the IVF Business Advisory Committee, and Kirby Laing also from the BAC. Douglas Johnson should continue as secretary of the BRC.

When the Tyndale Fellowship Committee met two days later, it was agreed that Alan Stibbs, the vice-chairman, should be acting chairman and that it had not been the best arrangement to have the same person as chairman of the Fellowship committee and Warden of Tyndale House. For want of someone involved in research, the General Secretary himself, Douglas Johnson, would continue to serve as secretary. A report was given on a meeting of the Friends of Tyndale House, when a hundred had been present to hear Professor Bruce give 'an inspiring and concise statement' of its history. The audience had included C. F. D. Moule, Lady Margaret Professor of Divinity and great-nephew of Bishop Handley Moule. It was noted that Howard Marshall's Tyndale Lecture had been published as a Tyndale Monograph, *Eschatology and the Parables*, and that several others were in process of production, including

D. F. Payne, *Genesis One Reconsidered*, and A. S. Dunstone, *The Atonement in Gregory of Nyssa*. Works by F. D. Kidner and R. A. Finlayson (*The Study of Theology*) were to appear, along with one particularly notable publication, Donald Guthrie's *New Testament Introduction*.

The primacy of biblical research

A recurring refrain in this period, 1957–66, was the reassertion of the primacy of Biblical Studies. The research arm of IVF had begun with the establishment of the *Biblical* Research Committee in 1938; W. J. Martin's dream at the Kingham Hill conference was the establishing of a school of *biblical* research and a *biblical* research library. Even James Packer, who had pled for recognition of the significance of Theology and Church History, had argued in *'Fundamentalism' and the Word of God* that Evangelicals were distinguished from Catholics (both Roman and Anglo) and Liberals in their united stand on the final authority of *the Bible*. But were Theology and Church History second-order disciplines requiring lesser skills than first-class, front-line, objective, technical and linguistic biblical research? One can hardly imagine such an assumption in Scotland or Germany!

Or was there behind this the view that 'the Bible unites, but theology divides'? Certainly the debates of the early 1950s produced division over five-point Calvinism, even among those who regarded themselves as 'Reformed'. Or were the different viewpoints on the place of theology and history over against biblical studies influenced by the differing Evangelical traditions? Those who looked to Puritanism or stood in the Presbyterian or Welsh Calvinistic Methodist tradition might be expected to look to the Old Princeton tradition or to Calvin himself more than those whose traditions laid equal emphasis on Scripture and its exposition, but not so much on Systematic Theology. The latter might include the Anglican Evangelicals in the tradition of Charles Simeon and Handley Moule, the Christian Brethren and the Wesleyan Methodists. The protagonists tended to divide in a way which reflected these varying traditions.

But perhaps the strategy is simply to be taken at face value. The challenge to the Christian faith was seen to be coming not so much from those who were the church's declared enemies, but from some Christian preachers, apologists and theologians. Their 'liberal' approach to the Bible was held to compromise Christian truth, weaken the appeal of the gospel and undermine the faith of students and thinking Christian lay people. The sensation created by Bishop John Robinson's *Honest to God* in 1963 reinforced this belief. In this context, the fundamental need for the defence of the gospel was seen to be the re-establishing of a school of unimpeachable biblical scholarship, and, given the scarcity of resources, the strategy had to focus on that one point.

Yet to re-establish the original aim of biblical research, so clearly asserted at the Waverley Hotel day conference, was one thing. To take the first clear and practical steps to its realization through the long haul was another. Bridger had some creative ideas about how such a programme should be started, and Morris had himself made a significant contribution to Evangelical biblical scholarship. But having two Wardens serve for brief periods, unexpectedly terminated, had not been conducive to establishing long-term practices. If the readopted strategy was to have a chance of success, a period of stability was necessary at Tyndale House. It was essential to find a Warden with a long-term commitment to the priority which had been so clearly defined: biblical research.

5. REFOCUS

Wiseman, Stibbs and Kidner, 1964–70

The appointment of a new Warden and a new Librarian together with an extension to the library, the beginning of the annual publication of *The Tyndale Bulletin*, and the appointment of a part-time secretary of the Tyndale Fellowship all took place in the mid-1960s and marked the beginning of a new phase for Tyndale House and the Fellowship.

New developments

The new Warden was the Revd F. D. Kidner, an Old Testament scholar who had been a tutor at Oak Hill College since 1951. Derek Kidner had begun his career as a pianist, studying piano at the Royal College of Music and graduating ARCM. Sensing a call to the ministry, he had matriculated at Cambridge in 1937, served as President of CICCU in 1939–40, and graduated with a First the following year. As a student he had twice performed piano concertos at concerts arranged by CUMS (the Cambridge University Musical Society). After a period as Vicar of Felsted in Essex, he had gone to Oak Hill to teach Old Testament. His colleague Alan Stibbs encouraged him to take the appointment as Warden of Tyndale House, telling him that Leon Morris had been able to spend most of his time there in research and writing. When the Kidners arrived at the Warden's Lodge in the summer of 1964, Alan Millard had been part-time Librarian since the beginning of the year, also working as an assistant at the British Museum. In April he had become full-time Librarian.

A new committee structure

At the new Warden's first meeting of the BRC, held at the IVF office at 39 Bedford Square, London WC1, on 22 September 1964, the chairman, Professor Wiseman, explained the reorganization of committees. It had now been agreed to bring together under one committee, the Biblical Research Committee, the functions of (1) the original BRC; (2) the Tyndale House Committee; (3) the Awards Committee; and (4) the Friends of Tyndale House Committee. It was agreed that the BRC was now responsible to the Trust Committee for:

- The policy, administration and finance of Tyndale House, the library, residents and research projects
- The promotion of Evangelical scholarship, including the discovery of new scholars and assistance in their training
- The perpetuation of the Tyndale Lectures (with the inviting and remuneration of the lecturers)
- The increase of support through the Friends of Tyndale House
- The presentation of a written annual report, after having been approved by the Committee, to the Trust.

The Tyndale Fellowship Committee, which was composed of those most actively engaged in study groups, would be responsible (as a sub-committee of the BRC) for:

- The day-to-day promotion and coordination of the work of the study groups

- The selection and nomination of lecturers for the annual
  Tyndale Lectures
- The recruitment of new scholars of promise by means such as
  the sixth-formers' and theological students' conferences.

Different areas of the work were allotted to BRC members for
their oversight: New Testament research projects and workers to
F. F. Bruce; major finance to B. M. Harris; maintenance of the
House and associated provisions to F. A. Houlding; fabric of the
House to W. K. Laing; Old Testament research projects and
workers to D. J. Wiseman and W. J. Martin; Biblical Theology
and theological advisory functions to Martyn Lloyd-Jones and
A. M. Stibbs.

The BRC would meet three times each year. In October, they
would meet over lunch at Tyndale House on the Open Day, the
main business being the House, library and finance. A winter
meeting would be held in early January (when some of the more
distant members would be in London for the meetings of the
Society of Old Testament Studies). The main business then would
be future research projects. A spring meeting would be held in
April or May to find and encourage research workers and determine the awards.

Five 'research workers' who were receiving awards for 1964–65
were listed in addition to the Warden and Librarian. Two Old
Testament research projects were beginning, Alan Millard on
Genesis 1 – 11, and Ian Snook on Isaiah, and a New Testament
project was minuted: James Dunn's PhD research on the charis-
mata of 1 Corinthians 12 – 14. Reports were received on progress.
There was some discussion too of the new situation arising
because two grantees were married and would be living out of the
House. Since the Librarian also lived out of House, only fourteen
of the twenty rooms were occupied. It was resolved to explore
ways of attracting research students through contacts with head-
masters and headmistresses, sixth-formers and careers masters,
possibly arranging house parties.

When the Tyndale Fellowship Committee (now a sub-committee
of the BRC) met later that same day, 22 September 1964, with Alan
Stibbs in the chair, Mr Kidner was welcomed as the new Warden

of Tyndale House. The rationale of the reorganization was now explained to the TFC.[1] Since its wartime inception, there had been several stages of growth and change in the work of Tyndale House. One result had been the proliferation of committees and sub-committees with overlapping membership and functions. The appointment of the new Warden and the imminent retirement of Douglas Johnson as IVF General Secretary appeared to be an opportune time to clarify functions and reduce the number of committees. After resolutions of the IVF Trust, the IVF Council and the Business Advisory Committee, the following was the position. The IVF Trust, which owned Tyndale House, had reassumed responsibility and had reconstituted the original arrangement whereby the Biblical Research Committee (from whom Tyndale House and the Tyndale Fellowship had sprung) had overall responsibility for the research arm of IVF. The Tyndale Fellowship was now asked to concentrate upon its original and basic task of biblical research ('biblical' underlined!).[2] The Graduates' Fellowship had been asked to adopt the various groups for the study of Theology, Church History, and Apologetics (the last having just been started).[3] But the main point for the Tyndale Fellowship was that little 'basic scientific biblical research would get done unless the few available and equipped men and slender resources were concentrated upon it'.

When the BRC met only one month later for the October meeting, it established the annual pattern of meeting in the morning in Tyndale House to meet with members of the staff, and in the afternoon in the Warden's Lodge. At this meeting in

---

1. It is not clear from the minutes of this meeting of the TFC for 22 September 1964 who gave the following explanation, but it seems most likely that it was the retiring General Secretary, Douglas Johnson.
2. This seems to be contrary to the concession to James Packer at the Waverley Hotel conference that the Fellowship had a wider remit than the House (see pages 113–115f.).
3. Clark Pinnock, who had been a research student at Manchester under Professor Bruce, was to be secretary, and it was suggested that Professor MacKay of Keele should be asked to be chairman.

October 1964 they noted with regret the death of Dr Norval Geldenhuys of Pretoria, one of the original members of the committee.[4]

Johnson's retirement and the Frinton conference

The year 1965 was Douglas Johnson's last on the Tyndale Fellowship Committee. Having handed over to Oliver Barclay as General Secretary of IVF, he gave one more year to the Tyndale Fellowship. At the beginning of the year, the committee offered congratulations to F. F. Bruce on his election as President of the Society for Old Testament Studies. (He was later to achieve the rare distinction of also being elected President of the Society for New Testament Studies.) New TF members that year included James D. G. Dunn, George Carey, who was a curate at Islington, and M. E. J. Richardson. It was announced that the BRC had agreed to consider proposals to replace *The Tyndale House Bulletin* with an annual scholarly publication of 160 pages which would include Tyndale Lectures and papers from study groups. The Librarian, Alan Millard, would be the editor and the editorial board would be Bruce, Martin, Wiseman and Kidner. DJ's resignation as secretary of the Tyndale Fellowship was eventually accepted with regret at the meeting on 5 January 1966.

Dr Johnson continued to be a member of the BRC, but gave his apologies when they held a residential meeting on 6 and 7 January 1967 at The Cedars Hotel, Frinton-on-Sea, Essex. This was another of the 'strategy' sessions held from time to time, the first since the Waverley Hotel conference in 1961. Wiseman, Bruce, Stibbs, Martin and Oliver Barclay were all present (Bruce and Stibbs for part of the time), together with two of the IVF businessmen in the committee, B. M. Harris and F. Houlding, and the Warden. Frank Houlding was the owner of the hotel, and the committee expressed their thanks to the Houldings for their hospitality. Dr Johnson wrote to resign his membership, but the committee urged him to keep in touch by receiving agenda and

---

4. He was present at the first organizing meeting at St Luke's Vicarage, Hampstead, in June 1938 (see page 30).

minutes, even if he could not attend meetings. In fact, he continued to attend!

In a wide review, progress since the Kingham Hill conference of
1941 was recalled. (Of the members of that seminal conference,
Bruce, Stibbs and Martin were still present and active.) The
reasons for the establishment of the BRC and Tyndale House still
held good: the promotion of academic biblical research, the
encouragement of Evangelicals to obtain university posts, and
the promotion of theological publication. Progress was noted: the
founding of Tyndale House was now furthering research; there
were theological publications; and about fifteen Tyndale
Fellowship members were now members of faculties related to
biblical studies. The House was an internationally known focus of
Evangelical scholarship, and the library had a high reputation
outside Evangelical ranks. The very existence of a research centre
was a continual reminder of the importance of good scholarship.
As a place where ideas could be exchanged, it had a stimulating
effect on biblical research.

The blueprint

Following Douglas Johnson's proposal at the previous meeting, the
conference then attempted to identify a 'blueprint' of areas of biblical research which should have high priority for Evangelicals. The
new Tyndale Fellowship secretary, R. T. France, had prepared a list
of priorities in New Testament studies in consultation with
Dr Howard Marshall. The major need was to respond to the dom-
inating influence of Rudolf Bultmann and his followers. This
meant tackling the question of the Historical Jesus, together with
the nature and purpose of the Gospels. In addition there were the
presuppositions of the Bultmannian school and the criteria they
employed in determining the authenticity of sayings and the historicity of narratives. Tradition and the transmission of material in
the early church, the question whether there were different schools
of theology in the early church, Bultmann's existentialist interpretation of Paul and John, and the nature of first-century Gnosticism
and its influence on the New Testament all required research. In
addition to this, there was a list of other topics in historical-critical
studies, including the proto-Luke theory, the historicity of Acts,

the date and origin of several New Testament books, and the mutual interpenetration of the Jewish and Hellenistic worlds in New Testament times. There were also doctrinal topics on the list of priorities: sanctification, the church, authority and New Testament eschatology.

F. F. Bruce agreed with emphasizing the immediate importance of work on the Gospels in view of the Bultmannian attempt to de-historicize Christianity. But studies were needed not just on his-toricity, but on the significance of these issues for faith. Taking the long view, he said that they should aim to do for the late twentieth century what J. B. Lightfoot and others did for the late nineteenth century: that was, to provide thorough commentaries on the Greek text. Such constructive work would also have a defensive value. A commentary on Galatians, for example, would cover much of the ground disputed by the Bultmann school.

The committee then considered a list of Old Testament topics for research compiled by the Librarian of Tyndale House, Alan Millard. Heading his list was the significance of Ugarit for Old Testament studies: the evaluation of the linguistic, social and archaeological data. The book of Jonah required a large-scale study of linguistic, literary, historical and theological aspects. Then there was a need for a study of 'myth', the purpose of ancient myths and their place if any in the Old Testament, along with a similar study of ancient ideas about 'history'. Careful and basic study was needed on kingship, covenant, Hebrew law (no thor-ough recent study existed), and on the significance of the Dead Sea Scrolls. Probably the most important topic in the next few years, he believed, would be the study of literary methods and styles. Finding how ancient people wrote and edited books should lead to a revision of theories about the composition of Old Testament books from the Pentateuch all the way through. Finally, there was the Aramaic background of the New Testament. The committee agreed that thorough commentaries on the Hebrew text of the Old Testament were of primary importance and should be initiated.

But it was B. M. Harris, not one of the academics, who pointed out the discrepancy between the projects recommended by the committee and the theses actually produced at Tyndale House.

With a gross shortage of men [sic], he questioned whether they were making the best use of the talent available. Should they use their money differently? Should they perhaps send students to do research under selected supervisors or provide research assistants for senior scholars?

This led to further discussion of grants, grantees and finance. It was agreed that the present form of the BRC, including both businessmen and academics, was not a good structure, and at Mr Harris's proposal, it was agreed to alter the committee structure yet again. The BRC would be an academic body, and it should be partnered by a Finance Committee set up by the IVF's Business Advisory Committee. The BRC would present an annual budget to the Finance Committee, which would then allocate funds and indicate the money available over a longer period of three to five years. The Finance Committee would be responsible for the fabric of the House, and the two committees would meet together every two or three years or when major developments were in view. After some further discussion it was agreed that the BRC and the Tyndale Fellowship Committee should remain separate. Mr K. A. Kitchen and the Revd Dr I. H. Marshall were to be invited to join the BRC.

The library and the fellowship

Alan Millard as Librarian

The October meetings of the BRC at Tyndale House now became the annual occasion for meeting staff and grantees. In his first report in October 1964 Alan Millard reported that 186 books, including 41 second-hand, had been bought since he had come in January, at an average cost of thirty shillings each.[5] Another sixty had been received by gift or exchange. The number of religious books published in Britain each year was 1,470, but this included many not relevant to a research library. The present allocation for

---

5. Thirty shillings became £1.50 when the decimal currency was introduced in 1971.

library purchases was therefore adequate, provided prices did not rise too much. The recataloguing of the library following the simplified scheme devised by Dr Morris had been completed and, for the first time, there was a complete subject catalogue. (Thanks were expressed to the typist, Miss Plumbridge, for her persistent work, assisted by Mr Snook.) It was hoped to prepare a periodicals' subject index soon.

In October 1965, the Warden reported that twenty men were in residence, of whom twelve were studying theological subjects. In 1966 there were eighteen residents, leaving two vacant rooms, but this was only because of late cancellations. Eleven of these were engaged in various branches of theology, and there were several non-resident regular users of the library engaged in biblical research for higher degrees. That same October Alan Millard had reported a greater use of the library, and the reports over the next four years indicate a steady increase in demand. Some indication of the quality of scholarship being nurtured in the library is given by listing the occupants of the first six desks in the library in 1965–66: Alan Millard, the Librarian (later to be Rankin Professor of Hebrew at Liverpool); Harold Dressler (a German Old Testament and Ugaritic scholar who later taught at Regent College, Vancouver); David Catchpole (later Professor of Theology at Exeter after some time at Lancaster); R. T. France (later Principal of Wycliffe Hall, Oxford); James Dunn (later J. B. Lightfoot Professor of Theology at Durham); and Graham Stanton (later Professor of New Testament at King's College London and Lady Margaret Professor of Divinity at Cambridge).[6]

In 1967,[7] Millard reported that there were 12,000 volumes in the library, with an annual intake of around 350. Eighty-eight periodicals were received. There was an average of six readers *per diem* in addition to the Librarian and the Tyndale House residents. In the early part of 1967, the library had been almost full much of the time and the number of books in use numbered 250 per month. The

---

6. From a recollection of R. T. France in a letter of 21 January 2004.

7. From 1967, the annual written reports of the Warden and Librarian were incorporated in the BRC Minute Book.

Warden's report commented that most of the postgraduate research at the House was being done by non-residents: J. D. G. Dunn, R. Banks, G. Stanton, H. Hoehner, S. Travis, Dr R. N. Longenecker, and J. W. Mackay. Six postgraduate degrees had been completed in 1966–67 by those associated with the House: the Librarian himself, R. T. France, E. M. B. Green, P. Richardson, W. Stott and C. N. Hillyer. Four former residents or grantees had been appointed to academic posts: D. Catchpole, T. C. Mitchell, A. F. Walls and H. Willmer.[8]

Annually the House was reported to be generally full with all or most rooms taken, and in addition there were two flats for married students at 35 Eltisley Avenue. There was a drop in the number of residents in 1969–70, but that was offset by a fuller use of the House in vacations. Applications for residence in 1970–71 exceeded capacity, so that a waiting list had become necessary. The number of book purchases had dropped to 237 by this time, and the Librarian commented that constantly rising prices raised the question of the library's income. The use of the library by non-residents steadily increased. In 1968, Alan Millard reported that twenty Readers' Tickets had been issued, but by 1970 that had risen to thirty-five. The growth naturally presented problems – the problem of finance and the problem of pressure on space.

Finance

At the beginning of F. D. Kidner's service as Warden, the BRC demonstrated its vision of the future. Finances had now increased (it noted in a meeting on 17 April 1965), the library was expanding, and a periodicals room and a research room would be needed. The committee agreed to draft a plan for development over the next ten years and send it to the chairman of the IVF Trust for

8. At the meeting in 1967, thanks were expressed by Professor Bruce to the Domestic Bursar, Miss P. J. Allen, as she prepared to depart for Washington, DC, for her outstanding service over nearly ten years. She was succeeded by Miss J. M. Paterson, formerly a missionary in Nigeria with the Sudan United Mission.

comment. They envisaged two research fellowships of senior lecturer status and a senior fellowship for an established scholar on
sabbatical. They asserted:

> If the House were ever to achieve anything approaching the original aim
> of an 'Institute of Advanced Biblical Studies' where research would be
> regularly done by adequately trained and experienced workers there was
> need for the project to be planned and supported by a committee intent
> on this aim, able to make its own decisions and to budget for the future
> of such a project.

But two years later, they agreed at the Frinton conference that it
was neither practicable nor desirable for Tyndale House to be
financially autonomous. It was immediately after this conference
that they agreed to separate the BRC into an academic BRC and a
Finance Committee.

The BRC's first annual budget to be presented to the Finance
Committee was approved at the first meeting after the Frinton
conference, in May 1967. The total budget came to £3,780
(as compared to £2,430 the previous year), and the major items
were £2,605 for research grants, £940 for the library, and
£235 in the administration of the Tyndale Fellowship. Salaries,
coming direct from IVF, were not included in this. The figures
had not greatly altered by 1970, but it was a matter of concern to
the Librarian that rising prices meant fewer book purchases.
The major part of this expenditure was being borne by IVF,
a student organization, and its graduate supporters; however, it
must be borne in mind that this was offset by donations from John
Laing and others sent to IVF specifically earmarked for Tyndale
House.

D. J. Wiseman circulated a memo, which was discussed at the
BRC meeting of 2 January 1969, on the desirability of an endowment. The total annual expenditure in running Tyndale House
(including salaries) came to £7,000 per annum. Perhaps, he suggested, they could move gradually by first of all presenting the
need for an endowment for the library (including the employment
of the Librarian), then for research grants, and finally for the other
salaries. During 1969 an unsuccessful appeal was made to an

American foundation, and in January 1970 the matter was back on the agenda. The committee reaffirmed its belief that a fund should be established with the aim of making the minimum recurrent call on IVF funds. Since some potential benefactors were limited to educational projects, it would be beneficial to set up a sub-trust within the IVF (which had been set up originally, they noted, solely for the benefit of Tyndale House).

Building plans

The problem of the pressure on space due to the greater number of readers and married researchers was also a challenge. In January 1965 the BRC had considered plans drawn up by John Laing's architect to turn the upper floors of Tyndale House into flats for married students. But it was thought best not to introduce family life into the House and so the flats in Eltisley Avenue were procured. By the end of 1965, it was a plan to extend the library (again drawn up by the architects of Messrs Laing & Co.) which was being considered. Alterations to the Librarian's office plus a room to seat sixty adjacent to the library were in view, at a cost of £10,000. By the following May, two sets of plans were on view; the room had been extended to accommodate seventy-five, apparently a two-storey octagon. The committee wanted the stairway to be at its north-east corner, and wanted the architect to add a corridor on the upper storey, giving access from the residential upper floor of the library building. It was felt, however, that it was not the right time to appeal for funds. At the Frinton conference in January 1967, 'Mr John Webster's drawing of an octagonal conference room linked to the south-west end of the library received approval as to general conception.' But the time was not yet. By 1968 it had been decided to go ahead only with the work on the Librarian's office and the improvement of the heating.

The Tyndale Bulletin

The publication of *The Tyndale Bulletin* as a serious academic journal was a significant step forward. In January 1945, the IVF publication *Theological Notes*, edited and largely written by A. M. Stibbs and F. F. Bruce, had been renamed *The Tyndale Bulletin*,

but in 1948 it had been incorporated in *The Christian Graduate*.[9]
In 1956, Andrew Walls had begun the publication of *The Tyndale
House Bulletin*, and in April 1965 (as we have seen)[10] it had
been decided that the time had come to replace this with an
annual scholarly publication of 160 pages. This would include
Tyndale Lectures and papers from study groups and a limited
number of review articles. The Librarian, Alan Millard, would
be the editor and the editorial board would be Bruce, Martin,
Wiseman and Kidner. Ronald Inchley, the IVF publications
secretary, reported to the TFC on cooperation from the Literature
Committee. It was not thought that the new journal would clash
with *The Evangelical Quarterly*, which had a different readership,
and it was intended that it would rank with the best of technical
journals.

The first issue of the new *Tyndale Bulletin* consequently appeared in July 1965 and a thousand copies were printed, to be sold
at twenty-five shillings each.[11] An annual subscription of thirty
shillings would procure the *Bulletin* and membership of the
Tyndale Fellowship, but membership alone would be ten shillings.
Despite the name change from *The Tyndale House Bulletin* to *The
Tyndale Bulletin*, the numbering continued, so that the 1966 issue
was 'No. 17'.[12] In its brightly coloured cover, it included articles by
D. A. Hubbard, S. S. Smalley, K. A. Kitchen, R. A. Ward, F. D.
Kidner, A. R. Millard and S. G. Taylor. News of members and
of members' publications was transferred to the Members' Letter,
sent out by the TF secretary. In January 1969, the Tyndale
Fellowship Committee received a report of circulation. In 1966,
640 copies had been sold, 386 in 1967 and 291 in 1968. But standing orders were increasing.

9. See above, pages 55 and 89.
10. See above, pages 91 and 128.
11. Twenty-five shillings became £1.25 when the decimal currency was
    introduced.
12. The *Tyndale House Bulletin* had been published, usually twice yearly, from
    1956 to 1965, each issue being numbered separately up to 1961 (Nos 1 to
    7–8), and thereafter numbered together as one per year (Nos 9–16).

The visit of Dr Bruce Metzger

By the end of the 1960s, there were some clear signs that the long-term strategy of reviving biblical scholarship among Evangelicals at the highest and most exacting level was just beginning to bear fruit. The Warden's report to the BRC for 1968–69 told of a full complement of residents, and of research at the House by a group of very able young scholars. These included R. E. Davies, M. J. Harris, R. P. Gordon (who held the Tyrwhitt Hebrew Scholarship for 1969 and had taken the Mason Hebrew Prize), A. J. M. Wedderburn and R. T. France. The Librarian, along with W. G. Lambert, had had *Atra-hasis: The Babylonian Story of the Flood* published by the Clarendon Press.

One notable event in 1969 was the visit of Bruce M. Metzger, Professor of New Testament Language and Literature at Princeton Theological Seminary, as scholar-in-residence. Metzger, one of the editors of the United Bible Societies edition of the Greek New Testament, stayed at the House in the latter part of 1969. He delivered two lectures (chaired by F. F. Bruce) in the Divinity School at the university: 'Methods and Presuppositions in Biblical Research' and 'Historicity in the Gospels'. This was a notable development, since, at the end of the 1960s, Evangelical scholarship (despite the contribution of F. F. Bruce and others) was still somewhat suspect in the academic world.

There were both historical and intellectual reasons for this suspicion. Historically, Evangelicalism had suffered intellectual eclipse after the death of the turn-of-the-century generation – Moule, Denney, Orr, Forsyth and others – and had been associated with the obscurantist Fundamentalism in America. The IVF in particular had moved in a more conservative direction, compared with the SCM, and had been associated with the Graham 'crusades'. And intellectually, the world of scholarship still held to the nineteenth-century idea of 'objectivity', which seemed to many to be incompatible with a stated confessional position. Although Christian Dogmatics had university status in continental universities and in Scotland, Systematic Theology in the English universities more often took the form of philosophical theology or philosophy of religion (or the historical study of Patristics), in which it was easier to pretend to some kind of neutral, supposedly

'objective', scholarly position. To many English biblical scholars
therefore, the whole project of a biblical research library funded
by a student evangelistic movement seemed intellectually suspect.
Their presuppositions about scholarly objectivity made it very
difficult for some to accept the claim of Martin or Bruce (despite
their erudition) to be neutral scholars, simply recounting what the
New Testament documents said and arguing for their historical
reliability. Metzger's visit possibly helped to produce the first chink
in the armour of the supposedly neutral mindset of 'modernity'.
Here was another first-class scholar associated with Tyndale
House who was also committed to 'conservative' critical conclusions and a confessional, Evangelical position.

Alan Stibbs and the new committee

The late 1960s also saw the development of the Tyndale
Fellowship as somewhat more distinct from Tyndale House, for
when the Tyndale Fellowship Committee was constituted in 1961
as a distinct sub-committee of the BRC, it was in fact a new committee. Since the founding of the Fellowship when Tyndale House
was bought in 1944, the BRC had in fact been the committee
which ran the Tyndale Fellowship and was sometimes known as
the Tyndale Fellowship Committee. For a brief time under Martyn
Lloyd-Jones's chairmanship in the early 1950s, a distinct Biblical
Research Committee had been created as a sub-committee of
what was then called the Tyndale Fellowship Committee. That
structure seemed to indicate that the more specialized work of
biblical research was a sectional concern within the broader theological interests of the Fellowship. The ending of that two-tier
structure was part of the reassertion of the priority of biblical
research at the beginning of D. J. Wiseman's years in the chair. But
the new two-tier structure of 1961 made the Tyndale Fellowship
Committee a sub-committee of the more specialized committee
of senior academics (also usually including businessmen) whose
primary concern was the promotion of biblical research. The
wider theological concerns were largely removed to the province
of the IVF Graduates' Fellowship, and the Tyndale Fellowship
Committee was to be concerned largely with the Tyndale Lectures
and study groups. Although the membership of this new TFC was

identical with the previous BRC, it had in fact been turned into a new subordinate committee.

When Douglas Johnson resigned as secretary of both, the Warden became secretary of the BRC and Alan Millard acted as secretary *pro tem* at the January 1966 meeting of the TFC. R. T. France was already being approached for the job under a new arrangement which would link the TF secretary more closely to Tyndale House. The idea, adopted by the BRC in October 1965, was that a research student receiving a Tyndale grant should be appointed as TF secretary for three years and paid for his part-time work of administering the TF from an office in the House. R. T. France was already receiving a grant and had been one of the grantees interviewed by the BRC earlier in the day, and the Warden was asked to approach him. By January 1966, he had indicated that although his thesis was virtually completed, he would combine the position with his curacy at St Matthews, Cambridge, but it was the end of September before he was able to begin, devoting one day per week to his duties. He was welcomed to the Tyndale Fellowship Committee when they met on 27 September.

The same meeting received a letter from Howard Marshall calling (unsuccessfully) for the reinstatement of the former Church History Study Group as part of the Tyndale Fellowship; news of the publication of Kenneth Kitchen's *Ancient Orient and the Old Testament*; and a proposal for a revised edition of *The New Bible Commentary*.

In November 1967, Dick France published the first regular members' letter with information gathered from 'green forms' returned since July which, he hoped, would be of value simply for interest, for prayer and to enable members to discover who was working on kindred subjects. He listed nine new members elected during the year, including P. C. Craigie, Ward Gasque and G. J. Wenham. Under appointments he included G. L. Carey's appointment to Oak Hill College, D. R. Catchpole's to Clifton College, A. Morgan Derham to be General Secretary of the Evangelical Alliance, A. F. Walls to lecture in Church History at Aberdeen and H. Willmer at Leeds. Degrees included A. R. Millard's MPhil on the Atrahasis epic, E. M. B. Green's Cambridge BD for his book *The Meaning of Salvation*, H. H. Rowdon's PhD on the

origins of the Plymouth Brethren, and W. Stott's DPhil on the
origins of the Christian Sunday. Prof. D. J. Wiseman had been
elected a Fellow of the British Academy. Publications were listed
for six members, and current research projects for twenty-one, all
in Old Testament. When Members' Newsletter No. 2 came out
the following May, New Testament and Biblical Theology publications and research projects were listed. Altogether, these first
two newsletters listed twenty books and twenty-eight articles
published by Tyndale Fellowship members. The books included
J. W. Wenham's *The Elements of New Testament Greek* (Cambridge
University Press, 1965), a work which made him as well known
among theology students as (if not better known than) any other
member of the Fellowship!

In January 1967, the TFC noted that A. F. Walls was to chair the
re-formed History Group, assisted by D. F. Wright and H. H.
Rowdon. An Ethics study group had been proposed by Oliver
Barclay, and by May it was reported that it had been formed, also
under the Graduates' Fellowship, in cooperation with Latimer
House. It was to be chaired by J. I. Packer with R. T. France as
secretary. New members received into the Fellowship during the
year included Earle Ellis, Graham Stanton, D. J. A. Clines, Anthony
Thiselton, J. P. Kane and Bruce Milne. A request was reported
from the TSF for more books on the Old Testament and more
commentaries on the Greek text of the New. The New Testament
Study Group proposed a series of such commentaries when it
met in July, with Matthew and Ephesians as priorities. The Old
Testament group felt that they were already heavily committed to
the revision of the New Bible Commentary and the Tyndale
Commentary series.

In January 1968, Howard Marshall made another attempt to
promote Church History, proposing that the Tyndale Historical
Theology Lecture should be revived, but the TFC referred the proposal to the History Group of the Graduates' Fellowship. But
disquiet was expressed about the increasing separation of the
Fellowship's activities into the constituent groups. An occasional
meeting of the Fellowship as a whole would be desirable, and plans
should be made for such a meeting in London in January 1969,
when Carl Henry would be in the country. The meeting of May

1968 considered possible publications. A book of documents from New Testament times was under production. But a book on Christology was needed with reference to Bishop Robinson's *Honest to God*, along with books on revelation and communications, the Ten Commandments, the doctrine of 'man', hermeneutics, 'infallibility' (to 'lay the dust on this particular term'), and the doctrine of God. Additionally, responses were needed to Jürgen Moltmann's *Theology of Hope* and Rordorf's *Sunday*. In the September meeting, Oliver Barclay reported that the Theological Studies Group of the Graduates' Fellowship was about to be disbanded, and David Payne reported that there was a group planning to organize in Belfast on the model of the Scottish Tyndale Fellowship. The committee recommended, however, that it should *not* be called the 'Tyndale Fellowship'. Also in September, previous caution about accepting overseas members was formulated into a policy that members would be elected from outside the British Isles only when there was reason to hope that they would attend study groups from time to time. During the year new members included David Wenham and S. H. Travis.

1969 began with the winter meeting for the Tyndale Fellowship as a whole. It was held at the Whitefield Memorial Church Hall in London on 3 January and addressed by Dr Carl Henry. The committee met that morning and expected forty to fifty to attend in the afternoon. They heard of a conference for sixth-formers who might be interested in biblical research addressed by J. P. Kane, A. R. Millard, M. E. J. Richardson and R. P. Martin. They also received a report on the circulation of *The Tyndale Bulletin*[13] and on other publications. The Tyndale Commentaries on Deuteronomy, Ezekiel and Revelation were nearing publication, and an author had still to be found for the last New Testament commentary, on Luke. A. F. Walls resigned from the committee in January in the light of his distance from London and was replaced by D. J. A. Clines. A new secretary was also needed, since Dr France was about to leave to become a lecturer in Religious Studies at the Ife University in Nigeria, and Gordon Wenham accepted the post,

---

13. See above, page 136.

combining it with research at Tyndale House. Before he left, however, Dick France began a purge of the membership. Membership stood at 201, but only 100 had paid their subscriptions in 1968. There were still six known life members, and altogether fifty-eight members would be liable to termination.[14] Among the new members elected during 1969 were Donald Hagner, Peter T. O'Brien and Martin J. Selman.

Seventeen academic appointments were listed in the two Members' Newsletters that year, including three new principals: E. M. B. Green to the London College of Divinity, G. W. Grogan to the Bible Training Institute, Glasgow, and J. I. Packer to Tyndale Hall, Bristol. The books written by Tyndale Fellowship members and published during the year included J. N. D. Anderson's *Christianity: The Witness of History*;[15] I. H. Marshall's PhD thesis, *Kept by the Power of God*,[16] A. Skevington Wood's biographies of Martin Luther (*Captive to the Word*) and John Wesley (*The Burning Heart*),[17] John Stott's *One People: Clergy and Laity in God's Church*[18] and two Tyndale Commentaries, L. L. Morris on Revelation and J. B. Taylor on Ezekiel.

At the September meeting, Gordon Wenham, Alan Millard and Derek Kidner were asked to draw up a statement of purpose for the Tyndale Lectures. They were to include the following points: (1) that the lectures must be compatible with the IVF Basis of Faith; (2) that they must be of the highest academic quality and

---

14. This figure of 201 is puzzling in view of the fact that at the Waverley Hotel conference in 1961, a membership of 346 had been reported, 299 of these in the British Isles (see above, pages 111f.). But possibly this was the figure *after* the purge.

15. J. N. D. Anderson, *Christianity: The Witness of History: A Lawyer's Approach* (London: Tyndale Press, 1969).

16. I. Howard Marshall, *Kept by the Power of God: A Study of Perseverance and Falling Away* (London: Epworth, 1969).

17. A. Skevington Wood, *Captive to the Word* (Exeter: Paternoster, 1969), and *The Burning Heart: John Wesley – Evangelist* (Exeter: Paternoster, 1967).

18. John R. W. Stott, *One People: Clergy and Laity in God's Church* (London: Falcon, 1971).

must be addressed to scholars working in the field; and (3) that they must be of general interest in the theological world.

On 2 January 1970 A. M. Stibbs chaired his last meeting of the Tyndale Fellowship Committee and announced his resignation. Just over eighteen months later, the committee gave thanks for his life and work, along with the life and work of Dr B. F. C. Atkinson.

The 1960s had seen a significant cultural change. The increasing influence of the mass media and 'pop' culture and, above all, of what was called the 'permissive society', was challenging what was seen as the authoritarian Christian 'Establishment'. The changing mood was led by the revival of biting satire and a reaction against the culture of deference toward those in authority in church and state. Legislation on gambling, divorce, homosexuality, censorship, abortion and Sunday observance was sweeping away what had been a Christian consensus in the nation.

It was certainly true that there had been a considerable Evangelical resurgence. The National Evangelical Anglican Congress at Keele in April, 1967, when a thousand delegates led by John Stott participated in hammering out an agreed statement, was an outstanding success. Stott himself described it as 'a landmark, a watershed'.[19] With no compromise on the gospel or the authority of Scripture, the congress was notable for a new Evangelical confidence and vision. Prompted by Prof. Norman Anderson, the delegates embraced a new Evangelical concern for involvement in social issues. But meanwhile the growth in many Evangelical churches was far outweighed by the decline in total church membership and attendance. Further, the unity of the growing Evangelical movement had been shaken by the public appeal made by Martyn Lloyd-Jones for Evangelicals to leave 'mixed' denominations. His growing concern with a drift to Rome which he saw in the ecumenical movement led to his dramatic appeal in an address to the Second National Assembly of Evangelicals held by the Evangelical Alliance in the Methodist Central Hall in Westminster in October 1966. The drama of the occasion was heightened

19. Timothy Dudley-Smith, *John Stott: A Global Ministry* (Leicester: IVP, 2001), 97.

when John Stott, as chairman, rose to give a postscript expressing his profound disagreement. Lloyd-Jones's appeal failed, and
the next year the formation, on the one hand, of the new British
Evangelical Council by those sympathetic to the Doctor and
the success, on the other, of the Keele Congress of Evangelical
Anglicans seemed to cement the division.[20] The annual Puritan
Conference, which had begun in 1950 as a study group of the
Tyndale Fellowship and which met at Westminster Chapel, was a
casualty of the newly divisive atmosphere. James Packer not only
was an Anglican but had participated in the Anglican–Methodist
Unity Commission and had published *Growing into Union* in 1970
along with Colin Buchanan and two Anglo-Catholics, E. L. Mascall
and Graham Leonard. Lloyd-Jones terminated the Puritan
Conferences in 1969 and started the 'Westminster Conference' in
1971, excluding Packer and all those from 'mixed' denominations
from the committee and from participation.[21]

In the context of both church and nation, therefore, the role of
Tyndale House and Fellowship at the end of the 1960s was of
increasing significance. These were two of the institutions which

---

20. For the drama and significance of the event at the National Assembly of
    Evangelicals, cf. David W. Bebbington, *Evangelicalism in Modern Britain:
    A History from the 1730s to the 1980s* (London: Unwin Hyman, 1989), 267; Iain
    H. Murray, *David Martyn Lloyd-Jones: The Fight of Faith 1939–1981*
    (Edinburgh: Banner of Truth, 1990), 522ff.; Oliver Barclay, *Evangelicalism
    in Britain, 1935–1995* (Leicester: IVP, 1997), 83; John Brencher, *Martyn Lloyd-
    Jones (1899–1981) and Twentieth-century Evangelicalism* (Carlisle: Paternoster,
    2003), 92–106; and Dudley-Smith, *John Stott*, 65–71. The controversy over
    Lloyd-Jones's address continues: cf. Iain H. Murray, *Evangelicalism Divided:
    A Record of Crucial Change in the Years 1950 to 2000* (Edinburgh: Banner of
    Truth, 2000); also David F. Wright's review article of Murray in *Reformation
    and Revival*, 10.2 (spring, 2001), 121–136, Murray's response, 'Who is
    Misrepresenting Lloyd-Jones?' *Evangelicals Now* (November, 2001), 21,
    and David F. Wright's letter to the editor, '1966 and All That', *Evangelicals
    Now* (December, 2001), 23.
21. See Alister McGrath, *J. I. Packer: A Biography* (Grand Rapids: Baker, 1997),
    154–161; and Brencher, *Martyn Lloyd-Jones*, 114.

embodied continuing Evangelical cooperation and, as the research arm of what was now UCCF, the Universities and Colleges Christian Fellowship, they had the potential to strengthen and reinvigorate Evangelical thought at a time of declining Christian influence in society at large.

6. PROGRESS

Wiseman, Kidner and Millard, 1970–78

By 1970, the founding generation had largely given way to their successors. G. T. Manley, who belonged to an even earlier generation, had died in 1961. A. M. Stibbs retired from the chairmanship of the Tyndale Fellowship Committee in 1970 and died the next year. Martyn Lloyd-Jones had retired from Westminster Chapel in 1968 and no longer had any active involvement in the Tyndale Fellowship. Douglas Johnson had retired as General Secretary of IVF in 1965, and W. J. Martin had retired from his post at the University of Liverpool in 1970. F. F. Bruce, younger than all of these, became a Fellow of the British Academy in 1973 and was to be Rylands Professor of Biblical Criticism at Manchester until his retirement in 1978. There he continued to mentor a generation of Evangelical biblical scholars to staff the universities, colleges and seminaries of the English-speaking world, but he was no longer quite so active in Tyndale Fellowship activities. His main contribution to Tyndale House had been in its founding while he was chairman of the BRC, and he had chaired the New Testament Study Group until 1974, but his advice was still sought. Douglas Johnson was still attending

the BRC meetings and, along with Martin and Bruce, could inter-
vene decisively. Donald Wiseman, John Wenham and Derek
Kidner represented continuity between the founding fathers and
the new generation of younger scholars now appearing. John
Wenham had the longest involvement, having been the student
leader of the Theological Colleges' Prayer Fellowship at the initi-
ation of the BRC in 1938, but he now played more of a
background role.

Gordon Wenham, the son of John Wenham, succeeded Dick
France as secretary of the Tyndale Fellowship Committee in
September 1969 and served until taking up a post at Queen's
University, Belfast, in the summer of 1970. He was succeeded by
Donald F. Murray, who handed on the job to H. G. M. Williamson
in 1971 when he was appointed to Southampton.[1] J. B. Taylor succeeded A. M. Stibbs as chairman of the TFC, but made it clear
that his appointment was temporary and to be reviewed in two
years. So the early 1970s saw a quick succession of officers in the
Fellowship. Alan Millard provided stability by serving for fourteen
years as TF chairman when he succeeded J. B. Taylor in 1972,
but the rapid turnover in TF secretaries continued while the post
was linked to duties at Tyndale House and held by a research
student.

Theology again

A major development in the work of the Fellowship came about
largely at the initiative of Oliver Barclay, who had succeeded
Douglas Johnson as General Secretary of IVF in 1965. The relationship between Biblical Studies and Theology was perhaps the
underlying question in a long discussion in the TF committee about
the Tyndale Lectures and the Doctrinal Basis in September 1970.
Dr Barclay's initiative came at the meeting in May 1971, when he
raised the question of the need for greater strategic planning and
coordination of topics taken up by the TF study groups. Should
these not be more closely related to the burning issues of the day

---

1. Professor Bruce commented that this was the twentieth appointment in
   Biblical Studies of a member of the Tyndale Fellowship.

and to doctrines neglected in current debate? The implication was that the mission of the IVF demanded not only long-term scholarly biblical research, but also research into the more immediate issues addressed by theology and ethics. He was asked to present a paper at the next meeting in September.

The paper began with the role of the Tyndale Fellowship within IVF as a whole. The TF, he argued, should deal with a wider range of theological discussion than at present. In view of the movement in the universities to concentrate more on Religious Studies, he regretted that the TF did not give more of a lead and assistance in matters of doctrine, in apologetics and in applied theology. If the TF was not to be left out on a limb, it should consider broadening its front. After a long discussion, it was agreed to suggest to the IVF Council that another part-time secretary should be appointed to foster further study groups. By January 1972, A. N. S. Lane had been suggested for appointment as part-time secretary to organize study groups in fields such as missiology, ethics, comparative religion and the study of particular doctrines.

At the same meeting in January 1972 Graham Stanton introduced a discussion on policy governing material published by the Tyndale Press. Possibly controversial material was often not offered for publication by the study groups because of a fear that it would be rejected for doctrinal reasons. He asked whether the Tyndale Press (the imprint for academic works published by Inter-Varsity, which had been introduced in 1951)[2] could broaden its appeal to the academic world. Ronald Inchley, welcoming the discussion, responded on behalf of IVF publications, but he put the point that in view of its close affiliation with IVF, the Tyndale Press could not publish works whose whole approach challenged the doctrinal basis. After a full and open discussion of the issues, it was agreed that the General Secretary, Dr Barclay, should be asked to bring all interested parties together to discuss the issue in depth. Clearly further thinking had to be done about the relationship between a confessional theological

---

2. Above, page 68.

position and (in F. F. Bruce's phrase) 'unfettered studies and research'.[3]

At the same meeting in which Alan Millard was elected chairman of the TF committee in September 1972, the committee received a report from Tony Lane that he accepted appointment as organizing secretary of the Theology Project and had a list of fifty names from which he hoped to establish five study groups: one on faith and reason, one on ethics and three on doctrine. James Packer, who had resumed the chairmanship of the Biblical Theology Study Group from Geoffrey Grogan, then introduced a discussion about the group's future. It was rather different from the other study groups in that it was attended by few academics (there were no university posts in Britain in Biblical Theology), it had few regular attenders and its viability was called in question by Mr Lane's appointment. He proposed that it should either aim to keep clergymen informed, or perhaps drop out of the Tyndale Fellowship altogether and amalgamate with the theological studies groups of the Graduates' Fellowship. After extended discussion, it was agreed that the TF could not neglect its responsibilities in this area but that the group could plan to be more wide-ranging, to draw more than the other groups on non-members.

It was clear that, no matter how much some might want to narrow the aim of the IVF research department by concentrating resources on the foundational questions of Biblical Studies, the need for theological work in order to speak to the immediate issues arising in mission to the contemporary world just would not go away! As General Secretary of IVF/UCCF,[4] Oliver Barclay was

---

3. See the 'General Principles Governing Research Activity' drawn up by Bruce, Johnson and Stephens-Hodge in 1944 (above, Chapter 2, 'Plans and policies', pages 49–52).

4. IVF (Inter-Varsity Fellowship) had been renamed UCCF (Universities and Colleges Christian Fellowship) in 1975 to reflect the growing number of affiliated Christian Unions in the colleges of higher education. See Douglas Johnson, *Contending for the Faith: A History of the Evangelical Movement in the Universities and Colleges* (Leicester: IVP, 1979), 338f. The familiar 'IVF' continued in popular use for a time.

deeply aware of the demands of mission in the student world. But
the issue could be seen from the other side. The long-term strategy was not just to produce work of immediate value, but to
concentrate scarce resources on developing a school of first-class
biblical scholars who could present the often neglected position
that the Christian faith was in fact built upon historically reliable
documents. Such a generation of biblical scholars, once established on the grounds of their academic excellence in the
universities, could have a deep and lasting long-term effect upon
the church and provide a solid basis for mission to 'thinking
people' and thus turn the anti-Christian tide in the whole culture.
In the vision of W. J. Martin and others, that long-term goal must
not be sacrificed for short-term gain.

The threat from inflation

While the TF committee was re-examining the strategy for
effective and useful research and thinking about the relationship
between theology and scholarship, the BRC was beginning to face
new financial problems at Tyndale House. These were a consequence of the severe inflation in the British economy which began
in the early 1970s and continued throughout the decade, under
both the Conservative government of Edward Heath and the
Labour administrations of Wilson and Callaghan.

The decade began well. The Warden's report for 1969–70
noted that applications for the forthcoming academic year
exceeded capacity, making a waiting list necessary for the first
time in many years. He noted that several young scholars associated with the House had been appointed to academic posts:
R. T. France to Ife University in Nigeria, Robert Gordon to
Glasgow University, Graham Stanton temporarily to Cambridge
and then to King's College London, Stephen Travis to the
London College of Divinity and Gordon Wenham to Queen's
University, Belfast. But in his last Librarian's report, Alan Millard
drew attention to the way in which the rise in book prices was
affecting accessions to the library. In September 1970 he was succeeded as Librarian by C. N. Hillyer, and the following January,
having taken up his post at the University of Liverpool, he was
elected to the BRC.

By June 1971, the increasing inflation occasioned a presentation of the major problems facing the House from the chairman, Professor Wiseman. Tyndale House was becoming known as a distinctive Evangelical voice in the academic world and the most likely source of influential teachers in the next generation. In view of the rising costs, however, he believed that the committee were forced to consider several options: (1) an increased subsidy from IVF; (2) the subsidy being held at the present level, which would mean retrenchment; (3) the supplementing of the subsidy from other sources; and (4) securing support entirely from other sources.

In the subsequent discussion, other possibilities were considered. The first was dispersal: the closure of the House and library, sending students wherever they would best be taught. Against this were the value of fellowship and discussion, the library's service to members of the Tyndale Fellowship, and the importance of a known headquarters. Closure, it was said, would destroy a symbol which was internationally respected and the 'brain' of the IVF. The second possibility was a merger, but this was impracticable since there were no institutions with similar aims. The third possibility was a non-residential library, but it was residence which made full use of the library possible. It was agreed that the third of the original options, supplementing income from new sources, was the best course to pursue, and Douglas Johnson advocated the appointment of a fund-raising officer or sub-committee. He also suggested approaching Christian institutions abroad to endow scholarships at Tyndale House, but the chairman reported that this had been tried, so far with no success.

Meanwhile the daily life of the House continued, and in his report for 1971–72, Derek Kidner commented on the first-class service given by the secretary, Miss Jean Plumbridge, and informed the committee that the Domestic Bursar, Mrs Watson, would retire in May 1972, to be succeeded in September by Miss Brenda Heathcote. The Librarian reported the accession of 452 new books and that 114 periodicals were on order. The number of reader's tickets had risen from 21 to 35, and borrowings had risen by 60% in two years.

The Doctrinal Basis and academic freedom

The BRC and TFC began to hold joint meetings in 1972. The first 'Extraordinary Meeting' was in July 1972, when Howard Marshall proposed the amalgamation of the two committees. Douglas Johnson was opposed to this, but it was agreed (presumably as a compromise) that the two committees should meet together annually each January to discuss strategy for biblical research. This meeting also identified some priorities in Old Testament study (literary styles and methods; myth; covenant and law) and in New Testament study (the historicity of Acts; the sayings of Jesus with reference to Aramaic; and Christology). Dr Barclay suggested that Evangelicals should be making the running in Biblical Theology, but the academic world of Theology was of course by this time deeply influenced by James Barr's swingeing attack on the Biblical Theology movement in *The Semantics of Biblical Language*, published in 1961.

The first of the planned January meetings took place on 3 January 1973 at 39 Bedford Square, with D. J. Wiseman in the chair and H. G. M. Williamson acting as secretary.[5] Donald Guthrie and Tony Lane were welcomed as new members of the TF committee, and the latter reported that the first three of the new study groups – those on doctrine, historical theology and ethics – had met. Some discussion took place on priorities for research, but it was noted that there had been no success in encouraging members of the Fellowship to undertake research in areas felt to be of strategic importance. Discussion highlighted the difficulty of any such policy.

But the major discussion at this meeting was on the issue raised by Dr Graham Stanton in the TF committee; namely, the publications policy and, connected to that, the positions taken in

---

5. Those present included John Baker, Oliver Barclay, David Clines, Donald Guthrie, Norman Hillyer, Frank Houlding, Ronald Inchley, Douglas Johnson, Derek Kidner, Kenneth Kitchen, Sir Kirby Laing, Tony Lane, Howard Marshall, Alan Millard, David Payne, John Roberts and Graham Stanton. Apologies were received from F. F. Bruce, David Gooding, James Packer, John Taylor and David Wenham.

contributions made to study groups. There had been some reaction to contributions at study groups the previous summer which seemed inconsistent with the distinctive position of the TF, and a memorandum drawn up by Dr Marshall was distributed for discussion.

A MEMORANDUM TO T.F. CONTRIBUTORS

Readers of papers at the Study Groups may be glad to have some clarification of the Tyndale Fellowship's attitude to academic freedom. Perhaps it is best seen against the background of the professional societies which have no doctrinal tests, and which provide a forum for scholars of a great variety of views and presuppositions. Happily many of our members belong to such groups, and have good opportunity for debate on those terms. But the T.F. would have no *raison d'être* if it simply duplicated these societies: it exists to do research from an agreed starting-point of conservative evangelical faith, summarized in the Doctrinal Basis of the IVF. In particular, for its doctrine of Scripture it seeks to treat our Lord's attitude and pronouncements on the subject as normative.

Prof. F. F. Bruce pointed out in an article in *EQ* 19 (1947), in the early days of the Fellowship, that whereas some defenders of orthodoxy prescribe the conclusions that ought to be reached, we are content to define our premises, leaving each other free to state whatever can be shown to follow from them. It is, we believe, a first academic virtue to know and declare one's assumptions (to pretend that one has none is a form of obscurantism) and a second virtue to expose one's reasoning and conclusions to rigorous criticism. In the Study Groups we reckon to take the total authority of Scripture for granted, but nothing else; and would therefore hope to be adventurous but not arrogant; above all, to be accurate students of the Word.

This is not everyone's position, and it is not our wish to question the good faith of those who differ from us. But it is the position of the Tyndale Fellowship, and we count on those who contribute to our discussions to build their arguments on this foundation.

Despite some dissent on the joint committee, it was agreed to distribute the memo to study-group contributors. As far as publications were concerned, Ronald Inchley pointed out that Tyndale Press and what was now Inter-Varsity Press could only have the same policy, since it was the same publisher. Oliver Barclay gave some leeway, however, by pointing out that there was a difference between discussion and publication, and that issues could be raised and positions taken for the sake of discussion in study groups which might not, however, be appropriate in publications. Apparently not everyone at the meeting was fully convinced, but after further discussion it was evident that there was not sufficient support to recommend a change of policy.

Inflation and the viability of Tyndale House

In 1973, Norman Hillyer had completed three years as Librarian and revising editor of *The New Bible Dictionary*. He reported to the BRC that 418 books had been purchased in 1972–73 and that pressure on the library facilities continued to increase. Thirty-six readers' tickets had been issued and borrowing had increased by 84% in three years. The subject index begun by Alan Millard[6] continued to make progress, and Mrs Judy Lyon had typed 2,500 cards without charge in appreciation for her American husband's use of the library over the past year. Over the last three years, 5,000 cards had been added to the index. Dr Constant de Wit had been a willing fellow labourer in the August 1972 check of the library's 13,000 books, and the Librarian's son, Mr Philip Hillyer, had skilfully repaired many books during his university vacations.[7] Miss Jean Plumbridge, the secretary, was especially thanked 'for her never-failing wheel-turning behind the scenes'. Presumably this was intended to be a compliment! Norman Hillyer moved from the library to be TF secretary, continuing as revising editor of *The New Bible Dictionary*, and was succeeded as Librarian on 1 September by R. T. France, who had returned from Nigeria. Hugh Williamson, who had been TF secretary, left to pursue studies at the Hebrew University in Jerusalem.

---

6. Above, page 132.

7. A gratifyingly low number of books (seventeen) had been missing, but
   mysterious reappearances on the shelves had reduced the number to six!

Dick France was immediately aware of the financial stringency. He sold 'non-priority' books and duplicates, disposed of non-theological periodicals, invited TF members to sponsor periodicals and added to the exchange arrangements whereby *Tyndale Bulletin* was exchanged for other journals. But the thick stack of index cards requesting the addition of books to the library grew inexorably longer. Selection was painful.

In October 1973, the financial problems at Tyndale House caused by inflation led to a question from the businessmen, the Business Advisory Committee of the IVF: 'How important is it to have a private library for Biblical Research?' Just at the time that thirty years of pioneering seemed to be bearing fruit, the whole existence of Tyndale House was being forced on to the agenda by the economic conditions. A response to this question in the form of a draft memorandum had been prepared before the BRC meeting of 27 October, when only Wiseman, Barclay, Johnson, Houlding and Hillyer were able to be present. They discussed it point by point with the aid of written comments from the absentees (Bruce, Laing, Marshall, Harris, Kitchen, Millard and Roberts) and approved it as their response to the BAC.

They had given careful thought, they said, to the question raised by the Business Advisory Committee, and in Section A of their memorandum, they presented nine points for consideration. It was misleading to call Tyndale House a 'private library', since it was held under trust conditions and open to any qualified reader, and the following advantages of such an institution had to be noted:

1. As a Specialised Collection. The Tyndale Library makes the tools of biblical research highly accessible, perhaps uniquely so. This is a comment often made to us. Elsewhere the relevant material tends to be widely scattered and hard of access, since libraries which serve the whole field even of theology can seldom adequately cover a single area. So a specialist in biblical research may have to seek out his material in a number of different libraries and different universities. These difficulties are likely to increase on account of the current trend away from biblical studies as the backbone of theological courses towards an emphasis on comparative religion, or the sociology or psychology of religion – subjects whose own literature

competes for space and money with that of biblical studies, in the budgets of university and college libraries.

2. As an Evangelical library. It possesses certain scholarly books and periodicals which are hard to come by elsewhere. It would seem a pity to lose the benefit of good work by men of faith whose standpoint may be currently out of favour.

3. As a visible Research Centre. This fact draws the attention of
   (a) Evangelicals to the existence and importance of research; and
   (b) of other theologians to the fact that Evangelical scholarship exists and is seriously pursued. These things would be less obvious if our researchers were dispersed round the universities in ones and twos.

4. As a focus for the Tyndale Fellowship, with its scattered membership. An office scarcely fulfils this function.

5. As a residential library. It offers people the opportunity of doing concentrated study, perhaps for a few days, perhaps for several months, on their own projects. In this way it serves at times not only full-time research workers, but authors, ministers, university teachers, and others, including overseas visitors who want to deepen or extend their reading.

6. As an Information Centre. The Librarian is often able to draw readers' attention to new material related to their subjects and answer correspondents' questions on bibliographies, etc. The Warden receives many enquiries about the possibilities and facilities for doing biblical research.

7. As a Forum. Here readers meet one another and frequently discuss their work at some depth. But it is the Library which draws them together to this centre day after day; and there is special value in the fact that scholars who are at different stages in their careers (from beginners in research to lecturers on sabbatical leave) meet informally and often. One of the ablest of them remarked recently that his oral Ph.D. examination was less searching than many of the tea-time conversations at Tyndale House. He pointed out the stimulus of the theological interest found there, and the attention to Scripture as a unity, not only to its minutiae. He was fervently grateful to have done his research in this context, not in isolation.

8. As an example to Evangelicals in other countries. Conservative scholars in Australia, New Zealand and the USA owe not a little inspiration to it. Also the Biblicum Institute in Uppsala owes more

than a little to this pattern, studied on a special visit to Cambridge by
its founder, and at Tyndale House a file has been opened for enquiries
received from abroad about the possibility of creating similar
institutions. A recent article in *Christianity Today* (XVII/22, 1973),
entitled 'Evangelical Theology: The British Example', was largely the
outcome of its author's visits to Tyndale House.

9. As a witness in Cambridge and internationally. To close down an
institution which has become well-known, not only in Cambridge but
internationally, would be to create an almost unavoidable impression
that Evangelicals have discovered (what those who differ from them
have always maintained) that faith in an infallible Bible cannot coexist
indefinitely with serious scholarship.

Having presented the case for investing scarce resources in
Tyndale House, the memorandum then in Section B formulated
priorities in the light of the current financial difficulties. The library
itself, including book purchases, periodicals, bookbinding and
basic staffing and maintenance of the building, must be the first
priority. Residential accommodation was desirable, but open to re-
examination if minimum accommodation for library users could be
provided more economically. Bursaries came third in importance
and could be cut back if necessary. The Tyndale Fellowship as a
section of the Graduates' Fellowship should be regarded as a legiti-
mate expense for IVF rather than specifically for Tyndale House.

In Section C, responses were given to specific questions raised
by Sir Kirby Laing and Mr B. M. Harris. Sir Kirby had raised the
question of what would happen if the library were in the possession of a university or other library. The committee considered it
unrealistic to think that any university or evangelical body would
undertake to keep a biblical research library of this size and quality
up to date. Mr Harris had raised five questions. First, how far was
the work of the BRC and Tyndale Fellowship tied to a private
library? Rejecting the description 'private library', the committee's
answer was: 'indispensable'. Secondly, to what extent was the
library being used by Evangelicals to further the aims of the BRC?
The Librarian estimated that 90% of the use of the library was by
conservative Evangelicals. Thirdly, were they satisfied that the
money could not be put to better use financing research at various

universities? With the one exception of Dr Barclay, the committee
were so satisfied. Prof. F. F. Bruce had written:

> I can conceive of nothing that would be a greater disservice to this cause
> than the closure or dispersal of the Library . . . Better that the Library
> should never have been founded than that it should at this time of day
> be dismantled. That such a thing should even be contemplated or
> implied would be evidence of the subordinating of long-term strategy to
> short-term tactics.

Dr Marshall added:

> I would rather have the Library than the small number of extra grants
> that could be had in exchange for it . . . I would be strongly opposed to
> any plan that involved the dismantling of the Library and removing this
> permanent centre of Evangelical scholarship.

Fourthly, Mr Harris had asked whether, since the residential
part of the premises would require a subsidy of not less than
£3,000 per annum, it was being occupied by people who contribute most to the aims of the House. The committee replied that
residence was restricted to Evangelicals. Finally: were they satisfied
that the money devoted to bursaries was well spent? Should the
resources not be devoted to those producing books elucidating
Scripture rather than PhD theses? The committee recognized the
value of producing work that was immediately useful, yet their aim
was the long-term one of penetrating the academic world. If necessary, cuts could take place in bursaries.

Addenda were provided by Douglas Johnson, Alan Millard,
W. J. Martin and Derek Kidner. DJ compared the role of research
institutes in other disciplines such as Law, Science and Medicine,
and in industrial firms. Tyndale House was one of the few (almost
unique) *research* libraries in the whole of the British theological
world! W. J. Martin weighed in with two paragraphs in defence of
his brain-child:

> I would be exceedingly sorry to see anything happen to Tyndale House
> and I believe that the leaders of Christian thought all over the western

world would consider its loss a major set-back for evangelical scholarship. It has probably done more to encourage serious scholarship of an acceptable academic standard than any other institution in the world. It has done much to increase the credibility of the conservative approach and we owe it to the many who have benefitted from its facilities that the Evangelical voice is once again clearly heard in the academic market place. If the Christian faith cannot justify itself before those most competent to judge, then all other propaganda of it becomes suspect. We shall fail utterly in our Christian duty if we have nothing to say to thinking men and women. Our commission does not permit us to be selective, therefore, we may not, any more than Paul, by-pass 'Athens' – the academic world. If we do, then all our other propaganda activities will ring hollow, as, I believe, some of our highly publicized broadcasting would do to anyone with the linguistic ability to check results.

Tyndale House has done and could do little in the way of window dressing. But, as Sir John Laing saw so clearly, if industry and science need their 'back-room boys', then the Christian faith needs them too. We cannot and would not use the slick business methods and clever advertising that are not unknown in certain Christian circles. Surely, however, there are men of vision and of faith who see the need of fundamental research in the biblical field, without which the critical questions that arise could not be answered.

In April 1974 the General Secretary wrote to the chairman and secretary of the Biblical Research Committee giving the considered response of the Business Advisory Committee after long and full discussion:

First of all the committee reaffirmed its commitment to the programme of biblical research and made it plain that they had never been in doubt about the importance of this.

Secondly, the committee agreed that your replies had satisfied them that the continuance of the research library was of primary importance under this heading. They also agreed that every effort should be made to provide adequate funds for the maintenance of the research library.

Thirdly, they took note of the fact that the provision of residential facilities and the provision of bursaries 'while desirable and really helpful to the research programme were of a second order of importance.'

The BAC agreed that there was no place for thinking of selling any part of the House or grounds, but thought must be given to reducing costs. Fourthly, they had decided to give the BRC a budget for each year for the whole academic account and would hold the BRC responsible for balancing the books.

Tenants and an Appeal Committee

The IVF Business Advisory Committee had done no more than exercise its responsibility of Christian stewardship to ensure that Tyndale House was giving value for the scarce resources which were being channelled into it. It had to be sure that the biblical research scholars were not simply using up scarce resources on their own pet projects without being aware of the need for their scholarship to advance the cause of Christian mission, for which so many people were giving their money. The exercise was worth while, therefore, and galvanized the BRC into finding ways of safeguarding the work of Tyndale House during the decade of severe inflation.

Two strategies were adopted. First of all, at its meeting in January 1975, when Wiseman, Barclay, Johnson, Millard and Kidner were present, the BRC considered contingency plans for economies. Four schemes were considered: providing accommodation but with no catering; letting out the two top floors of Tyndale House to a college; letting out the entire main house; and letting out the Warden's house. Secondly, fund-raising was considered. Estimated costs from a fund-raising agency were too high, but DJ informed the meeting of an offer to pay £200 for a brochure and suggested setting up an Appeal Committee. By February, negotiations with a college had failed, but negotiations with an evangelical church group wishing to start a residential community had begun. It was agreed to cease catering and to ask the BAC to continue the negotiations which the Warden had begun. By the summer, when the Warden gave his report, a two-year lease had been agreed with the local church group, the St Matthew's Fellowship, of the main house except the secretary's office and the lounge. This left the library building with twelve study-bedrooms, but regrettably it made the Domestic Bursar, Miss Heathcote, and the cook, Miss Nightingale, redundant. Arrangements were made for residents to eat at Newnham College, and later at the University Centre, and, by

moving the secretary up to room 11 above the library, a tiny residents' kitchen was created beside the front door of the House.

At the April meeting in 1976, the Warden was able to report
that, up to the beginning of March, the Appeal had brought in
£11,912.11, leaving £11,433.99 once expenses were paid. In his
report for 1975–76, given that summer, the Warden paid tribute to
the Appeal's Secretary – none other than the 'retired' Douglas
Johnson – and spoke of the 'immense debt of gratitude' owed 'to
Dr Johnson's tireless energy'. Gratitude was also expressed to
Dr Ward Gasque, who had written at his own initiative to several
hundred friends in North America. The Warden also reported that
the part-lease of Tyndale House was working well and the tenants
were excellent neighbours.[8] Gerald Bray, who had been appointed
as Librarian when Dick France returned to Nigeria in February
1976, reported that the library was filled almost to capacity. There
were eight Americans, three Australians, one Canadian, one Finn
and four British students renting desks, all but two of these being
PhD students. But he also underlined the serious threat from
inflation and the sinking pound. It had been difficult to get an
accurate statement because of the removal of the UCCF offices
from 39 Bedford Square to Leicester, but he noted that although
donations to the library had trebled to £2,070, fewer books had
been bought, since the cost per item had increased by a third.

The Tyndale Fellowship under A. R. Millard
While the BRC was fighting to save Tyndale House, the work of
the Tyndale Fellowship continued, with some significant new additions to the ranks and continuing discussion about the relationship
of its doctrinal position to genuine, open scholarship. As we have
seen,[9] Alan Millard was elected chairman in succession to John
Taylor in September 1972. Norman Hillyer succeeded Hugh

---

8. He also reported that the indefatigable Miss Plumbridge had moved to
the IVCF headquarters in Canada after twelve years of excellent service.
She was replaced by Miss Ann Bradshaw, who served right through Dick
France's time as Warden.

9. Above, page 147.

Williamson as TF secretary in May 1973, and at that same meeting
Dr Barclay announced that, with regret, IVF had decided to drop
the 'Tyndale Press' imprint. Plans were laid for a joint meeting of
the study groups at Tyndale House in mid-July 1974, with overflow
accommodation in neighbouring colleges. By May it was clear that
attendance would have to be limited to fifty or sixty members.
Although appointed to the staff of London Bible College in 1973,
Tony Lane continued to oversee the study groups in the Theology
Project. He reported in September 1973 that the three existing
groups were discussing 'Sunday', 'Man' and 'Development of
Doctrine', but by May 1974 the group studying 'Man' was in
abeyance and the other two groups had polarized. At that same
May meeting, news was received of the founding of an American
equivalent of the Tyndale Fellowship, the Institute for Biblical
Research, under the leadership of Earle Ellis, Ralph Martin and
Edwin Yamauchi, and Professor Bruce was at last allowed to resign
from the committee. The resignation was accepted in view of his
continued inability to attend meetings, but with great regret. The
committee 'recorded its immense debt to Professor Bruce's giving
of his time and thought over a very long period'. The following
year, Members' Newsletter No. 18 recorded his coming installation
as President of the Society for New Testament Studies, ten years
after serving as President of SOTS, noting that only Prof. Matthew
Black had previously filled both positions.

Among the new additions to the Fellowship in the mid-1970s
were Richard Bauckham, Peter Toon, Bruce Demarest, Don
Carson and N. T. Wright. A new Historical Theology group was
begun under the Theology Project, with David F. Wright of New
College, Edinburgh, as chairman and Richard Bauckham of the
University of Manchester as secretary. It held its first meeting in
Dunblane during the Easter break in 1975 on the subject of
'Heresy', with fourteen attending. James Packer resigned as chair-
man of the Biblical Theology Study Group,[10] to be succeeded in

---

10. In 1973, Packer had delivered the Tyndale Biblical Theology Lecture,
    'What Did the Cross Achieve? The Logic of Penal Substitution',
    published in the *Tyndale Bulletin*, 25 (1974), 3–45, showing a warm

1975 by Dr George Carey, who had lectured at Oak Hill and St John's, Nottingham, and was the new vicar of St Nicholas' Church, Durham. At the same meeting in May 1975, David L. Baker was welcomed to the committee as TF secretary in place of Norman Hillyer.

The new IVF Literature Committee, initiated by Dr Barclay to advise on suitable publications, and to be chaired by Tony Lane, was discussed. At the meeting in January 1976, Dr Barclay spoke about its role, and Ronald Inchley gave his last report on publications. A new series entitled 'Issues in Contemporary Theology' was under way, and two new series of Bible expositions were to be published under the title 'The Bible Speaks Today'. Alec Motyer would edit the Old Testament volumes and John Stott the New. The Tyndale Commentaries were being reprinted in Hong Kong and some of the volumes were being rewritten. Ronald Inchley was being succeeded by the Revd Frank Entwistle, who would attend the TF committee from the next meeting. The first book in the 'Issues in Contemporary Theology' series appeared the following year: *The Origins of New Testament Christology*, written by the general editor of the series, Howard Marshall.

There was also discussion on the membership basis of the Tyndale Fellowship. In September 1975 it had been agreed to circulate a note to the membership expressing the hope that all were in accord with the Doctrinal Basis, but leaving it to the initiative of members to resign if they were not. By January 1976, such a note had been drafted for inclusion in the next Members' Letter:

> The need to reprint the membership application form of the Tyndale
> Fellowship has raised the question of the suitability of the present
> membership declaration. As a Fellowship we wish to affirm our doctrinal
> position unambiguously and with enthusiasm. Therefore the committee
> has decided that it would be appropriate to ask prospective members to

---

acceptance of the idea of 'models' as opposed to 'theories' of the atonement, but continuing to move by logic to a doctrine of limited atonement. This is reprinted in *Celebrating the Saving Work of God: The Collected Shorter Writings of J. I. Packer*, Vol. 1 (Carlisle: Paternoster, 1998).

indicate their agreement with the theological outlook of the Tyndale Fellowship, as expressed in the UCCF doctrinal basis, rather than to sign the simple declaration of faith which has been used in the past. This is not intended as a change in policy, but simply to make explicit what was previously implicit and thus to clarify the theological position of the Tyndale Fellowship and its members. The Theological Students' Fellowship in particular has suggested that it would be helpful for students to know more precisely the theological position of Tyndale Fellowship speakers. A copy of the new form is enclosed for information, and it is hoped that it will meet with approval of present members. The committee assumes that any whose beliefs no longer accord with the Fellowship's doctrinal basis would not wish to continue in membership.

Evidently some disquiet had been expressed in the committee of the Theological Students' Fellowship about the positions of some members of the TF. At the May meeting of the TF committee, a letter was received from D. F. Wright expressing unease about a circular letter which he had heard was to be sent out by the TSF to staff in theological faculties about discrimination against Evangelical students. James Mynors, the TSF secretary, now attended the TF committee meetings and informed the committee that the letter had not yet been sent out. The TF secretary was instructed to write a strongly worded letter to the TSF committee about this 'potentially dangerous plan which might well be counter-productive'.

In May 1976 it was decided that the Librarian of Tyndale House should serve on the TF committee, and the new Librarian, Gerald Bray, was invited to attend. In September, C. J. H. Wright succeeded D. L. Baker as TF secretary and discussion took place on accommodation and catering for study groups under the new regime at Tyndale House. It was also reported that efforts had been made to collect overdue subscriptions from TF members. Information was received in January 1977 about the newly formed Fellowship of Evangelical European Theologians.

By 1977, doctrinal issues were on the agenda again, this time more specifically about the authority of Scripture. At the September meeting it was reported that the TSF had added a paragraph to their

PROGRESS: 1970–78

165

constitution explaining the article on Scripture in the UCCF
Doctrinal Basis:

> In speaking of the divine inspiration and infallibility of Holy Scripture,
> we accept as authoritative the witness of the Lord Jesus Christ in his
> testimony to the entire trustworthiness of Scripture in all that it affirms,
> whether for example concerning matters of its own composition,
> doctrine, history or the cosmos.

The Historical Theology study groups had already expressed
concern at this addition, and several members of the TF committee added their voices. James Mynors presented a letter from the
TSF Executive in which they expressed their desire to distinguish
two issues. On the one hand, they did not want to allow a distinction between two different levels of affirmation in Scripture
(theological *versus* historical/scientific), since they were concerned
to withstand the existentialist climate. But, on the other hand, they
did not assume that all traditional Evangelical interpretation of
doctrine, or of the literary character of different parts of Scripture,
was necessarily correct. The TF committee was not happy with this
and a proposal was made that the TF committee write to the UCCF
Universities Committee. This was ruled out of order by the acting
chairman, Derek Kidner, however, since the TF had no jurisdiction
over the TSF. Members could write privately.

Discussion of the TF's doctrinal position represented by the
UCCF Doctrinal Basis, particularly its view of Scripture, and how
this related to academic freedom, continued throughout the 1970s.
This was the decade when a great debate among Evangelicals in
the United States over 'inerrancy' was provoked by Harold
Lindsell's *Battle for the Bible*,[11] and American Evangelicals polarized
on the issue. The developing tension between those who were
genuinely alarmed that the authority of Scripture was being threatened and those who wanted to affirm the authority of Scripture
but believed that open and honest biblical criticism was being
threatened led to considerable division and not a little personal

---

11. Harold Lindsell, *The Battle for the Bible* (Grand Rapids: Zondervan, 1976).

pain for many biblical scholars.[12] Quite clearly, the theologians and scholars of the Tyndale Fellowship, while willing to profess their belief in the 'infallibility' of holy Scripture as the supreme author-ity in matters of faith and doctrine, were not prepared to affirm (nor, for that matter, to deny) its 'inerrancy' in other matters in their joint doctrinal statements. There were some who wished to affirm inerrancy, but the tradition of James Orr lived on in British Evangelicalism, and there was no consensus on the question.[13] Derek Kidner's refusal to allow a letter to be sent to the TSF no doubt contributed to the refusal of British Evangelicals to start a painful civil war on the issue.

In January 1978 John Bimson succeeded Chris Wright as TF secretary, and at the March meeting the latter took over the coordi-nation of the Theology Project from Tony Lane. Also in March, a letter was received from the chairman and secretary of the Scottish Tyndale Fellowship, Geoffrey Grogan and Peter White, outlining the history of the Scottish TF and requesting closer links with one subscription and joint publicity. A letter was also received from Howard Marshall proposing the formation of an Irish TF. There was hesitancy on the TF committee, however, since the Scottish Tyndale Fellowship had been formed before the member-ship of the Fellowship was more rigorously restricted to those engaged in research.[14] At the September meeting a further letter was received, this time from David Wright, proposing the region-alization of the Tyndale Fellowship, with Tyndale Lectures being

---

12. For this whole American debate, see George Marsden, *Reforming Fundamentalism* (Grand Rapids: Eerdmans, 1987). The American debate became the more strident because of the embrace of inerrancy by the widespread and influential fundamentalism (also embracing dispensation-alism and 'creationism'), a viewpoint hardly represented in Britain.

13. James Orr, Professor of Theology at the United Free Church College in Glasgow, had taken a different line from his American contemporary, B. B. Warfield. In *Revelation and Inspiration* (London: Hodder & Stoughton, 1910) he had affirmed the infallibility of Scripture, but accepted the presence of minor inaccuracies.

14. See above, pages 86f., 89 and 104.

held in Manchester, Birmingham, Bristol and Edinburgh. This was proposed as a way of dealing with the issues raised by the Scottish TF and the suggestion that an Irish TF should be formed. The committee was not, however, sympathetic to these suggestions from those resident in Glasgow, Edinburgh and Aberdeen![15] The south-eastern bias of the Cambridge–London–Oxford triangle would continue to dominate.

The Tyndale House Council

Meanwhile, in Derek Kidner's last two years as Warden, the financial stringency prompted some creative development at Tyndale House. At the same meeting of the BRC in April 1976 at which it was reported that over £11,000 had been raised, some crucial decisions were taken.[16] Mr R. Madeley, who had been co-opted onto the committee, outlined proposals for the next stage of the Appeal. The chairman announced the Appeal Committee's recommendation that the Biblical Research Committee should be renamed to express its function as the governing body of Tyndale House, and after discussion the BRC agreed that it should become 'The Tyndale House Council'. The change in name, however, was tied to an emphasis on the close connection between research and the spread of Christian truth. It was noted at the meeting that some of the most widely used IVP publications, such as the *New Bible Dictionary*, owed their existence to the basic research fostered

---

15. Actually all four of these representatives of Scotland are Englishmen! Grogan (at the Bible Training Institute in Glasgow), Wright (at New College, Edinburgh) and White (then parish minister of St David's, Broomhouse in Edinburgh) were Englishmen who had adopted Scotland as their homeland. Even Howard Marshall at King's College, Aberdeen, claims (to this writer's dismay) to be an Englishman, his mother having crossed the border to the family's home town of Carlisle at the appropriate time.

16. Professor Wiseman was in the chair, and Professor Bruce, Sir Kirby Laing, Drs Oliver Barclay and Douglas Johnson, and Messrs B. M. Harris, A. R. Millard, J. C. W. Roberts and the Revd F. D. Kidner (secretary) were all listed as present.

by Tyndale House and the Tyndale Fellowship. It was also noted that the Bible was increasingly under attack as irrelevant and unreliable (a swing away from the comparative conservatism of the Biblical Theology movement which had flourished in the early days of Tyndale House). It was therefore necessary, it was concluded, 'to direct some of our research to the areas under attack', and some proposals were laid before the committee for some specific research projects.

Although it is not explicit in the minutes, the close connection between money raising and apologetics seems to have been grasped. It seems to have been understood that the Evangelical constituency would be more likely to give money to research projects meeting perceived needs in the theological battle than simply to a biblical research institute which might merely be a cosy retreat where scholars could pursue their own interests. Mr Madeley outlined the next stage of the Appeal, when a statement of the objects of Tyndale House would be presented to trusts and major subscribers along with a brief description of specific research projects, with the expected costs of each.

The chairman put before the meeting a plan for three research projects: one in Old Testament, one in New Testament and one in Biblical Theology. In the Old Testament priority should be given to problems in Genesis (including the patriarchal narratives), but the needs for an Old Testament Theology and an enquiry into the validity of various current techniques of study were also noted. In the New Testament priority should be given to the reliability of the record of the words and deeds of Jesus, and in Biblical Theology retributive justice was a neglected subject calling for a new study. Professor Bruce agreed to draft the New Testament project in consultation with Dr Marshall, and the chairman undertook to draft an Old Testament project in consultation with Mr Millard. Each project would be directed by its own project committee and would be carried out by a full-time Research Fellow or research team with secretarial help. It would work to a three-year programme in order to produce articles during the three years and a book or symposium at the end, giving an Evangelical assessment of the subject. Mr Madeley had already estimated that the grant for a well-qualified Fellow might need to be £4,000 per annum.

The first meeting of the new Tyndale House Council took place on 22 March 1977 at 39 Bedford Square. Its constitution had been approved by the IVF Trust, and it was to act on behalf of the Trust as the governing body of Tyndale House, meeting normally only once a year. The Business Advisory Committee, as the financial agent of the Trust, would retain its responsibility for Tyndale House finances as long as money was needed from the UCCF General Fund. In accordance with the practice of the IVF Trust, members of the Council would be required to sign the UCCF Doctrinal Basis upon appointment and every three years thereafter.[17]

Mr Vernon Cobb, the Hon. Treasurer, estimated that the total annual cost of the work of the House and library was approximately £20,000, of which £8,000 would represent the cost of the Old and New Testament research projects. In the current financial year, £8,203 had been received as donations to the Appeal Fund. The Warden pointed out that there were other sources of income, including rent and charges for residence and library facilities. In the first half of the financial year, only £1,392 had been needed from the Appeal Fund.

D. J. Wiseman and A. R. Millard directed the Old Testament project, with D. W. Baker as research assistant. Dr R. T. France was employed as full-time director of the New Testament project from

---

17. The council appointed as its officers Professor Wiseman as Chairman, Sir Kirby Laing as Vice-Chairman, Mr V. Cobb as the Hon. Treasurer and the Warden, the Revd Derek Kidner, as Secretary. Two committees were appointed. The Business Committee would include Sir Kirby Laing and Messrs Cobb, Madeley, Roberts and Stradling. The Academic Committee would include Professor Wiseman, Drs Guthrie, Kitchen, Marshall, Milne and Thiselton, Mr Millard and the Warden. Prof. Sir Norman Anderson, Dr Johnson and the *ex officio* members (the chairman of the IVF Trust and the General Secretary of UCCF) would have no committee duties. It was reported that the following had agreed to be members of the Council of Reference: Profs. R. L. F. Boyd, F. F. Bruce, Norman Hunt, Dr David Ingram, Prof. B. M. Metzger, Canon L. L. Morris, the Revd Dr J. I. Packer, the Revd J. R. W. Stott and the Bishop of Norwich (the Rt Revd Maurice Wood). Dr W. J. Martin was also to be invited.

September 1977, at Tyndale House. But by October, when the Council met again with Sir Kirby Laing in the chair and apologies for absence from half the members, Dick France was interviewed for the post of Warden, which would fall vacant with Derek Kidner's retirement the next year.

The achievements of the Kidner years

Derek Kidner presented his last annual report as Warden in the summer of 1978. He noted that gifts amounting to £17,750 had been sent to Tyndale House, not counting those sent to the UCCF offices in Leicester. Mr Baker had handed over the Old Testament project to Dr John Bimson in order to devote himself to the completion of his own PhD thesis, and more than a dozen scholars were writing for Dr France in the New Testament project. He noted that four library users had secured academic appointments that year and that five had completed research degrees. The exterior of the House and library were to be repainted and the oil-fired boiler replaced with a gas-fired boiler, and the Warden's Lodge was to be redecorated for the new occupants. He expressed thanks to the IVF Trust, the Tyndale House Council, the succession of Librarians and domestic and secretarial staff. He also expressed particular thanks ('if so personal a note may be allowed'!) to his wife 'who has accepted this work as a vocation and has done much to make Tyndale House something of a haven, and not just a hive'.

He was also asked to give another report summarizing the developments over the fifteen years of his term of office. He estimated that thirty-eight former readers or residents during that time had gained doctorates in biblical or closely related subjects. Nineteen of those had proceeded to university teaching posts, and most of the rest to appointments in theological colleges in Britain or abroad. But if one 'product' of Tyndale House in these years was lecturers, another was literature. For the general reader, several portions of the revised *New Bible Commentary* had been written or rewritten at Tyndale House, including the sections on Isaiah, Jeremiah, Hosea, Amos and Corinthians, as well as at least four of the Tyndale Commentaries and a number of paperbacks in various series. (The Tyndale Commentaries, which he did not specify, included his own commentaries on Genesis and Psalms.) At a more rigorous level there had been many articles published in academic journals and longer works of scholarship. He mentioned as examples A. R. Millard and W. G. Lambert, *Atra-hasis: The Babylonian Story of the Flood* (Clarendon, 1969); R. T. France, *Jesus and the Old Testament* (Tyndale, 1971); D. L. Baker, *Two Testaments, One Bible* (IVP, 1976); and H. G. M. Williamson, *Israel in the Book of Chronicles* (Cambridge University Press, 1977). To these he added symposia arising out of study groups meeting at the House: *Notes on Some Problems in the Book of Daniel*, by D. J. Wiseman et al. (Tyndale, 1965); *New Testament Interpretation*, edited by I. Howard Marshall (Paternoster, 1977); and *This Is the Day: The Biblical Doctrine of the Christian Sunday*, edited by Roger Beckwith and Wilfrid Stott (Marshall, 1978).

'We believe,' he concluded, 'that we have had God's good hand upon us, perhaps most noticeably at the times when circumstances have been most difficult. And this is encouraging, since the theological scene is turbulent, and the work to be done both exacting and extensive.'

7. PROJECTS

Wiseman, Millard and France, 1978–81

When R. T. France moved into the Warden's Lodge to begin his duties on 1 October 1978, it seemed as if the financial problems of Tyndale House had largely been solved, at least for the time being. At the meeting of the Tyndale House Council at the House on Saturday, 14 October, the Hon. Treasurer, Mr Vernon Cobb, reported that in the financial year 1977–78 there had been an excess of income over expenditure of £19,789. After deduction of expenses on books, binding and bursaries, there would still be a surplus of £12,071 for the year, compared with £6,094 for the previous year. Donations had increased by 61% and expenditure for the year had been exactly as budgeted. However, rent amounting to £4,200 plus a further £2,500 or so for household costs had been received from St Matthew's Fellowship, so that news of the imminent ending of the tenancy meant that there would be a substantial reduction in income. A budget was approved giving £5,375 to research through grants and through the two research projects in Old and New Testaments, and £5,500 to library accessions and expenses.

The council discussed the future use of the main house and noted that there was no demand for any additional single study-bedroom accommodation. Providing accommodation for research students with young families would be desirable, but there would be considerable costs in altering the upper floors of the House to create self-contained flats, and the income from rents would not compare with the income from the present tenants. It was agreed that the House should not become financially dependent on UCCF again and that the possibility of selling the main House to finance the extension of the library wing should not be excluded.

At the same meeting the appointment of the new Librarian, Gordon McConville, was formally approved. When he and the grantees were interviewed, he indicated his intention of completing his PhD at Queen's University, Belfast, in another year. D. W. Baker was also in the final year of PhD research at London, and G. K. Beale hoped to have completed his Cambridge thesis in two years. Dr John Bimson, the Tyndale Fellowship secretary and Old Testament research project assistant, was unable to be present, but had sent a report of his own research on the date of the exodus.

Professor Wiseman reported on progress on the Old Testament project, which had been held up by the pressure of editorial work on Mr Millard and himself in the revision of *The New Bible Dictionary*. Dr France submitted a list of the thirty-two papers which had been promised for the New Testament project, and reported that negotiations were under way for publishing probably four volumes as supplements to the new *Journal for the Study of the New Testament*. In view of his new responsibilities as Warden, it was agreed to relieve him of the responsibility for the project by appointing Dr David Wenham as the new director from July 1979. That was just as well, for there was an acute shortage of staff. Apart from a part-time cleaner and occasional gardener, the Warden had the Librarian and one secretary-typist (for both library and House administration). There was no maintenance staff; the Warden had to do maintenance himself or call someone in. And he also acted as bursar.

At one point the council meeting was adjourned to welcome Mr and Mrs Kidner. Professor Wiseman paid warm tribute to their outstanding contribution and made a presentation to them as a mark of the council's appreciation. A collection among TF members and friends enabled them to visit the Holy Land for the first time.

Re-enter Theology

While progress was being reported to the Tyndale House Council on the Old and New Testament projects, the Theology Project, begun by the Tyndale Fellowship Committee at Oliver Barclay's initiative, was leading to the forming of additional study groups.[1] At the meeting in March 1978, when Chris Wright succeeded Tony Lane as coordinator of the project, he reported that he was planning to meet the six Tyndale Fellowship members who would be participating in the National Evangelical Conference on Social Ethics at High Leigh conference centre from 11 to 15 September. Altogether, seventeen members of the TF had expressed an interest in forming a study group in Christian Ethics. At the meeting on 22 September he reported that Joyce Baldwin, Howard Marshall, John Gladwin, David Field, David Cook, Ian McGregor, David Holloway and Jim Punton had been the nucleus which had met during the High Leigh conference. The 'Doctrine of Man' group and the 'Doctrine of Scripture' group were also meeting and there was the possibility of forming a Religious Studies group. Some inconclusive discussion also took place at this committee meeting about whether there was an understanding that Inter-Varsity Press would have first choice in publishing study-group papers, but it was agreed that Tyndale Lecturers should be made aware of their commitment to submit their manuscripts to The Tyndale Bulletin. It was also agreed that the secretary should remind members in the next newsletter that copies of papers should be lodged in the library.

Dr Barclay announced a £10,000 grant for five years for research in Theology and Christian Education. But he also raised the disquiet expressed by the committee of the Theological Students' Fellowship about the doctrinal stance of the Tyndale Fellowship. The TSF particularly questioned whether the stance of some of the contributors to the symposium New Testament Interpretation, published with the name of the Tyndale Fellowship attached, represented the

1. Above, Chapter 6, 'Theology again', pages 147, 149f. and 162.

Fellowship's doctrinal basis.[2] Tony Lane (who was not able to attend this meeting) had written suggesting a joint meeting with the TSF executive to clarify the whole stance and purpose of the work of the Tyndale Fellowship, but Donald Guthrie doubted the wisdom of this. It was agreed that papers on the question be requested from Dr Barclay, the TSF and Frank Entwistle.[3]

When the TF committee met again, on 5 January 1979, Chris Wright reported that the first meeting of the Ethics Study Group would be at Tyndale House in July, when they would discuss the relationship of the Old Testament to the New and the whole question of biblical authority in the field of Ethics. It was also reported that the Old Testament Study Group were to be considering papers for the Patriarchs project, and the New Testament group, papers for the Gospels project. The Historical Theology group would meet at St John's, Durham, at Easter on the theme of Justification. It was also reported by Frank Entwistle that the *New Bible Dictionary Revised* would be published in two forms: a one-volume version, and a three-volume version highly illustrated. *A Bibliographical Guide to New Testament Research*, to which Alan Millard, Graham Stanton and Dick France (as editor) were contributors, was to be published by *JSOT* Press with an acknowledgment that it was sponsored by the Tyndale Fellowship.[4] It was also announced that J. I. Packer was

---

2. I. Howard Marshall (ed.), *New Testament Interpretation: Essays on Principles and Methods* (Exeter: Paternoster, 1977). This was one of the works cited by Derek Kidner as a significant publication (above, page 171) and contained essays by many prominent members of the Tyndale Fellowship: Bruce, Marshall, Stanton, Thiselton, Guthrie, Drane, D. Wenham, Travis, Catchpole, Smalley, Ellis, R. Martin, France, Dunn, Nixon, Goldingay and Hillyer.

3. The same meeting also received the resignation of S. Barton Babbage (the secretary of the Biblical Research Committee, 1942–43) from the Fellowship, and news of a legacy left to the TF by E. D. Scott.

4. The *Guide* had originally been circulated as a duplicated paper in 1968 when Dick France was TF secretary. It was reprinted in *Themelios* in 1969, and a second edition published by TF in 1974. The *JSOT* publication of 1979 was thus the third edition.

resigning from the committee in view of his imminent departure to
Canada.

Doctrine and academic freedom

A letter was also read from the executive of the TSF expressing
concern about recent trends in TF scholarship, and about the fact
that not all members of the TF had signed the full Doctrinal Basis.
A reply drafted by the chairman was edited and approved. The
committee then set a date for a special meeting to discuss the doctrinal stance, and it was suggested that papers other than those
already requested and circulated should be requested from
members actually engaged in biblical research. France, Goldingay
and Marshall were suggested, and a specific question was agreed as
a focus for discussion: 'In what way and to what extent should
work encouraged by the Tyndale Fellowship be distinctively
Evangelical?' Donald Guthrie was asked to contribute a paper on
the intention of the TF's Doctrinal Basis. A letter from a member
of the Fellowship expressing concern about *New Testament
Interpretation* and James Dunn's *Unity and Diversity*,[5] and threatening
to withdraw his articles from the *New Bible Dictionary Revised*, added
point to the planned discussion.

The issues being raised were no doubt sharpened not only by
the American debate sparked by Harold Lindsell's *Battle for the
Bible*,[6] but also by James Barr's book *Fundamentalism*, published by
SCM in 1977. Already notable for his attack on the Biblical
Theology movement in *The Semantics of Biblical Language*, Barr now
turned his guns on another 'conservative' movement. A curious
mixture of insight and misunderstanding, the book began with a
chapter almost totally lacking in any documentary evidence, in
which Barr defined Fundamentalism in terms of three characteris-
tics: a strong emphasis on the inerrancy of the Bible; a strong
hostility to modern theology and critical study of the Bible; and an
assurance that those who did not share their viewpoint were not

5. J. D. G. Dunn, *Unity and Diversity in the New Testament: An Inquiry into the
Character of Earliest Christianity* (London: SCM, 1977).
6. See above, page 165.

'true Christians' at all. In his second chapter he identified the main enemy specifically as the Inter-Varsity Fellowship, which had recently (he understood) changed its name to the Universities and Colleges Christian Fellowship. Barr claimed that he had done thorough research into the substantial amount of literature published by this classic example of an 'exclusive and non-cooperative' Fundamentalist organization, but in fact he had already set up his own framework of interpretation in his first chapter.

James Barr's attitude and impressionistic understanding have to be understood as a reaction to his own Evangelical upbringing. His grandfather, the Revd James Barr, had been a notably successful evangelist to working men, and his father, the Revd Professor Allan Barr, had been one of the leading figures in the small minority of the United Free Church of Scotland which had refused to go into the historic union with the established Church of Scotland in 1929.[7] The younger James Barr had identified with his Evangelical heritage as a student, becoming president of Edinburgh University Christian Union, and, no doubt, he had encountered many grass-roots 'Fundamentalists' fitting his definition both in churches and among university students. But throughout the book Barr was determined to assert that all conservative Evangelicals, and specifically those in the IVF/UCCF, were 'Fundamentalists', and there is no mistaking the animosity he felt. To him, conservative Evangelical scholarship was deceitful, since it allowed its presuppositions about the Bible to affect the conclusions which it claimed to reach by the historical critical method. His later book, *Escaping from Fundamentalism*, suggests even more strongly that his attitude was the result of his own youthful struggles to reconcile the historical critical method with his Evangelical heritage.[8]

---

7. James Barr (grandfather) was also a Labour MP. Cf. the article by A. C. Ross in the *Dictionary of Scottish Church History and Theology* (Edinburgh: T. & T. Clark, 1993). See the obituary for Allan Barr in *Steadfast*, the magazine of the UF Church, for September 1988.

8. James Barr, *Escaping from Fundamentalism* (London: SCM, 1984). Cf. the illuminating review of *Fundamentalism* by David F. Wright in *Themelios*, 3.3 (1978), reprinted in *Solid Ground*, ed. Carl R. Trueman,

Given Barr's attack on 'Fundamentalism' on the one hand, and the question raised by the TSF executive on the other, the whole *raison d'être* of the Tyndale Fellowship was at issue. Was it possible to reconcile the authority of Scripture as the infallible word of God with genuine academic freedom in issues of biblical criticism? The Tyndale Fellowship Committee held its special meeting in the vestry of St Giles-in-the-Fields in London on Friday, 30 March 1979. The chairman, A. R. Millard, was delayed by a late train and Donald Guthrie took the chair. Apologies were received from G. L. Carey, I. H. Marshall and D. J. Wiseman. Dr Guthrie then asked those who had prepared papers to summarize their main concerns. Gordon McConville spoke for the TSF: some Tyndale Fellowship publications were no longer distinguishable as Evangelical scholarship, and it was feared that this was because of a departure from the authority of Scripture. Dr Barclay raised the question whether there were any distinct Evangelical presuppositions, and if so, in what sense could we approve of Professor Bruce's phrase 'unfettered scholarship'? If not, did the Tyndale Fellowship serve any purpose? Frank Entwistle of IVP also questioned whether some of the writings of TF members were compatible with the UCCF Doctrinal Basis. Dick France raised the question how far a doctrine of biblical infallibility committed them to a certain approach to scholarship. He suggested a fresh statement equivalent to Professor Bruce's paper of 1947,[9] this time owned by the whole committee. John Goldingay wondered how best they could develop a Chalcedonian doctrine of Scripture, taking account of both its inspiration and its humanity.

James Packer was asked to state his views. The Tyndale Fellowship, he said, had generally concentrated on historical questions, but now had a stunted product, strong on historical exegesis but weak on theological exegesis and on the theological controls of

---

Tony J. Gray, Craig Blomberg (Leicester: Apollos, 2000), 208–213. See also R. T. France, 'James Barr and Evangelical Scholarship', *Anvil*, 8 (1991), 51–64.

9. This was the article on the Tyndale Fellowship in *The Evangelical Quarterly* (see above, page 63, note 39), reprinted as Appendix G to this book.

scholarship. A clearer doctrine of Scripture was needed to give such directive and controls, and the distinction between inspiration (which concerned the givenness of Scripture) and interpretation/ exegesis (which concerned how to live by the truth gained) needed clarification.

The chairman arrived at noon, and having established that no-one had any reservations about the Doctrinal Basis, he posed Dr Barclay's question: what, if anything, distinguished Evangelical from non-Evangelical scholarship? Derek Kidner made a distinction between passages of Scripture where issues were sharp, for example where Jesus attributed the authorship of Psalm 110 to David, and those where scholars were free to arrive at a differing conclusion, such as the authorship of Matthew or Ecclesiastes. But John Goldingay pointed out that an earlier generation would have regarded even these authorship questions as crucial. Dr Kitchen spoke against compartmentalized thinking. Dr Packer saw the need for historical perspective, for earlier generations had been dogmatic over Genesis 1 or the authorship of Ecclesiastes because they misunderstood the literary genre. Dr Barclay remarked that Professor Bruce's phrase 'unfettered scholarship' should not be taken to mean that they were free to disregard evidence such as the authoritative statements of Jesus. Dr C. J. H. Wright drew an analogy with Christian and non-Christian research on the human body: their descriptive works might be identical, but they would differ drastically when they wrote on what it meant to be human. For Dr Packer, scholars had to be equipped for a dual task: scholarship which would stand up in the academic community, and scholarship which defended Evangelical presuppositions. For Mr Kidner, the distinctiveness of the Evangelical scholar's task was that his prior obligation was to his weaker brother.

After lunch, Dr Guthrie was asked to initiate a discussion on the role of presuppositions in Evangelical scholarship. He began by posing the question whether the biblical text should be examined as any others. Should presuppositions about inspiration be suspended? He argued that one could not wholly suspend one's presuppositions, for if we came to the conclusion that Paul had contradicted himself, or that there was a historical error, then our presuppositions would lead us to question the conclusion. Different scholars come to different conclusions because of different presuppositions. David Wright argued that Scripture must be seen to be *sui generis*, and Derek Kidner that exegesis without presuppositions was impossible. David Wright saw a change in Evangelical scholarship from the suspending of judgment over a problem in the text, to saying in effect that the Gospel records cannot be historical in a simple sense, and this was causing a turmoil of faith in the pew. Various other comments on the pastoral dimension followed, before Donald Guthrie posed the question where the line lay beyond which scholarly conclusions left the Doctrinal Basis behind. Dr Packer responded immediately that each TF scholar must draw that line for himself, but must be able to defend it. Peter Toon and David Wright suggested that different scholars had different models of biblical unity, not all harmonistic, but Donald Guthrie felt that some had gone beyond alleging diversity to alleging contradiction. Dick France and John Baker felt that the *veracity* of Scripture was the more fundamental issue, since some thought that contradiction implied error. James Packer distinguished between Warfield's view of inspiration, which involved infallibility, and the 'instrumental' view, which did not. It was not enough for the TF to send people back to Warfield, since that carried no weight with the TF's critics. The TF had failed those it served by not bringing the distinction into the open and offering its own defence. Discussion then turned to the formulation of a statement from the committee to TF members. There was agreement that members should sign the Doctrinal Basis annually and that the statement should aim to keep the work of the Tyndale Fellowship distinctively Evangelical and to explain their work to the 'plain man'. This was James Packer's last meeting before leaving for Regent College, Vancouver, and he was asked to close the meeting with prayer.[10]

---

10. According to Alister McGrath, Packer felt marginalized in England. His exclusion from the Westminster conferences by Lloyd-Jones; the declining interest in Puritan spirituality in the Church of England along with the rise of charismatic influence; and his unhappiness with the second National Evangelical Anglican Conference at Nottingham in 1977, when Anthony Thiselton put hermeneutics on the Evangelical agenda, all

John Baker had suggested at the meeting that the chairman (Alan Millard), Dick France and James Packer should collaborate to draw up a statement from the secretary's notes to be approved by the committee at the next meeting for circulating to TF members. The memorandum they drew up began by alluding in the first paragraph to the disquiet over the range of views on both critical and doctrinal issues which members of the Fellowship had expressed in recent years. The second paragraph was the heart of statement:

> The *raison d'être* of the Tyndale Fellowship is 'to promote biblical research in a spirit of loyalty to the authority of the Bible'. It has always been assumed that members approach their studies from an agreed starting point of evangelical faith as expressed in the Fellowship's doctrinal basis. Without such an agreed starting point the TF would have no reason to maintain a distinct identity in relation to parallel professional societies which have no doctrinal commitment. Acceptance of the doctrinal basis is to us not a regretted restriction, but a glad affirmation of the common faith which underlies and informs our study of the Bible, and is nourished by it. We desire to help one another to maintain and to refine this faith as we explore the ways in which it relates to the methods, techniques and findings of biblical scholarship, and they to it.

The third paragraph proceeded to spell out the implications of 'the divine inspiration and infallibility of Holy Scripture, as originally given'. This implied the 'inner coherence and unity' of the Christian Bible, 'the truth of all it declares, and its freedom from both self-contradiction and error'. This did not call for, or lay down, a corpus of 'acceptable' interpretations and critical views, since within the Fellowship 'we do not presume to define limits for each other in advance'. Members were asked to bear in mind that their work was likely to be read outside the academic circle and by Evangelical students in their early days of theological study, and to avoid ways of expressing themselves which could cause needless disquiet.

---

contributed to his decision to go to Canada. Cf. McGrath, *J. I. Packer: A Biography* (Grand Rapids: Baker, 1997), 217ff.

At the next regular meeting of the TF Committee, on 11 May 1979, further discussion followed on the memorandum. Howard Marshall had written suggesting a redrafting of the third paragraph, which sounded 'like an adoption of the American notion of "inerrancy", a word which . . . [is] open to misunderstanding'. David Wright had also written questioning the wording of this paragraph, which suggested 'a *strict* notion of inerrancy' which had not been in view in the committee discussion. But no changes were made on this point. Both letters also questioned wording which seemed to imply the adoption of a censorship role by the committee. The wording was consequently amended to say that the committee did not presume to set itself up as a censor, but that if work published by members seemed to conflict with the common basis, there was 'a responsibility to ask the authors to justify their methods and conclusions in terms of the Fellowship's position'. The object, Dr Barclay stressed, was not to conceal scholars' views, but to make clear where the Tyndale Fellowship stood. It was agreed to circulate the memorandum to all TF members.

A decade later, Dick France expressed surprise that he had approved the memorandum. While he still thought that the second paragraph expressed very well the reason for the existence of the Tyndale Fellowship, the memorandum did not really address what were essentially hermeneutical issues.[11] He had actually drawn up a memorandum himself for the meeting on 30 March in which he had defined the distinctiveness of Evangelical scholarship as its 'submission to scripture, properly interpreted, as in its entirety the authoritative word of God'. But the key question was what implications this had for the use of critical methods. Evangelical tradition was clearly not a sufficient basis for clinging to views of date and authorship, and he noted that some such views which had been regarded in earlier years as vital positions to be defended were now questioned or openly rejected. The issue was whether critical conclusions contradicted proper exegesis of Scripture's own statements. As far as 'alleged errors and contradictions' were

---

11. Letter of 2 August 1988 to the TF Secretary, Martin Selman, with the memorandum he had prepared in 1979 attached.

concerned, these were not self-evident categories and depended on the interpretation of language. Before one could speak of doctrinal inconsistency, therefore, it was necessary to resolve the hermeneutical issues.

Scots and study groups

At the same meeting of the TF Committee on 11 May 1979 a letter was read from the secretary of the Scottish Tyndale Fellowship stating that the Scottish TF was not prepared to change its name. They believed that it was the TF which had changed its aims and conditions of membership (to the more restricted area of research). It was agreed that Dick France, David Wright and Howard Marshall would meet with the Scottish committee at their next conference. By September, the dispute was apparently still brewing, since the secretary (David Wenham) was asked 'to reply to a letter from Mr Cameron (STF secretary) explaining the committee's concerns in as eirenic a tone as possible'!

A new study group in Systematic Theology was being proposed by Dr Bruce Milne, and by January 1980 it was announced that David Field had agreed to chair the new Ethics group. Peter Toon had given the royalties from *The Development of Doctrine* and *One God in Trinity*[12] to endow the Tyndale Lecture in Historical Theology. It was agreed that this would be kept as a genuine endowment and not absorbed into general TF funds. Further discussion took place about the new requirement that TF members sign the Doctrinal Basis annually. One member in the Christian Brethren tradition had scruples about signing a doctrinal statement at all, but was willing to sign it once. Another senior New Testament scholar had alleged that this requirement was changing the basis of membership, and this led to discussion whether membership had always *implied* acceptance of the Doctrinal Basis, or whether, since there

---

12. Peter Toon, *The Development of Doctrine in the Church* (London: James Clarke/ Grand Rapids: Eerdmans, 1979); Peter Toon and James D. Spiceland, *One God in Trinity* (London: Bagster, 1980). Members' Letter No. 28 (April 1980) advertised the books, commenting that six of the chapters in the latter had been papers read at the Historical Theology Study Group in 1978.

had been no such requirement, the conditions of membership had been the same as in university Christian Unions.[13]

A new constitution was approved for the Tyndale Fellowship at the January 1980 meeting, naming it as 'The Tyndale Fellowship for Biblical and Theological Research'. Its relationship to UCCF was clarified as being through the Tyndale House Council (with its committee as a 'sub-committee') and the UCCF Associates,[14] and the statement of aims included a reference to the Doctrinal Basis, with which the members now had to indicate their agreement. Committee appointments were to be approved by the Tyndale House Council, and the TF chairman and secretary were to be appointed by the Tyndale House Council on the recommendation of the TF committee. At the same meeting congratulations were sent to A. F. Walls and Howard Marshall on their professorial appointments at Aberdeen.

In April 1980, the Tyndale Fellowship Committee expressed its regret at the news of the death of W. J. Martin. Oliver Barclay retired that year, and the new UCCF General Secretary, Dr Robin Wells, attended his first meeting of the committee in September. The September meeting learned that the Scottish Tyndale Fellowship had reconstituted itself as the Scottish Evangelical Theological Society. Congratulations were sent to Professor Bruce on his seventieth birthday. At the April 1981 meeting it was announced that Professor Wiseman was resigning as chairman of the Old Testament Study Group after thirty years, and at that same committee meeting it was decided to invite Dick France to continue to serve on the committee despite the end of his three-year service as Warden of Tyndale House.

Patriarchs and Gospels
Dr France's three years as Warden saw the maturing of the two research projects in Old Testament and New Testament begun in

---

13. In the Christian Unions, members must sign a declaration of faith, but only committee members have to sign the Doctrinal Basis.
14. The new name for the Graduates' Fellowship. It later became 'Professional Groups'.

1976. The first volume of *Gospel Perspectives*, edited by R. T. France and D. Wenham, was published by JSOT Press of Sheffield University in March 1980. *Essays on the Patriarchal Narratives* was published by IVP in 1981, and that same year the second volume of *Gospel Perspectives* by JSOT Press. At the July 1981 meeting of the Tyndale House Council, it was agreed that if the third volume (on Jewish historiography and the Gospels) was to appear as *Gospel Perspectives III*, then it too should be offered to the JSOT Press.[15]

In his report for 1978–79, the Warden recorded the appointment of two former library readers and members of the Fellowship (Drs Graham Davies and Robert Gordon) as lecturers in Old Testament Studies at Cambridge. He himself and the Revd Tom Wright, chaplain of Downing College, had been appointed members of the Divinity Faculty. D. W. Baker had been appointed Assistant Professor of Biblical Studies at Bethel College, St Paul, Minnesota, and research degrees had been completed by Wayne Grudem, David Seccombe, Sven Soderlund and John Wood. He also reported that the Tyndale New Testament Lecture, given at Tyndale House in May during the university term by Bruce Metzger on 'Basic Questions Concerning the New Testament Canon', had been packed out and attracted several senior members of the Divinity Faculty.

Gordon McConville completed his PhD in 1980 and was appointed lecturer in Old Testament at Trinity College, Bristol. Gregory Beale was appointed to Grove City College in Pennsylvania, and Tom Wright to McGill University in Toronto. Dick France reported all this in his 1980 report and also wrote of the very generous new grants from the J. W. Laing Biblical Scholarship Trust. A non-repeatable grant of £10,000 had been given towards the cost of alterations at the House, and a total of £17,000 in recurring annual grants. Other donations in the financial year came to £16,846, compared with £10,964 the previous year. The full cost of the alterations had been met and research grants increased. The alterations which the Laing Trust paid for were the creation of three flats in the upper storeys of the

---

15. See below, pages 192 and 196.

main House. Dick France reported that families from Australia, Canada, South Africa and the USA had been in residence already for research or sabbatical study in the library and he felt that the presence of married couples had been a valuable addition to the life of the House.

In his second and final report as Librarian, Gordon McConville mentioned the addition of a new annexe to the library (in the room in the main House which had originally housed the whole library). The Church History and Classics sections had been moved there, leaving valuable space in the main library building. With four extra desks, there were now twenty-one desks, all booked for the coming year. On 10 June, he commented, they were occupied by sixteen PhD candidates, three overseas scholars on sabbatical, and the TF secretary. Those comprised eight Americans, six Britons, two Australians, one Canadian, one Dutchman, one Nigerian and one Indian. The number of readers who were neither British nor American was thought to represent a new trend, and he thought that the raising of fees for overseas students might lead to a decline in the number of Americans, whereas the increase in grants might lead to an increase in British PhD students.[16] Forty-six readers' tickets had been issued during the academic year to undergraduates. Colin J. Hemer was appointed Librarian in succession to Gordon McConville and took up his duties on 1 October 1980.

By January 1981, Professor Wiseman was reporting to the Tyndale House Council that Dr France had accepted an invitation to join the staff of London Bible College and had therefore tendered his resignation to take effect from 31 August. A sub-committee was appointed including the chairman, Drs Gordon and Guthrie and the General Secretary of UCCF, Dr Robin Wells, to select and approach suitable people in consultation with Dr France. An initial appointment would be for three years, although it would be desirable for a Warden to stay longer, and a

---

16. The Conservative government of Margaret Thatcher, elected in 1979, eventually conquered the severe inflation of the 1970s, but the rigorous financial remedies in their economic policy included a sharp increase in fees for overseas students.

more senior scholar might be given a longer appointment from the beginning.

At the July meeting of 1981, it was decided to invite Dr Murray J. Harris for interview for an initial three-year appointment with the hope of extension. It was agreed that the *Tyndale Bulletin*, edited by A. R. Millard until 28 (1977), and then by R. T. France, should be a responsibility of the staff at Tyndale House and that the new Warden would take responsibility as editor for Volume 33 (1982). In his final report, given to this meeting, Dick France noted that six grants had been given and a further ten approved for the coming year. This was particularly valuable, given the decrease in the number of government grants and the dramatic increase in university fees. The J. W. Laing Biblical Scholarship Trust was increasing its total grants from £17,000 to £27,000 in the coming year, and other donations in the past year had come to £14,370. He reported that Tyndale House readers had received appointments at Gordon-Conwell Seminary, Seattle Pacific University, and Notre Dame University in Indiana. Gerald Bray, a former Librarian, had been appointed to Oak Hill College, and six readers had completed their doctorates.[17]

Dick France left to become Donald Guthrie's successor at LBC as head of the Department of Biblical Studies and (a little later) Vice-Principal. He was later to become Principal of Wycliffe Hall, Oxford. One of the innovations he had introduced at Tyndale House was the admission of the first single female residents from 1980 onwards, something unthinkable a generation earlier! He had appreciated Sir Norman Anderson's presence in the House. Retired and living in nearby Gough Way, Sir Norman was a constant library user and wrote his later books there. Dick France also valued Colin Hemer's presence. He later wrote:

> He is among the most significant of the TH residents I have known,
> a meticulous and respected scholar, who never held a teaching
> appointment except for a brief spell at Manchester, and whose life really

---

17. In addition to G. K. Beale and N. T. Wright (already mentioned), they
    were D. Carr, R. W. L. Moberly, M. M. B. Turner and R. A. Whitacre.

seemed to revolve around Tyndale House. He was a delight to know and to consult with, and very good at bringing people in who would benefit from the fellowship.[18]

Dick France noted that most people who used the House were North American, while the funding was almost entirely British, but an attempt to appeal to known friends in North America was a dismal failure. Nevertheless, the number of British researchers was increasing. Colin Hemer's Librarian's Report of 1981 gave evidence of this, as well as bearing out the international value of Tyndale House. Nineteen of the twenty-one 'carrels' were occupied, sixteen by PhD candidates, two by overseas scholars on sabbatical and one by the TF secretary. Eight of these were British, four American, three Canadian, and there was also one each from Australia, the Netherlands, Nigeria and South Africa. It was encouraging (he noted) to see the increase in British students, fostered by the increasing Laing research grants. He also commented on the international visibility of the House as evidenced by the stream of visitors:

I write in a week when visitors on brief stays in England called here from Canberra and Melbourne on successive days, when a Norwegian missionary in Japan has just arrived and a Filipino is due in residence, an Ethiopian student has been using the Library, and a query has been received about an Iraqi scholar. The needs of biblical and theological research and training in the Third World are clearly of crucial importance, and it is gratifying if many recent contacts represent a trend and point to a yet wider usefulness.

By 1981, forty years after the Kingham Hill conference which led to the establishing of Tyndale House and the Tyndale Fellowship, vision was turning to reality. A school of Evangelical biblical scholarship was emerging at the highest level, as advocated so strongly by W. J. Martin, and the scholars were taking their place in the academic world. The influence of the House was also being

<hr>

18. Letter of 21 January 2004.

felt internationally in the growing young churches around the world which were the fruit of Evangelical missions, not least the student missionary movement of a century before. But theological issues remained, particularly continuing questions about the relationship of biblical scholarship to biblical inspiration. The questions of biblical 'Introduction' (historical questions, questions about the authorship and dating of the biblical books) were still on the agenda, but to these were now added questions of hermeneutics. The work of Anthony Thiselton and others was raising in a new way the relationship of biblical studies to theology.

8. EXTENSION

Wiseman, Millard and Harris, 1982–86

The new Warden, Dr Murray J. Harris, a New Zealander who had completed his doctorate on Pauline eschatology under F. F. Bruce at Manchester, was present and fulfilling his role as secretary at the meeting of the Tyndale House Council on 29 January 1982. He had taught for some years at Trinity Evangelical Divinity School in Deerfield, Illinois, and was working on a book on resurrection and immortality.[1]

---

1. Murray J. Harris, *Raised Immortal: Resurrection and Immortality in the New Testament* (London: Marshall, Morgan & Scott, 1983). The members of the council whom he met there included Professor Wiseman, Dr Barclay, Dr Donald Guthrie, Dr Douglas Johnson, Sir Kirby Laing, Mr R. Madeley, Mr A. R. Millard, Mr D. G. Stradling and Dr R. J. Wells (the UCCF General Secretary). Apologies were received from Sir Norman Anderson, Mr V. Cobb, Dr R. P. Gordon, Mr B. M. Harris, Dr K. A. Kitchen, Prof. I. H. Marshall, Dr D. B. Milne, and Mr J. C. W. Roberts. Among these the businessmen were Sir Kirby Laing (the son of Sir John Laing), R. Madeley, D. G. Stradling, senior manager

Taking stock

The major items of regular business at Murray Harris's first council meeting concerned finance, staffing, publications and library matters. First, on finance, thanks to the Laing Trust, the picture remained healthy. An expected deficit of £7,500 had been turned into a surplus of £4,658, and the Appeal Fund had held a total of £25,589 at 31 October 1981. A 'break-even' budget approved by the UCCF Business Advisory Committee assumed that income would increase by 17% (£11,000) in the coming year and that expenditure would increase by 25% (£14,000). The Warden was requested to write a letter of thanks to the trustees of the J. W. Laing Trust, who had indicated that gifts of not less than £40,000 would be given each financial year up to June, 1986. Concern was expressed about considerable under-spending in the library for the current year, so that spending would have to be increased in the coming year to £10,000.

Secondly, on staffing, a job description for a new administrative assistant to the Warden (to be known as the bursar) was approved, and Murray Harris reported the appointment of John H. Martin to a part-time post of twenty hours per week. Professor Marshall raised the question by letter whether the Bursar might not relieve the Tyndale Fellowship Secretary of some duties.

Publications

Thirdly, discussion turned to publications. Now that the *Essays on the Patriarchal Narratives* had been published, the council discussed the next Old Testament project. A letter from Frank Entwistle was considered along with comments of the IVP Theological and Reference Publications Committee on a proposal from Gordon McConville for a symposium on the relation between Jeremiah and Deuteronomy. Professor Wiseman drew attention to the proposal first put forward in 1966 and recently adopted by the council. It had emphasized the need for detailed and careful study

---

at John Laing & Son, Vernon Cobb, the company secretary of EMESS plc, B. M. Harris, and J. C. W. Roberts, the managing director of C. P. Roberts.

of what the text of Genesis 1 – 11 actually said and of the legiti-
mate range of interpretations, before the relation of science and
Scripture could be usefully investigated. There was agreement that
the project was an urgent necessity and that until there was an Old
Testament specialist working on the project at Tyndale House,
progress would be frustrated. Dr Gordon Wenham was to be
asked to coordinate the project, and Mr Desmond Alexander to
engage in the work at Tyndale House either full-time or part-time
for three years. A. R. Millard reported that the papers being
prepared from the next Old Testament Study Group would contribute to the 'History in the Old Testament' project.

Still on publications, David Wenham had sent a written report
that *Gospel Perspectives II* had received its first two reviews, which
were favourable; that three essays out of ten had been received for
Gospel Perspectives III (on the Gospels and Jewish historiography);
and that Volume IV, dealing with traditions about Jesus outside the
Gospels, would be ready for the publishers by the end of 1983. He
had received a proposal from the publisher, the JSOT Press,
regarding a continuing *Gospel Perspectives* series jointly sponsored by
JSOT and Tyndale House and edited by him. This led to considerable discussion of the pros and cons, but the council's consensus
was that it did not wish to launch a monograph series in conjunc-
tion with the JSOT Press, and wished to retain the *Gospel
Perspectives* title. Dr Wenham was to be thanked for his 'sterling
service' as acting Warden during the vacancy.

The same meeting in January 1982 also considered a conference
for potential researchers to be held at Tyndale House during the
summer vacation for promising second- and third-year theological
undergraduates. Following a report from the Librarian, Colin
J. Hemer, they also agreed to recommend to the UCCF Business
Advisory Committee that the books in the library should be
insured for £150,000, subject to investigation into the insurance of
comparable coverage at the University of London.[2]

---

2. Amazingly, there does not appear to be any previous minute referring to
   insuring the library collection. (The author is reminded of two
   redoubtable old ladies who used to run a certain Christian guest house

Six months later, in the summer of 1982, the new Warden's report listed the usual number of academic appointments for library readers: four on this occasion, one to Western Kentucky University, two to the Biblical Seminary of Columbia, and one to Belhaven College in Mississippi. Two readers had completed their Cambridge PhDs (John Webster and Stephen Farris) and four more were awaiting results. Circulation of *The Tyndale Bulletin* had averaged 560 for the last five volumes. Colin Hemer's last report as Librarian informed the Council that the subject index (some 80,000 cards) had been reorganized, that all twenty-one carrels were in use (by ten Americans, eight Britons, and one each from Canada, Japan and South Africa). Regular readers included a scholar from Yugoslavia and postgraduate students from America, Canada, South Africa and New Zealand. Readers from Australia, Greece, France, Hong Kong, Japan and Norway had worked in the library in the past year. An account of the library had appeared in the *Bulletin of the Association of British Theological and Philosophical Libraries*, 21 (June 1981) and members of the association had visited the library in March.

Overall theological strategy
The new Warden's first meeting of the Tyndale House Council in January 1982 had also initiated a discussion on 'Overall Theological Strategy' introduced by Dr Barclay. The Tyndale Fellowship Committee had had a similar discussion three weeks earlier, on 8 January: a 'wide-ranging' discussion on 'future policy and long-term planning'. Their minutes indicate, however, that discussion was mainly on the dissemination of the Tyndale Lectures and the falling attendance of senior members of the Fellowship at the study groups. At the April meeting of the TFC, their discussion widened to the communication of Evangelical

---

in Harrogate in the 1970s. They took out no insurance, but simply prayed to the Lord every night to protect the property and the guests from all harm and danger! Apparently he did.) It is possible that insurance was previously handled by the BAC of the IVF, but there is no indication of this in the THC minutes.

theological research to the church at large. A multidisciplinary approach, with all groups studying one theme (an idea credited to David Wright), might give a multidisciplinary perspective. By the September meeting, they had agreed to plan a first joint conference of all the study groups on the theme of 'War'. They also planned a leaflet, *Serving Christ through Biblical and Theological Research*, and a seminar to attract students to research.

But Oliver Barclay's concern about 'strategy' expressed in the Tyndale House Council was also about the influence of Evangelical theology and thought in the wider arena: not only in the church but beyond it. He was concerned 'that there should be a group of Evangelical leaders alert to current theological trends and issues so that challenges to the faith could be anticipated or could receive convincing replies'. He drew attention to the relative failure of the Evangelical response to Bishop John Robinson's *Honest to God* and to the dearth of Evangelical experts in the study of comparative religion, 'a subject gaining popularity in universities and in Religious Education teaching in schools'. He was asked to prepare a paper for the next meeting of the Council.

By January 1983, Dr Barclay returned to strategic questions with a paper entitled 'Tyndale House Policy: Some Questions'. He began by quoting a 'well-respected, academic member of the Tyndale Fellowship' who had said: 'It is unfortunate that the Evangelicals have become the new bastions of much irrelevant scholarship.' This remark should not be dismissed, he said, without considering some of the topics for which they had given grants for research. He instanced four topics which seemed rather abstruse to him,[3] although accepting that most of the research

---

3. One of these apparently abstruse topics was the 'The Poetic and Compositional Techniques in Jeremiah'. But Gordon McConville had proposed an Old Testament project to examine the relationship between Jeremiah and Deuteronomy which would have built on his foundational work on the relationship between the so-called prose and poetry of Jeremiah, the issue upon which questions about the unity and integrity of the book hung. A seemingly abstruse study of poetry and prose in Jeremiah, therefore, was an essential part of a study with wide

topics were good on the whole. Secondly, it seemed that most of
the PhD researchers went on to teach. And thirdly, he raised the
weakness of Biblical Theology in the work of the House and
Fellowship, a problem given the influence of theology on, and its
inseparability from, exegesis. He made three suggestions. First,
they ought to consider how to strengthen the work in Biblical
Theology: the idea of a combined conference in 1984 was a step in
the right direction. But were there other ways in which academic
studies could be 'related to the actual business of discovering
the meaning and application (both intellectual and practical) of the
teaching of scripture'? Secondly, could they do more to help
research students to get better supervisors and better research
topics? Thirdly, could they do more to help people into more constructive work once their PhD research was complete? Should
they establish more Tyndale House Fellowships? Surely some able
people would develop in the direction of Biblical Theology,
Ethics, Applied Theology, Comparative Religion, Systematic
Theology and other disciplines where good scholars were desper-
ately needed. He also made the practical point that while there
were scarcely any jobs in Old or New Testament, London Bible
College and Spurgeon's had recently been crying out for good
people in Philosophy and Ethics. He admitted that the opening
criticism he had quoted was very much exaggerated, but the 'well-
respected academic member' had laid his finger on a danger which
must be watched.[4]

His predecessor as General Secretary, Douglas Johnson, also
had a proposition to push at the same meeting of the Council. He
was concerned that the Genesis 1 – 11 project should be given

---

implications for its relation with Deuteronomy and thus for the whole
of Old Testament theology. But undoubtedly Dr Barclay was right that
specialized research should be able to demonstrate its wider significance for
theology and the church, as envisaged by those who originated the House.

4. In a final thought, Dr Barclay noted how many university Theology
faculties were dependent on students training for the ministry. Should
Evangelical students not therefore begin calling the tune a little more in
what is regarded as worthwhile Theology?

priority. He regarded it as 'the single most important and needed subject for research'. He argued:

> For forty-four years, from the original planning meeting of the first Biblical Research Committee in 1938, through the fruitful BRC conference of 1941, the purchase of the House in 1943 and at many intervals since, this precise need has been pin-pointed, called 'urgent' and everyone agreed 'something must be done immediately'.

Clearly the importance he attached to such a study of the text, literary structure and historical background of Genesis 1 – 11 was connected to its strategic apologetic significance. The reigning paradigm of the evolutionary development of Israel's religious development from polytheism to monotheism needed a powerful scholarly challenge. This was to be Douglas Johnson's last significant contribution to the committee he had called together in 1938. He was the last surviving original member of the BRC still serving on what was now the Tyndale House Council in 1982.

Entering the fifth decade

While attempts were being made to look with vision at the long-term aims of research to further the influential presentation of the Evangelical Christian perspective to the church, the university world and the wider society, more immediate and practical vision was also required for the development of Tyndale House and the ongoing work of the Fellowship as they completed forty years of activity. As we have seen, there had been significant progress in publications with the success of the Gospels project. In July 1983 David Wenham completed his 'distinguished contribution' as director of the Gospels Project for four years. Volume III, *Midrash and Historiography*, had just been published, and Volume IV, *The Rediscovery of Jesus' Eschatological Discourse* (his own volume) was almost ready for the publisher. He would continue editorial work on Volume V, *The Jesus Tradition outside the Gospels*, and Volume VI, *The Miracles of Jesus*, and secretarial help would be made available. Other publications were also progressing. A special grant was given to Dr Hemer for a year to complete *The Seven Churches of Asia* and begin research and writing on the historicity of Acts. Mr

John L. McGregor was also given a special one-year grant to assist in the Genesis 1 – 11 project and engage in his own research for that. A one-year Fellowship was also to be recommended for Dr Craig Blomberg to produce a popularization of the *Gospel Perspectives* series.

There was some progress too with the Genesis 1 – 11 project. No suitable applicant was available for appointment as director, but a consultation had been held at Tyndale House on 13 May 1983 and a list drawn up of areas to be examined. The proposal was that there should be three volumes, one dealing with literary and historical issues, one with theological matters, and one aimed at a popular audience and including discussion of all the questions frequently asked about Genesis 1 – 11. Alan Millard also reported that papers were being written and presented with a view to inclusion in the 'History and the Old Testament' project.[5]

The Warden's annual report for 1982–83, given at that same meeting in July, detailed the changes in personnel. Mr Craig C. Broyles had taken up his duties as Librarian. David Wenham was leaving to take up a New Testament lectureship at Wycliffe Hall, Oxford, and John H. Martin was to lecture in Biblical Studies at All Nations Christian College. Miss Ann Bradshaw was moving to a legal firm after seven years as secretary. Five readers had obtained academic posts: at Oak Hill College; Trinity Evangelical Divinity School in Deerfield, Illinois; St Bede's Theological College in Umtata, South Africa; Westmont College, California; and the University of Witwatersrand. Six library readers had

---

5. At this meeting in July 1983, Dr Bruce Milne was warmly thanked for his leadership of the Systematic Theology group (see page 183) and assured of the council's prayerful interest as he took up pastoral duties in Vancouver. The Warden also reported that Sir Norman and Lady Anderson had been presented with a book from Tyndale House Council on the occasion of their Golden Wedding. Attention was also drawn to the fortieth anniversary of the purchase of Tyndale House, which would be recognized in the September Appeal letter. 'The matter of a possible writing of a history of Tyndale House was deferred.' To the best of this author's knowledge, it was never raised again.

completed their PhDs. The Warden also reported that the annual Trust grant of £40,000 had been increased by £25,000, enabling the House to support eleven additional researchers. Twenty grants were made in all, mainly to PhD students. Dr Harris summed up progress:

> As we are now able to reflect on the first forty years of the ministry of Tyndale House to the Church, we marvel and give thanks for God's gracious prospering of the work. As the House enters the fifth decade of its existence, we are poised on the threshold of some important developments, in particular the formation of a team of post-doctoral researchers at the House, the possible extension to the Library, and the possible wider influence of the House and the Tyndale Fellowship in helping to foster and co-ordinate on a worldwide scale evangelical research and writing in the area of biblical and theological studies.

But perhaps the wider short-term picture was not so positive. The following month, Prof. Howard Marshall wrote a confidential note for the consideration of the Tyndale House Council at the first opportunity. In it he commented that, while there were senior members of the Fellowship holding university posts, no 'junior' members had recently gained university appointments. This seemed to be reflected in the number of overseas scholars attending study groups and obtaining Tyndale grants. Indeed, these comments might also have been supported by the number of overseas appointments obtained by library readers on completing their doctorates.

But the mid-1980s not only saw Tyndale House and the Tyndale Fellowship taking stock and strategizing; there were also some significant developments.

New developments

The Hexagon
For Tyndale House, the major challenge of Murray Harris's years as Warden was the need to extend the library, and he presented the rationale for an extension to the Business Committee of the council

in 1982. First, there was the need for additional accommodation for readers. The twenty-one rented desks were always in use and a further six to ten could easily be filled. Secondly, additional shelving was needed. Five hundred books and five hundred issues of journals were added every year, and shelving reached almost to the ceiling. There was nowhere for a book display. Thirdly, like most academic libraries, they needed to have a periodicals bay for current periodicals, separate from the bound volumes. Fourthly, a larger Librarian's office, an interview room, an office for the Warden and office space for other staff were all needed. There was nowhere for supervisors to talk to students, and the TF secretary and Gospels Project director worked from an ordinary library desk.

This initial brief presentation of the rationale was followed by a fuller paper which detailed the needs. With the growing number of Tyndale House research grants, the demand for space was going to increase. In addition to the extra offices mentioned in the initial paper, the Warden now also mentioned the need for a seminar room holding up to fifty people. Various short-term solutions were reviewed, but all had disadvantages. There were several possible long-term solutions. The first was to revive the 1966 plans for the extension of the library 'from the garden door southwards', which it was estimated would now cost between £130,000 and £200,000. The second was to use the 1966 plans (without the additional living accommodation) for an extension at the east end of the library. That would preserve more open space. Another suggestion was to expand the library southwards along its entire ground-floor length.

Sir Kirby Laing, as chairman of the business committee, reported to Tyndale House Council on 16 July 1983 on a feasibility study done by Mr Burden of Cusdin, Burden and Howitt. He had prepared plans with such great sensitivity and creativity that the Cambridge city planners and the Fire Department had responded positively. The business committee agreed with Mr Burden that the main House should be retained. Examination of the second floor of the library building showed that it could not support the extra loading for library use. The plans included four phases: first, alterations to the ground floor of the library to give extra stack space; second, alterations to the main House to meet administrative needs; third, the building of a hexagonal[6] library extension on the south side, giving additional reading space; and finally, alterations to the first floor of the library building. (The original idea of an octagon had been changed to a hexagon.) Several suggestions were made at the council meeting, including six reading bays on the north side of the library, accommodating four desks in each bay, and duplicating the bays in the south side. It was agreed that Sir Kirby and J. C. W. Roberts should form a sub-committee and send their recommendations on the various options to members of the council for their comments.

The meeting also agreed to make the post of Bursar full-time and approved a job description.[7] It was agreed to recommend the Revd Iain B. Hodgins to the UCCF Council and the IVF Trust for appointment, commencing 1 September 1983. Miss Ruth M. Otway was also recommended for appointment as secretary.

The building of the library extension began in April 1984. Twelve reading bays were added to the library, each accommodating from two to four readers. The two-storeyed hexagon included a periodicals room, a reading room with a new book display, additional desk and shelving space and offices on the ground floor, and a seminar room on the first floor. For a year, research had to live with the upheaval of building construction.

War: The first TF Joint Conference

It was quite convenient that the Tyndale Fellowship study groups did not meet that summer in Tyndale House, but at the High Leigh

---

6. See page 135.

7. The Bursar would keep the financial records (excepting the library funds), supervise domestic staff and the maintenance of the property, answer general inquiries, arrange accommodation, acknowledge gifts and have general responsibility for the physical welfare of all in Tyndale House. He would also assist the editor of *The Tyndale Bulletin*, take care of advertising and practical arrangements for lectures, seminars and Open Days, produce publicity material, purchase household supplies, determine rents, supervise cleaning, assist the Librarian in annual stocktaking, assist the Tyndale Fellowship secretary in all administrative and practical tasks, and travel as asked to make the work of the House known.

conference centre. For, while the major development at the House was the building extension, the major development for the Fellowship was the first plenary conference since the early 1950s, planned for 9–12 July 1984.[8] The theme of war was topical, since in April 1982 the junta in Argentina led by General Leopoldo Galtieri had invaded the British colony of the Falkland Islands, 400 hundred miles offshore in the South Atlantic, and the British had been amazed to find themselves at war, sending a task force 8,000 miles away to reconquer the islands.

Five main papers were delivered at the conference and later published, four of them in the *Evangelical Quarterly*. Derek Kidner's paper, 'Old Testament Perspectives on War', considered three kinds of war in the Old Testament; the nature and purpose of the *ḥērem* (what was 'devoted' to God); the 'holy war'; the effects of the monarchy on war; lessons for the present era; and finally the Old Testament vision of peace.[9] Howard Marshall's paper, 'New Testament Perspectives on War', looked at the use of the language of war in the New Testament, gave most space to the teaching of Jesus, and considered briefly the rest of the New Testament.[10] David Wright's paper, 'War in a Church-Historical Perspective', summarized Christian views on war in the 'Age of the Martyrs', the development of the 'Just War' theory by Ambrose and Augustine,

---

8. Iain Hodgins, the new Bursar of Tyndale House, was present at the Tyndale Fellowship Committee meeting in September 1983 and assumed his responsibilities for correspondence with members and for finances. Since no new TF secretary had yet been appointed, he also took the minutes. Once appointed, the new secretary would be responsible for correspondence with Tyndale Lecturers, the biannual Members' Letter and 'the general guidance of the Fellowship', and it was hoped that this lighter role would enable someone other than a research student to take the position. By March 1984 still no appointment had been made, and the Warden brought a list of names to consider. The joint conference therefore took place with David Wenham and Iain Hodgins carrying the administrative load.

9. *EQ*, 57 (1985), 99–113.

10. *EQ*, 57 (1985), 115–132.

thinking in the medieval period, and the views of Luther and Calvin.[11] George Carey, who was chairman of the Biblical Theology Study Group and now Principal of Trinity College, Bristol, was given the task of looking theologically at the biblical and historical material and considering the hermeneutical approaches and interpretations of some recent theologians.[12] He considered 'Yahweh – the Warrior God'; the impact of the teaching of Jesus; the early church view of the Christian as a citizen of two communities; and then at the debate between pacifism and 'Just War' theories in the modern era, looking specifically at the writings of Jean Lasserre and John Macquarrie. John Stott's final paper considered contemporary issues and perspectives; the material was incorporated in his book *Issues Facing Christians Today*.[13]

In addition to the plenary sessions, the study groups had three sessions (as opposed to their normal seven), and Professors Bruce and Wiseman were asked to speak at a special session on the past and future of the Tyndale Fellowship. Several Tyndale Lectures were also delivered. Dr Nigel Cameron, Warden of the newly founded Rutherford House in Edinburgh, preached at a concluding celebration of the Lord's Supper.

In reviewing this first attempt at a plenary conference at their meeting in September 1984, the committee agreed that the interaction between the study groups had been very valuable. However, there was some feeling that there had been inadequate time for the study groups to pursue their specialist interests, and the conference programme had been very full. Further, attendance at the annual study groups usually came to a total of about one hundred, and since 140 participants were required to meet the costs at High Leigh, the conference had sustained a financial loss. Lessons from the experiment would have to be carefully noted if another plenary conference were to be held.

---

11. *EQ*, 57 (1985), 133–161.
12. George L. Carey, 'Biblical-Theological Perspectives on War and Peace', *EQ*, 57 (1985), 163–178.
13. John Stott, *Issues Facing Christians Today* (London: Marshall, Morgan & Scott, 1984).

By that same committee meeting in September 1984 the chairman was able to announce to the TF committee that Dr M. J. Selman of Spurgeon's College was willing to accept an invitation to become secretary of the Tyndale Fellowship. The TF secretary would therefore no longer be based at Tyndale House, and practical and administrative work would be cared for by the Bursar as Administrative Secretary of the Fellowship.

New guidelines for proposing new members of the Fellowship were suggested by the chairman, Alan Millard. Only those established in research for a year should be proposed for membership, and sponsors should have been members for at least three years. Instead of a second sponsor, there should be a referee who would testify to the applicant's Christian commitment in a local church, and recommendations should be circulated in writing to the chairman and the Warden of Tyndale House before coming to the committee.[14]

David Deboys, newly appointed as Librarian at Tyndale House, attended the next TF Committee meeting on 22 March 1984. R. W. L. Moberly had agreed to succeed John Goldingay as secretary of the Old Testament group, and T. A. Noble to succeed R. J. Bauckham as secretary of the Historical Theology group. Gerald Bray

---

14. Since the adoption of the constitution in January 1980 the Tyndale House Council had already approved all the TF committee members now serving. In January 1981, they had approved Dr George Carey and the Revd Ron Davies as chairman and secretary of the Biblical Theology group, Professor Wiseman and the Revd John Goldingay for the Old Testament group, Professor Howard Marshall and Dr Max Turner for the New Testament group, and the Revd David Field and the Revd Chris Wright for the Ethics group. In July 1981 they had approved Mr D. F. Wright and Dr Richard Bauckham for the Historical Theology group and Mr A. R. Millard (also chairman of the TF committee) as chairman of the Biblical Archaeology group. M. J. Selman, D. B. Milne, A. N. S. Lane and R. T. France had also been approved as additional members. John Barclay replaced Chris Wright in January 1982. A new chairman was found to succeed D. J. Wiseman in the Old Testament Study Group when Gordon Wenham agreed to assume that responsibility in March 1983.

recounted the history of the Systematics group, which had met with Bruce Milne, and David Wright suggested that the Historical Theology group should expand to become the Historical and Systematic Theology study group. After further discussion, it was renamed the Christian Doctrine study group.

Financial support

Some concern had apparently risen in Tyndale House Council discussions from time to time about the reliance of Tyndale House upon one generous Trust, and in July 1984 Vernon Cobb presented a short paper to the council on the matter. He noted that in 1980, 47% of the running expenses and bursaries granted by Tyndale House had come from the Laing Trust. In 1981 that had risen to 93%; in 1982 it had been 71%; in 1983, 84%; and in 1984 it would be 78%, according to the budget. He addressed three questions. The first was about the effect on support from others. On that he noted that individual Christians tended to give money to workers known to them personally, but that the council should seek wider support.

> However [he continued] because the work of TH appears remote from evangelism, many Christians have little conception of its value. Its contribution tends to be recognized by a relatively small number of Christians who have seen the benefits of research in the spheres of business and education. The Trust represents that recognition on the part of one man!

Secondly, Mr Cobb asked, 'To what dangers does it expose Tyndale House?' In theory the trustees might seek to exert undue influence on its work, but there was no hint of that. Another possibility was that Tyndale House could be financially embarrassed if the trustees should suddenly withdraw their support. But that was not likely to happen, since no grants were awarded until the funds were available or promised. Thirdly, he asked what view the trustees took, and concluded that they had shown no reluctance to give. Indeed, for the extension 'they themselves showed considerable enthusiasm and promised massive financial support so that the work could be completed in one stage'. Mr Cobb wrote:

> Having now considered the matter, I have concluded (a) that my
> previous misgivings were based more on emotion than on prayerful
> consideration and (b) that the trust's generosity is not to be feared: rather
> it is cause for gratitude to the God Who liberally provides all that is
> needed for the blessing of His people and the furtherance of the gospel.

But the council did not sit back and rely on the Laing Trust. They
requested the Warden to make a fund-raising visit to North America
to publicize the newly expanded library facilities and to present the
immediate financial needs. Over 60% of library users over the previous five years had been from North America, but only 6% of
donation income had come from there. The Library Extension
Appeal Fund still needed £35,000 to reach the target of £250,000;
since gifts were tax-deductible and the dollar had never been
stronger against the pound, it seemed a very appropriate time to go.

Murray Harris made his visit to North America in November
and December 1984 and reported to the council that response
everywhere was warm and positive. Most people were unaware of
the strategic importance of Tyndale House for Evangelicalism
worldwide. Two large churches and several individuals were considering Tyndale House for their giving in 1985 or 1986. A friend
from his time as a research student in Manchester, Dr Paul
E. Leonard, was eager to establish a North American support
group and had also formed the opinion (as chairman of an IBR
steering group) that IBR would do better to support Tyndale
House than to attempt to duplicate it.[15] Since the Warden had been
asked to serve on the NIV Committee on Bible Translation, which
met annually in the USA, there would be further opportunities to
undertake publicity for Tyndale House.

Library report, 1985
David Deboys submitted his first report as Librarian in June 1985.
Craig Broyles had guided the library through the upheavals of the
extension in the earlier part of the academic year, and since taking

---

15. For the formation of the American IBR (Institute for Biblical Research),
see page 162.

up office the new Librarian had been trying to catch up with book ordering, which was behind because of a two-month interregnum. The library had been fortunate to be guided over the years by a variety of highly dedicated and gifted scholars, but a variety of systems had been used in cataloguing books and a consistent approach had to be developed. A significant part of the Librarian's time was taken up in helping readers. Of the twenty-four regular long-term readers, eight were from Britain, eleven from the USA, two from Canada, two from Australia and one from Scandinavia. Six were on sabbatical, eleven engaged in doctoral research, two were the Tyndale House Research Fellows (Colin Hemer and Craig Blomberg) and two were missionaries from Bangladesh. Over thirty short-term readers were also using the library. As in previous years, the number engaged in NT research outnumbered those in OT research by four to one.

A research degrees proposal

At their meeting on 31 January 1986, the Tyndale House Council considered a proposal from Gordon Wenham that they should apply to the CNAA, the Council for National Academic Awards, to be approved for the supervision of research degrees. He began by defining the two problems he saw. First, 'despite the good flow of Evangelical research students over the last few decades, relatively few have tackled key areas of controversy in modern debate'. Their theses tended to deal with fringe questions, and therefore the products of Evangelical scholarship seemed remote to concerned laymen and there were few Evangelicals who could speak out in the current theological debate. Secondly, he noted that some able Evangelical research students were weaned away from conservative positions by their supervisors. The reason for both problems could be the same: namely 'the TF policy of encouraging students to research under liberal scholars'.[16] In order to do acceptable theses they therefore tended to avoid areas where conservatives and liberals were at loggerheads.

---

16. There was of course no such formal policy, but it had always been accepted that doctoral students would seek the best-qualified supervisors.

His proposal was therefore that Tyndale House should investigate the possibility of its staff supervising PhD research, probably
in affiliation with the Council for National Academic Awards. With
its library facilities and location, Tyndale House would be very
attractive to Evangelical students, and as some Anglican colleges
had moved in an Evangelical direction in order to attract more students, so the universities would find themselves under pressure to
appoint staff who would attract conservative research students. The
Warden was asked to prepare a paper on this proposal to be considered at the Tyndale House Academic Sub-committee.

The UCCF Research Council

The Tyndale House Council spent much more time at this meeting
(on 31 January 1986) considering a report from the UCCF Trust on
the relations of the UCCF Trust, the UCCF Council, Tyndale
House and the Tyndale Fellowship. Mr Brian Harris, who had
served as IVF Treasurer and then as chairman of the Business
Advisory Committee, indicated that discussion in the Trust
Committee had been prompted by a concern that theological
research (as distinct from biblical research) fell outside the terms of
reference of Tyndale House. The Trust Committee had held four
meetings on this and had reported to the whole Trust. He presented
a document entitled 'Memorandum to the Tyndale House Council:
The Organisation of UCCF', explaining that it came with the unan-
imous approval of the Trust Committee and the UCCF Council.

The Trust Committee had considered three options: a total separation of research from the student work; a single council
controlling both; and a compromise. They had opted for the compromise: to set up a UCCF Research Council, to which the
Tyndale House Council would be responsible, along with a new
parallel body, the 'Theology and Education Committee'. The latter
would be concerned with areas of research other than Biblical
Studies. The UCCF Research Council and the UCCF Council,
the body which oversaw the student work, would both be responsible to the UCCF Trust. The Trust would continue to be a non-
executive holding body.

There was then some discussion about the role of the Tyndale
Fellowship in the new structure. Three options emerged: that the

TF Committee should be responsible to the Tyndale House Council as at present; that the TF study groups in Biblical Studies should be responsible to the Tyndale House Council and the others to the new Theology and Education Committee; or, thirdly, that the TF Committee could be responsible to the new Research Council. After discussion, there was agreement with the new structure in principle, and some minor amendments to procedure and nomenclature were suggested. A better name should be found for the Theology and Education Committee, and the third option was recommended for the Tyndale Fellowship Committee: that it should be directly responsible to the new Research Council. Meanwhile, since Dr George Carey had resigned as chairman of the Biblical Theology Study Group, approval was given for the Revd Roger Beckwith, the Warden of Latimer House, Oxford, to succeed him.

The end of an era

By July 1986 the Tyndale House Council was considering a double resignation, and indeed the end of an era. At the end of February, Murray Harris had submitted his resignation as Warden to take appointment as Professor of New Testament at Trinity Evangelical Seminary, Deerfield, Illinois, from September, and Donald Wiseman had announced his decision to retire as chairman, after almost three decades. In response to an advertisement six persons had expressed interest in the post of Warden, but none was considered suitable. Some others had been approached, but were not available. An attempt had been made to find an acting Warden, but so far without success. Three Research Fellowships were awarded for the next year: to Dr Richard Hess for work on 'Personal Names in Genesis'; to Dr Donald Carson (provided no funding was available from the USA) for work to complete his *A Syntactical Concordance to the Greek New Testament*; and to Dr Colin Hemer for his research into the historicity of Acts. Eleven research grants were also awarded, and the chairman reported that three Research Fellows would be working at Tyndale House on the Genesis 1 – 11 project during the 1986–87 academic year. Dr Craig Blomberg reported on his popularization of the *Gospel Perspectives* series, and the Warden was asked to convey to him the warm gratitude of the council for that and for his editing of the sixth volume, on *The Miracles of Jesus*.

In his last report, Murray Harris announced that Mrs E. Eggo had retired after almost twenty years' devoted service as house-keeper, and Mrs Audrey Disney had now assumed responsibility for all domestic affairs. Six library readers or research grant recipients had been appointed to academic posts: Kevin J. Vanhoozer, Craig L. Blomberg, Iain W. Provan, Barry G. Webb, Ernest C. Lucas and Christopher Marshall. Eight library users or grant recipients had completed PhDs. Volume V of the Gospel Perspectives series, *The Jesus Tradition outside the Gospels*, had been published in October 1985, and Volume VI, *The Miracles of Jesus*, was to be published in the autumn. The series was a robust, informed defence of the reliability of the Gospels by thirty-three New Testament scholars from seven nationalities. Craig Blomberg's popularization of the main findings *The Historical Reliability of the Gospels* had been completed during his year as a Research Fellow. Colin Hemer, also a Research Fellow, had revised for publication his major work *The Letters to the Seven Churches of Asia* during his first year at the House and was now working on a two-volume work on the historicity of Acts, which he hoped to complete by July 1987. Two Research Fellows, Dr Leslie McFall and Dr David D. Tsumura, would start work in the autumn on the Genesis 1 – 11 project. Grants totalling £35,350 had been awarded to nineteen researchers. A fortnightly seminar had been held at the House, usually with a visiting American scholar, and some twenty-two undergraduate and graduate students had attended a conference on the need and opportunities for biblical research. The weekly chapel service on a Tuesday morning was now being held in the seminar room of the hexagon. All of the thirty-two desks in the extended library had been in use throughout the year. Five hundred and twenty-six books had been processed in 1985, and a further three hundred and thirty-eight in the first four months of 1986.

The chairman also reported that the Warden had submitted a proposal to the Academic Sub-committee giving the pros and cons of PhD supervision at Tyndale House through the CNAA, but that the consensus was that the scheme was interesting but impracticable. It would change the function of Tyndale House, and students taught there might become suspect in some unsympathetic circles. Sir Kirby Laing reported from the Business Sub-committee that final accounts had still to come for the extension and that £2,500 had been received from the will of Mrs E. M. Houlding, whose late husband had served on the UCCF Business Advisory Committee and as one of the businessmen on the Biblical Research Committee. Inquiries were to be made about the policy of the University Library on fire insurance; currently the library contents were insured for £235,000.

At the conclusion of the meeting two presentations were made. Professor Wiseman presented Dr and Mrs Harris with a gift in appreciation of their service to the House during the previous five years. But before that, he himself was presented with a gift, marking his resignation as chairman, by his successor, Alan Millard, who commented with warm gratitude on the magnificent contribution he had made in nearly three decades. Those three decades had indeed seen several significant achievements. First, there had been the reassertion of the focus on biblical research at the Waverley Hotel conference of 1961, with the aim of producing significant publications and the nurturing of a new generation of biblical scholars. There had been steady progress towards those goals under four Wardens at the House, the financial storms of inflation had been weathered, and the library building extended. The Tyndale Fellowship had maintained its commitment both to the Evangelical faith and to 'unfettered research' (although not all the issues there had been resolved), and, largely at the initiative of Oliver Barclay, had begun to address the need for contemporary Evangelical thinking in the wider areas of Theology and Ethics.

9. WIDER HORIZONS

Millard, Wright, Cook and Winter, 1986–94

Although he had retired as General Secretary in 1980, Dr Oliver Barclay continued to take a vital interest in biblical and theological research and its role in the mission of the UCCF. The biblical research promoted at Tyndale House was now bearing fruit in publications and in the emergence of a new generation of biblical scholars who were committed both to the highest standards of scholarship and to the Evangelical faith. That was full of hope for the future. But Oliver Barclay was still concerned about the present influence of the Evangelical voice in wider areas such as Ethics, Theology and Education.

New agencies

The Whitefield Institute
By 1986, the Theology Project which he had initiated was in its eighth year of operation, and in 1985–86 awarded £18,000 to eleven researchers, mainly to complete research degrees in Education or Theology. Four former grantees had been appointed during the year

as lecturers and one as an editor. The new UCCF Research Council was established that year[1] and set up the new Theology and Religious Education Committee, which met for the first time in January 1987. It was chaired by Dr David Cook of Green College, Oxford, and included A. N. S. Lane, Philip May, David F. Wright, and Oliver Barclay acting as secretary. Its remit was to establish a new research institute in Oxford to perform a parallel function to Tyndale House, but without establishing a library. All its finance was to be devoted to research grants and the work of its Director. Whereas grants from Tyndale House were for Biblical Studies, the new institute would finance work in five areas: Doctrine, Philosophical Theology, Apologetics, Ethics and Religious Education. By the second meeting in April, the new committee had selected the name 'Whitefield Institute' in honour of the great eighteenth-century evangelist George Whitefield, who had been recruited into the Wesleys' 'Holy Club' while a student at Oxford and had later led them into evangelism by 'field preaching'. David Cook took up his post as Director of the institute that same month and so became secretary of what now became the Whitefield Institute Council. Oliver Barclay took his place as chairman of the council and presented a paper on the policies which had governed the awarding of grants by the Theology Project up to 1986. An office was established in Oxford.

At their third meeting, in September 1987, the new Whitefield Institute Council approved a job description for the Director. He was to promote and encourage research aimed at producing literature; supervise sabbatical study; organise seminars for academic teachers, ministers and lay people; identify the issues of the day calling for swift response; and guide research students in the selection of topics and supervisors. Meanwhile, the Tyndale Fellowship Committee had set up a working party, David Cook with Dewi Hughes and Martin Selman, to investigate ways to stimulate and coordinate Evangelicals in the field of Religious Studies. In consultation with Trevor Cooling of the Association of Christian Teachers, they had already identified a significant contemporary issue: namely, religious pluralism. A consultation was planned to

1. See pages 214ff.

tackle such questions as the nature of 'religion'; whether Christians
can teach world religions with integrity, and the eternal destiny
of people of other faiths. More widely, the council agreed that
Philosophical Theology and Ethics should be priorities, with particular attention to anthropology and sexuality. The possibility of a
textbook in Systematic Theology was discussed, and an inaugural
lecture by Alvin Plantinga was arranged. Plantinga delivered the
lecture on 'Justification and Theism' at the Examinations Schools in
Oxford on 4 May 1988.

David Cook was already in wide demand, as his very busy
schedule in his report to the council for the three months of
January to March 1988 illustrates:

> I spoke at Cuddesdon College on the Philosophy of the Social Services,
> to the Genetics Department of Oxford University on genetic
> engineering, did a series at Wycliffe Hall on Sociology of Religion, a day
> conference for lay readers on sexuality for the Guildford Diocese,
> preached at St Aldate's, Oxford, Dean Close School, Monmouth School,
> Mutley Baptist (Plymouth), Tenterden Baptist, Orpington Baptist,
> St Barnabas (Kensington), Regent's Park College, did a conference for
> ministers at Willersley Castle on ethical issues, did a weekend conference
> on [moral] decision making in Kingsbridge and Portsmouth, spoke in a
> doctor series for Cirencester Deanery, to the sixth form at King Edward
> VI School, Southampton, at the Southern Regional TSF conference in
> Oxford, at a day conference with Partnership in Northampton on
> medical issues. I also lectured at a LICC three-day conference on
> Practising Ethics for health care professionals, and a series of six lectures
> for Southampton School of Christian Studies on 'Thinking about Faith'
> and presented a paper to the Philosophy Society at Keele University.

In addition to his speaking engagements, the Director had published articles on homosexuality, suicide and AIDS, finished a first
draft of a book for IVP, and seen the third edition of his book *The
Moral Maze*[2] published. He had made two radio programmes on

---

2. E. David Cook, *The Moral Maze: A Way of Exploring Christian Ethics*
(London: SPCK, 1983).

embryo research, surrogacy and abortion and taken part in a Kilroy television show on mercy killing. He had been consulted by the BBC on questions about genetic engineering; Christian art; forgiveness and Nazism; and animal rights. He had been invited to do 'Thought for the Day', a three-minute slot on the BBC Radio 4 morning current affairs programme *Today*. In addition to these media engagements, he had run a Whitefield Institute day seminar in London, attended the RTSF national committee and organized a conference for those teaching Philosophy of Religion in the theological colleges. He had completed a CNAA validation exercise on possible federation for theological colleges and visited Spurgeon's College to advise on graduate courses. In addition to several other activities, he was preparing to lecture in the United States, visiting seven major cities, lecturing at the Billy Graham Centre for Ethics and taking a faculty conference at Gordon College.

By September 1988, there were ninety-two 'Friends' of the Whitefield Institute, some giving particularly generous support. By then, Timothy Bradshaw, Fred Hughes and Keith Watson had joined the council. Dr Watson presented a list of eight pressing issues for Christians in education, in addition to strictly religious education issues. The council soon added another twenty. But the major issue had arisen at the education consultation held in London in July 1988 for thirty-five leading Evangelicals in education, including university and college teachers, inspectors and education advisers. The educationalists were well aware of the practical implications for Evangelicals of contemporary thinking in Religious Studies, but they constantly felt themselves hampered by the lack of any serious foundational work on the theology of Religious Studies from an Evangelical perspective. Arising from that, a steering committee had been called, including David Cook, Dewi Hughes, who lectured in Religious Studies, Martin Selman, the TF secretary, and Trevor Cooling, the Director of Stapleford House.

The UCCF Research Council

Since the Whitefield Institute Council was really a development of work which had been initiated under the Theology Project, it very quickly got into its stride. The UCCF Research Council, on the other hand, was a completely new committee and had been introduced more to fulfil a need in the structure of UCCF than to perform a specific function. The Christian Unions in the universities had been the origin of the whole movement, and these had linked together voluntarily to form the Inter-Varsity Fellowship (now UCCF) in 1928. It was out of the mission to students by students that the publishing arm (now IVP) and the Graduates' Fellowship (now the Professional Groups) and the research arm had developed. In contrast to the WSCF and SCM, where former students such as John R. Mott and Tissington Tatlow had retained leadership and control,[3] the principle in the IVF/UCCF had always been that it should be a student organization operated by the current generation of students. True, there was a General Secretary, who began as a student, but who remained in office for almost forty years, and there was the UCCF Trust, senior figures who held the property and guaranteed faithfulness to the Evangelical aims, thus keeping faith with the many donors and supporters. And it is true that the structure had indeed grown around Douglas Johnson, the long-serving first General Secretary. But he had insisted on a background role as secretary, essentially as a facilitator, and this had continued to operate well under his successor, Oliver Barclay, who had grown with the organization and so was formed in its 'culture'. But now, with the continued growth of the work of UCCF, and with the advent of a new generation of leaders (including a General Secretary from outside the movement), some rationalization of the structures appeared to be necessary. Clear lines of organization and responsibility were needed which related the different agencies and recognized the primacy of the student work, and the major issue appeared to be the relationship between the student work and the research arm.

The Research Council was therefore invented as a compromise in preference to two other options: a more unified structure bringing research under the UCCF Council, or a complete separation of the research arm from the rest of the organization. The compromise was to give the UCCF Trust Committee, previously a fairly inactive

---

3. See Chapter 1 above, 'The Student Volunteer Movement', pages 21f.

body, a more active role supervising and coordinating three bodies: the UCCF Research Council, the UCCF Council and IVP. The Research Council would then supervise and coordinate the work of three committees: the Tyndale House Council, the Whitefield Institute Council and the Tyndale Fellowship Committee.

Dr R. T. France, who was now Principal of Wycliffe Hall, Oxford, served as the first chairman of the Research Council. According to the Terms of Reference approved by the UCCF Trust Committee on 9 October 1987, the council would include a representative of the Trust, up to two representatives of the UCCF Council, the chairmen (or other representatives) of the three constituent bodies, the General Secretary of the UCCF and other members they wished to co-opt. The Warden of Tyndale House or the Director of the Whitefield Institute was to act as secretary. The new council's main function was to give primary attention to the strategic appraisal of the state of Evangelical scholarship, rather than to the details of the operation of the dependent committees. It was to coordinate applications by the Tyndale House Council and the Whitefield Institute Council to the Laing Trust, and it was to have the responsibility of appointing the Warden, Librarian, and senior staff at Tyndale House and the Director and senior staff of the Whitefield Institute, upon the recommendation of the respective councils, and approving the officers of the Tyndale Fellowship Committee.

One of the first actions of the new Council was to conduct a survey of forty-three Evangelical leaders, asking them to identify areas of current discussion in Biblical Studies, Theology, Ethics and Education where there was a need for an Evangelical contribution. The council was particularly interested in areas where a biblical or theological evaluation of secular thinking was needed, and the results of the survey were considered at the council meeting on 18 September 1989. Twenty-nine replies had been received, and in the field of Theology and Biblical Studies religious pluralism was away out in front as the most significant issue, with eighteen votes. Interestingly, the doctrine of the church came second, being selected by eleven. Thereafter, the numbers dropped to six (Liberation Theology), five (the unity of the Bible and Theology), five (women issues) and four (the missionary role of the Church at home and abroad). In the field of Ethics, medical ethics, specifically genetic engineering, was considered the most significant issue by fourteen, and no other issue attracted any more than six votes.

Bruce W. Winter

During the year in which the Whitefield Institute and the Research Council were set up, Dr Don Carson of Trinity Evangelical Seminary in Deerfield, Illinois, was serving as acting Warden at Tyndale House. Since Alan Millard had become chairman of the Tyndale House Council, the Tyndale Fellowship Committee nominated David Wright of New College, Edinburgh, to succeed him as their chairman and the Tyndale House Council approved his appointment in January 1987. Douglas Johnson's final retirement from the Tyndale House Council was announced at the same meeting. He had served on the BRC/THC for one year short of fifty years. At the same meeting the name of the Revd Bruce Winter was placed before the council as a possible Warden. An Australian who had been vicar of St George's Church, Singapore, and Warden of St Peter's House, Singapore, and had taught at Moore Theological College, Sydney, he was currently working in Cambridge and was just completing a PhD thesis at Macquarie University under Professor Edwin Judge. By the July meeting of the council, he was present, but only as Warden designate, since a work permit still had to be issued.

The July meeting of the THC also heard of the sudden death of Dr C. J. Hemer, who had been Librarian from 1980 to 1982 and was currently a Research Fellow. A meticulous and respected scholar, who had held an academic teaching appointment only for a brief time at Manchester, Colin Hemer's working life (as Dick France wrote)[4] seemed to have revolved around Tyndale House. The community there was as a family to him, and he had a genius for drawing residents and readers into the fellowship of the House, taking a particular pastoral interest in overseas students. As acting Warden, Don Carson had given pastoral care during his last weeks, and his death left a painful gap. Members and friends

---

4. See pages 187f.

contributed to a bench, which was carved with a simple tribute and placed in the Tyndale House garden.

The committee agreed that Conrad Gempf, a Fellowship member who had recently submitted his PhD, completed under Prof. Howard Marshall in Aberdeen, should be invited to edit Dr Hemer's unfinished manuscript on the book of Acts and to prepare the camera-ready copy for publication under the joint supervision of Professors Marshall and Bruce. Only Dr Hemer's views would be stated, and in place of the final chapter, on which he had not begun work, there would be a summary of what he had already written.[5] The cost would be met from the balance of the funds for his fellowship, and if necessary from Dr Hemer's estate, the bulk of which he had left to Tyndale House. He had given the responsibility for determining its use to the Academic Sub-committee, his own preference being that it should enable developing-world biblical scholars to come to Tyndale House for doctoral or post-doctoral research.

At the meeting of the THC in February 1988 Bruce Winter, now officially appointed, fulfilled the Warden's role as secretary. The acting chairman of the Business Committee, D. G. Stradling, reported that the Lodge had been redecorated and a new scullery and kitchen installed in the House. An Ibycus scholarly computer had been purchased, and Tyndale House Library was now linked to the University of Cambridge mainframe computer. Later that year the members of the council signed an atlas of the Bible as a gift for Sir Kirby Laing, in thanks for his service as chairman of the Business Committee.[6]

In the Warden's report for 1988–89, Bruce Winter reported that

---

5. Conrad Gempf's research had been on a similar topic. Dr Hemer's manuscript was originally entitled 'The Historicity of Acts' and there were
   several chapters which had not been completed or even started. Some of
   those were omitted and others published as articles in the *Tyndale Bulletin*.
   The title was changed to *The Book of Acts in the Setting of Hellenistic History*
   to reflect better the reshaped manuscript.
6. Under the new structure, the Tyndale Fellowship Committee was no
   longer responsible to the Tyndale House Council but to the Research

on 1 March the first copy of Colin Hemer's volume, *The Book of Acts in the Setting of Hellenistic History*, published by J. C. B. Möhr of Tübingen in their prestigious New Testament monograph series, had been delivered to Tyndale House. The 480-page work had been set up on the Tyndale House desktop printing facilities and had been recommended to Möhr by Prof. Martin Hengel, who had visited Tyndale House in August 1988. The Warden thanked Conrad Gempf, the editor, and Professors Marshall and Bruce, both of whom had read all of the draft versions. At the launching of the book on 3 April, Professor Graham Stanton of King's College, London, had spoken of it as one of the five most substantial books in New Testament studies published in recent years. The Warden also reported that camera-ready copy of another book by a Tyndale House Research Fellow, Dr David Tsumura, working on the Genesis 1 – 11 project, was in the hands of Sheffield Academic Press.[7] Three other Research Fellows were currently working at the House: Prof. Lion Cachet from South Africa, Dr David Peterson from Australia and Dr Jonathan Chew from Singapore.

The Librarian, David Deboys, reminded the same May meeting of the THC that the recent expansion of the library would suffice only for a decade, and that it would do so only provided some measures were taken. He proposed bringing top shelves into use and disposing of the Church History collection. Even with these measures, further expansion would need to be considered in five years.

D. J. Wiseman's assessment of progress

Professor Wiseman thought it was an appropriate time to re-examine the purpose of Evangelical research and its future

---

Council. But in view of the close working relationship, it was agreed that a TF representative should serve on the THC, and that the TF secretary, Dr M. J. Selman, already a member of the council, should fill that role.

7. David Tsumura, *The Earth and the Waters in Genesis 1 and 2* (Sheffield: Sheffield Academic Press, 1989). Another publication resulting four years later from the Genesis 1 – 11 project was R. S. Hess, *Studies in the Personal Names of Genesis 1 – 11*, Vol. 234 of the series *Alter Orient und Altes Testament* (Neukirchen-Vluyn: Neukirchener Verlag, 1993).

direction, and prepared a paper which was considered at the next meeting of the THC on 17 January 1990. In it he concluded that the aim in founding Tyndale House had been, and still was, good. Though the development of Evangelical scholarship had been slower than hoped, the supply of appropriate university and college teachers over the previous forty years had been a distinct advance over the situation before the Second World War. Publications had been fewer than hoped for, largely because of the difficulty of finding suitable researchers for projects and directed research. Nonetheless, volumes produced, including the *New Bible Dictionary* and the work on Daniel, the Gospels, the Patriarchal narratives and Genesis, had produced books of lasting worth. The library was first class, augmented now by computer provision, but the expansion of the building had been piecemeal and achieved at increasing cost. Vision and boldness was needed for a new additional building with adaptable facilities. Just adding shelf space would not be enough. In the future the House should continue to concentrate strictly on Biblical Studies and to focus on new British scholars. With the passing of the founding generation, a new generation needed to be challenged, and some hitherto neglected areas should be considered, including Bible translation and Linguistics (perhaps an endowed place for a scholar from Wycliffe Bible Translators), Intertestamental Judaism and Biblical Archaeology.

'Disseminating the useful results'

When David Wright became chairman of the Tyndale Fellowship Committee in 1987, one of the first issues which he had to handle was a change in the Doctrinal Basis of the Fellowship. Members of the TF were still giving their assent to the 1960 Doctrinal Basis of the IVF/UCCF, but that had been slightly expanded in 1981. In a final informal report to Tyndale House Council in July 1986, Murray Harris had suggested that the changes would create unnecessary disquiet, not because TF members would disagree with the changes (which were all additions), but because many would disagree in principle with the idea of altering a Doctrinal Basis. In August 1987, however, the new chairman wrote to members of the Fellowship to tell them that the committee had agreed to the changes in principle and inviting any comments. The additions included a new article on Christology, totally omitted from the original:

> The full deity of the Lord Jesus Christ, the incarnate Son of God; his virgin birth and his real and sinless humanity; his death on the cross, his bodily resurrection and his present reign in heaven and earth.

There was also a new article on Justification:

> Justification as God's act of undeserved mercy, in which the sinner is pardoned all his sins, and accepted as righteous in God's sight, only because of the righteousness of Christ imputed to him, this justification being received by faith alone.

The article on the indwelling of the Holy Spirit was expanded to speak of gradual sanctification and power to witness in the world, and the article on the personal return of Christ was expanded to include the future judgment 'executing God's just condemnation on the impenitent and receiving the redeemed to eternal glory'. The introduction of these amendments to the Doctrinal Basis did not produce any debate in the Tyndale Fellowship, but the issue of biblical authority and biblical criticism surfaced once again.

Future directions and biblical authority

In March 1988, David Wright circulated what he called a 'green paper' on 'Future Directions' for the Tyndale Fellowship. He began from the aim of the Tyndale Fellowship as defined in its constitution:

> To advance the Christian faith by promoting biblical and theological studies and research and disseminating the useful results of such study and research for the public benefit in a spirit of loyalty to the Christian faith as enshrined in the consensus of the historic creeds, the confessions of the Reformation and the Doctrinal Basis of the Fellowship.

Clearly, this statement of the aim of the Fellowship meant that it was not simply a research society. Its overall purpose was 'to advance the Christian faith', and in order to do so it was not only to engage in research but to 'disseminate its useful results'. The paper mooted various suggestions for fulfilling the aim, such as promoting interdisciplinary discussion; making Biblical Theology central to the whole enterprise rather than a distinct study group; and concentrating on projects. He also had suggestions for fulfilling the second aspect of the aim, disseminating the results of research. The third aspect, loyalty to the historic faith and in particular the Doctrinal Basis, led him to redistribute to the TF Committee the paper drawn up by Dick France, Alan Millard and James Packer in 1979.[8] This third aspect of the aim constituted the distinctive necessity of the Tyndale Fellowship, and the significance and relevance of this to research had to be continually clarified. He quoted one correspondent who had replied to a request for comments, writing that there was 'an urgent need for a review of what constitutes a specifically evangelical approach to biblical study'. The whole issue had surfaced once again six years previously, when James Dunn's two-part article on the authority of Scripture in the Anglican Evangelical journal *Churchman*[9] was one of the factors leading to a new, more conservative editorial board and the sacking of the editor, who established the new journal *Anvil*.

The recurring question of the relationship of biblical authority and academic freedom in matters of biblical criticism came up again in the Tyndale Fellowship Committee three years later. Steve Singleton, the RTSF secretary, wrote to David Wright on 11 November 1991 conveying the concern which had been expressed by postgraduate Theology students in the RTSF about a perceived inconsistency between the theological position of some Tyndale Fellowship members and their commitment to the UCCF Doctrinal Basis. He forwarded a letter from Kevin Ellis, the

---

8. See above, pages 181f.

9. James D. G. Dunn, 'The Authority of Scripture according to Scripture', *Churchman*, 96 (1982), 104–122 and 201–225. There were already differences of opinion on a range of issues.

North-West of England representative on the RTSF Executive, raising specific questions about two TF members who were professors of standing. One advocated a form of reader-response hermeneutic, while the other openly differed from the interpretation of the Doctrinal Basis put forward in the definitive UCCF publication *Evangelical Belief*. While Kevin Ellis could understand how younger scholars would go through periods of struggle, and understood too that there was 'tremendous diversity' among Evangelicals and was not in favour of a purge or a witch-hunt, he did believe that there was a problem here. He was surely right in that the diversity of opinion could only go so far without dissolving the unity of the Evangelical position represented by UCCF, and at the heart of that unity was the common position on biblical authority and the implications for biblical interpretation. Evangelical Christianity affirmed the authority of Scripture in continuity with the Reformation confessions; but the UCCF position was differentiated from fundamentalism by simultaneously affirming the validity of biblical criticism. But could scholarship be totally 'unfettered', as F. F. Bruce had insisted, or were there limits on biblical criticism implied by the unique status of the Bible?

Religious pluralism

It was not this recurring issue, however, but the question of religious pluralism which was the major item on the agenda as David Wright took the chair of the Tyndale Fellowship. The consultation of educationalists arranged by David Cook of the Whitefield Institute in July 1988 had identified the pressing need for an Evangelical theological basis for approaching religious pluralism, particularly as it affected the discipline of Religious Studies in schools and colleges. The topic presented itself as a challenge which the three constituent bodies united under the UCCF Research Council – the Whitefield Institute, the Tyndale Fellowship and Tyndale House – should tackle together. The steering committee set up after the education conference had put it this way:

> It is crystal clear that there is a desperate need among those involved in education at every level for a Christian theology of pluralism from an evangelical perspective. It is also certain that Christians in general are

facing a major crisis of confidence in expressing their faith in our multi-faith contexts both in evangelism and in mission. The urgent need is for a biblically based theological framework for understanding and responding to religious pluralism and its fundamental challenge to our generation.

They identified the Tyndale Fellowship as the Christian organization best placed and most qualified to respond to that kind of challenge. Here was an opportunity for the research arm of UCCF to link research and mission by 'disseminating the useful results' of research undertaken in response to a request for help in what was seen as the most pressing and vital aspect of contemporary mission.

TF study groups had already laid plans for their 1990 conferences, but questionnaires were sent out to TF members and almost all of the forty-two replies received expressed support for the idea that the 1991 study groups should tackle the topic. It was agreed at the TF committee meeting in April 1989 that the Pluralism Project Steering Committee would arrange a preliminary conference in the spring of 1990 to clarify the precise issues that the study groups should be addressing.[10]

The preliminary planning conference took place at Stapleford House, the conference centre of the Association of Christian Teachers, on 22 and 23 March 1990. Six short papers were presented: Old Testament perspectives from John Goldingay; New Testament perspectives from Steve Motyer; the pluralist position of John Hick, presented by David Cook; a paper on issues of 'Love, Truth and Judgement' by Stephen Williams; a paper on sociology of pluralism by the sociologist Greg Smith; and a final paper on mission and evangelism by Colin Chapman, the Principal of the CMS Training College in Selly Oak, Birmingham, Crowther Hall. The missiologist Andrew Kirk and Ken Gnanakan of the South Asia Institute for Advanced Christian Studies in Bangalore also participated in the preparatory conference. At the end, the

---

10. That meeting was Martin Selman's last meeting as TF secretary, but he continued to act as secretary of the steering committee. By the November meeting of the TF committee, T. A. Noble had taken over as TF secretary.

Steering Committee met with all the members of the TF committee who were present and agreed to produce a list of the key
questions which had been established. It was agreed that the study
groups would need to meet together the following summer and
that, following that conference bringing together the expertise of
biblical scholars and theologians, the next step would be to receive
further comments on the published papers from practitioners,
probably at a further conference.[11]

Second plenary conference: Oak Hill, 1991

The second plenary conference of the Tyndale Fellowship,
'Evangelical Responses to Religious Pluralism', met from 8 to
11 June 1991 at Oak Hill Theological College, attended by over a
hundred participants. There were major papers given by Bruce
Winter, Richard Hess, John Goldingay, Stephen Williams, David
Cook and David Wright. Major papers were also given by two
guest speakers: Dr Shirley Dex on the sociology of pluralism and
Dr Robert Song on 'Pluralism and the State'. In the final plenary
session, Colin Chapman spoke on 'Mission/Evangelism' and
Martin Goldsmith of All Nations Christian College responded.

Interspersed with the plenary sessions were four sessions for
the regular study groups, with interdisciplinary discussion groups
meeting simultaneously. Two transatlantic participants, Bruce
Demarest of Denver Seminary and Clark Pinnock of McMaster
Divinity College in Ontario, enlivened the Christian Doctrine
Study Group with a hammer-and-tongs debate. The six Tyndale
Lectures were also delivered, and Gerald Bray led the concluding
celebration of the Lord's Supper using the Book of Common Prayer.

Thanks to an arrangement Bruce Winter had made with
Eerdmans, a selection of papers from the conference was published

---

11. Following a further telephone conference of the Pluralism Committee
in July in which David Wright, David Cook, Tom Noble, Martin Selman
and Bruce Winter participated, the outline of the joint study group
conference in the summer of 1991 was formulated. The proposal was
approved at the TF committee meeting in June and the final details left
to the Pluralism Committee.

rapidly in a volume planned as a supplement to the *Tyndale Bulletin*. Entitled *One God, One Lord in a World of Religious Pluralism*, the book contained the plenary session papers by Richard Hess, John Goldingay (combined with Chris Wright's response), Bruce Winter, David Wright and David Cook, along with five other papers.[12] The steering group arranged to meet again the following January to consider the other papers for publication. There was already some criticism, however, that the conference and its aftermath had not been completely successful. Colin Chapman had expressed his unease after the earlier planning conference, and in the final plenary session Martin Goldsmith had expressed quite pungently his dissatisfaction with the way that missiology had simply been tacked on to the end of the conference programme, as if all it could do was take the findings of the other disciplines and 'apply' them. Colin Chapman wrote to express surprise that several of the plenary session papers had not been included in the book and that there was no preface or introduction, and indeed no mention of the undertaking of which the conference was simply a part.

In addition to the two missiologists, David Atkinson wrote a full letter to the TF committee to express his concern and disappointment. There were two main reasons why he thought the conference was only a limited success. First, the planning of the conference was based on the premise that the authority of the Bible required a move from Bible through doctrine and associated disciplines to application, but this was a serious misconception. In fact the serious study of any contemporary issue demanded a sophisticated move back and forward between the issue and secular disciplines on the one hand and a firm biblical and theological perspective on the other. Secondly, there had been an irredeemable generality in the use of 'religious pluralism'. He made a plea that, in addition to 'biblical research' in the narrow sense (which, he agreed, must remain at the heart of the Tyndale Fellowship), there must be an attempt to relate biblical research to the wider questions of the day, and this must encompass the wider

---

12. Andrew D. Clarke and Bruce W. Winter (eds.), *One God, One Lord in a World of Religious Pluralism* (Cambridge: Tyndale House, 1991).

disciplines of Systematics, Ethics, Missiology and so on. Without that, biblical research risked the danger of a certain scholarly irrelevance. He would be deeply concerned if it were thought that the work of the conference could provide any answers for people such as Christian teachers.

The TF secretary attempted to meet the criticisms in the Members' Newsletter No. 50 in October 1991 by making it clear that the conference was not the whole process. The project had begun with issues posed by educationalists. Moreover, the publication of *One God, One Lord* (which TF members received with the newsletter) was not yet the end-product:

> The conference papers were (as intended) by specialists for specialists.
> The steering committee is now considering how the work of the
> conference can issue in publications specifically relevant to Christian
> teachers and others facing similar questions. It would be foolish to think,
> however, that even that is the end of the line. We have by no means
> answered all the questions. But the project is prompting research and
> serious reflection on a pressing issue for the mission of the Church.

In short, once the conference was understood as only part of the whole project, it could be seen that there had in fact been 'a sophisticated move back and forward between the issue and secular disciplines on the one hand and a firm biblical and theological perspective on the other'. Plans were laid for a substantial book to be written by the Directors of the Whitefield Institute, David Cook and Stephen Williams. The manuscript was then to be submitted to a further conference of educationalists, missionary thinkers and strategists and those involved in pastoral ministry, particularly with ethnic minorities. It was envisaged that a more popular book would follow. Regrettably, neither of these publications eventually appeared.

Associates
Participating in the Pluralism Project was not the only development widening the work of the Tyndale Fellowship in the early 1990s. In August 1988 the Revd David Kingdon, a former Principal of the Irish Baptist College who attended the TF committee as

theological books editor at IVP, drew up a proposal that the Fellowship should launch an associate membership. The case had to be argued carefully, since, decades before (in the mid-1950s), the membership of the Tyndale Fellowship had been deliberately restricted to those engaged in research to provide a place where Evangelical biblical specialists could consult.[13] The Fellowship was not meant to be a theological debating society open even to all graduates. David Kingdon argued, however, that there were two new factors. First, there had been a great increase in the number of theologically educated ministers and others since the Fellowship had been formed; secondly, there were fewer teaching posts available. But, crucially, he did not propose that those not eligible should be able to attend study groups for specialists, but that they should have their own group meetings and conferences. The stated aim of the Fellowship, after all, was not just to promote biblical studies and research, but also to engage in 'disseminating the useful results of such study for the public benefit'. The TF committee mulled over the question and eventually approved the formation of an associate membership in 1991. The Revd Peter Read of Monmouth, a former TSF secretary, agreed to act as associates' secretary.

An international secretary had also been added to the committee in 1989, a task undertaken by Dr C. J. H. Wright. In June 1990 he reported that of the 293 members of the Fellowship, 122 lived outside the United Kingdom. He proposed sending out a circular letter, and was encouraged to contact in particular those in Australia, where the TF seemed to be dormant. He was also encouraged to communicate with colleagues in other countries involved in FEET, the Fellowship of European Evangelical Theologians. The TF committee also agreed to the request of the Revd Peter Walker to join the sponsors of a conference, 'Christian Perspectives on Jerusalem', being organized at All Nations Christian College in April 1991. The volume of conference

---

13. That did not restrict membership to those holding academic positions: several ministers and laymen (such as John Lilley and Alan Willingale) engaged in serious research leading to occasional publications.

addresses was published as a supplement to the *Tyndale Bulletin* the
following year.[14]

Archbishop Carey

1990 also saw the surprise appointment of Dr George Carey as
Archbishop of Canterbury, the second since the Second World
War from the Evangelical wing of the Church of England.[15] He
had become Principal of Trinity College, Bristol, in 1982, and had
been Bishop of Bath and Wells only since 1987. Since he had
served for ten years on the TF committee as chairman of the
Biblical Theology Study Group (1975–85), had delivered the
Tyndale Biblical Theology Lecture for 1980, 'The Lamb of God
and Atonement Theories',[16] and had been one of the plenary
session speakers at the 1984 Tyndale Conference on War, the TF
chairman wrote to congratulate him on his appointment. In his
reply Dr Carey wrote:

> I will never cease to be grateful to God for the resources of the Tyndale
> Fellowship which have helped me to benefit from the riches of Scripture
> and the Christian tradition.

Although he was no longer a member of the Fellowship, the TF
secretary commented in Members' Newsletter No. 48 that 'even
those of us who are not Anglicans' would have noted the appointment with delight. He encouraged the members to pray for Dr Carey
in his public role with the media and in the influence he would exercise in church and national affairs and in the Anglican communion
worldwide. Nonetheless, although there were cordial relations with
the new Archbishop, it was pointed out by the General Secretary
that Dr Carey had distanced himself from his Evangelical roots to

---

14. Peter W. L. Walker (ed.), *Jerusalem Past and Present in the Purposes of God*
     (Cambridge: Tyndale House, 1992).
15. The other, Donald Coggan, had been involved in IVF as editor of the
     Inter-Varsity Magazine and had written *Christ and the Colleges* (London: Inter-
     Varsity Fellowship, 1934).
16. *Tyndale Bulletin*, 32 (1981), 97–122.

some extent in an article in the journal *Theology*.[17] He had stated that, although his heart beat in time with the 'evangelical love of Jesus', his head could not 'go along with received evangelical teaching'. Although he had 'started out from a very definite, conservative, evangelical, Protestant' position, he wrote that he was nowhere near that now, and that 'no one will ever hear me call *myself* an evangelical'.[18]

Obituaries

In addition to losing the participation of Dr Carey a year before he became Bishop of Bath and Wells, the Tyndale Fellowship also lost several significant members through death in the late 1980s and early 1990s. In December 1985, Members' Newsletter No. 39 carried obituaries for Professor Peter C. Craigie and Canon J. Stafford Wright. Peter Craigie, who was Vice-President of the University of Calgary, died as the result of a road accident. He was a leading Old Testament and Ugaritic scholar who had delivered two Tyndale Lectures and had published *The Problem of War in the Old Testament*, in addition to commentaries on Deuteronomy and Psalms 1 – 50.[19] Stafford Wright had been a member of the Kingham Hill conference in 1941. He had contributed to *The New Bible Handbook* (IVF: 1947), his Tyndale Lecture had been published as a Tyndale Monograph (*The Date of Ezra's Coming to Jerusalem*, 1947) and he had written the article on Ezra and Nehemiah in *The New Bible Commentary* (IVF, 1953) and various articles for *The New Bible Dictionary* (IVP, 1962). He had taught Old Testament at Oak Hill and in Bristol at a time when Evangelical scholarship was at its nadir. The obituary recalled that he came to Tyndale House in its early days when facilities were minimal and pitched his tent in the garden to attend study groups.

---

17. 'Parties in the Church of England', *Theology*, 91 (July, 1988), 269–270.
18. See also George Carey, *Know the Truth: A Memoir* (London: HarperCollins, 2004). This autobiography does not mention Dr Carey's participation in the Tyndale Fellowship.
19. *The Problem of War in the Old Testament* (Grand Rapids: Eerdmans, 1983); *Deuteronomy* (NICOT, 1976); *Psalms 1 – 50* (Word, 1983).

In May 1988, Members' Newsletter No. 43 carried obituaries for
John P. Baker and Roger Cowley. John Baker, who was rector of
Newick in Sussex, had been secretary of the Biblical Theology
Study Group for fourteen years in total, and died at the age of 51
after suffering with leukaemia. Dr Roger Cowley was 48 and had
been a missionary in Ethiopia; he had completed *Ethiopian Biblical
Interpretation* (Cambridge University Press, 1988) at the time of his
death. The death of Prof. R. A. Finlayson of the Free Church
College in Edinburgh at the age of 93 was reported in the newslet-
ter of May 1989, and that of Gösta Erikson, a Swedish Old
Testament scholar who had participated regularly in the Old
Testament Study Group, in the newsletter of March 1991.

The same newsletter of March 1991 also carried a tribute by
Howard Marshall to F. F. Bruce, who had died on 11 September
the previous year, just a month before his eightieth birthday:

> Fred will be remembered first and foremost as the biblical scholar who
> by his personal contribution and his teaching did more than anybody
> else in his generation to establish conservative evangelical scholarship as
> an intellectually respectable and coherent discipline.

Recalling details of his academic career, Professor Marshall
continued:

> His gifts won wide acclaim: he is one of the very few persons to have
> been called to be President both of the Society for Old Testament Study
> and of the Society for New Testament Study. Possessed of outstanding
> intellectual ability and love for learning, a phenomenal memory, an
> encyclopaedic knowledge, a colossal capacity for work, and a limpid style,
> he produced a remarkable output of books and essays which will
> continue to be read for years to come, and he trained directly or indirectly
> many younger scholars now working in all parts of the world . . .[20] Yet he

---

20. W. W. Gasque, in his article on F. F. Bruce in the *Biographical Dictionary of
Evangelicals* (Leicester: IVP, 2003), 85–88, writes: 'Bruce's knowledge of
the Bible was prodigious. He seemed to have had the whole Bible, both in
the original languages and in several translations, committed to memory.

was no narrow academic: he was a couthy individual with a pawkie sense of humour and a vital interest in the world around him . . . He was a man of many talents, a modern Erasmus (but with an evangelical fervour that was sadly unknown to Erasmus), committed to the service of the Word of God, and we praise God for his life and witness.[21]

In Members' Newsletter No. 51 in March 1992, John Wenham contributed an obituary for Douglas Johnson. John Wenham thought that 'DJ' was almost certainly the greatest single influence on the course of British Christianity in the twentieth century, a remarkable tribute to one who was so single-minded in keeping out of the public eye. He thought indeed that he probably deserved the title of genius. When he had taken over as secretary of the IVF, Evangelical fortunes were at their nadir, but now, at the end of the century, there could be little doubt that Evangelicalism was the most dynamic force in the Christian scene. Wenham thought that this was owing to Douglas Johnson above others. He attributed this first to 'a simple desire to proclaim Christ', so that 'he worked with a passion that almost killed him'. Secondly, it was his organizing ability, 'making bricks without straw' and believing in 'the essential unity of all Bible-believing, gospel-preaching Christians'. Thirdly, he was a theologian, always reading widely and realizing that

---

When asked a question about the Bible, he did not have to look up the text. He would sometimes take off his glasses, close his eyes as if he were scrolling the text in his mind, and then comment in such an exact manner that it was clear that he was referring to the Hebrew or Greek text, which he either translated or paraphrased in his answer.'

21. The TF secretary included in the same Members' Newsletter a story about Bruce's unassuming character which he had been told after the memorial service at Brinnington Evangelical Church, Stockport. A building-site worker had been converted and joined the fellowship of the church, and had been confronted by his workmates with difficult questions about his new-found faith. He returned with the most excellent and well-informed answers, until at last his workmates asked him where all his answers came from. 'There's an old fellow in our church called Fred,' he replied, 'and he seems to know all about these things.'

Theology was essential to a healthy church. Fourthly, he was a personal worker, writing a thousand letters of encouragement a year
full of enthusiasm and meaty with ideas. Fifthly, he was a man of
humility who avoided the limelight.[22]

In October, 1992, Members' Newsletter No. 52 carried Dick
France's tribute to Donald Guthrie, who had been Vice-Principal
and later President of London Bible College and was chiefly noted
among New Testament scholars for his magisterial *New Testament
Introduction* (Leicester: IVP, 1970). He had served on the Tyndale
Fellowship Committee from 1973 to 1991, and on the Tyndale
House Council from 1977 to 1991. Dr France commented:

> Donald has been a valiant fighter for evangelical truth, never afraid to be
> unfashionable, but always open to new ideas and approaches, which he
> would criticise with scrupulous fairness and scholarly caution . . . It was
> typical of Donald that at a time when it had become decidedly
> unfashionable to set out a New Testament Theology under the
> traditional categories of Systematic Theology rather than studying the
> writers individually he nonetheless chose the traditional model for his
> great *New Testament Theology*, because he believed that it would be of
> more practical use as a tool for Christian ministry, and accepted with
> equanimity the inevitable criticism from some in the academic fraternity.

The same newsletter carried the information that in the last
weeks of his life, the Council for National Academic Awards (just
before its own demise) had conferred the degree of DLitt on
Dr Guthrie at his last public appearance at the LBC graduation cer-
emony. In the same letter there was news that the Archbishop of
Canterbury had conferred a Lambeth DD on Roger Beckwith (who
had succeeded him as chairman of the TF Biblical Theology Study
Group) and that the ranks of the TF had three new professors: Paul
Helm as Professor of Philosophy of Religion at King's College,
London; Anthony Thiselton as Professor of Christian Theology at

22. D. J. Goodhew, in his article on Douglas Johnson in the *Biographical
Dictionary of Evangelicals* (333–334) comments that he was 'intensely shy of
publicity' and 'almost phobic in his aversion to appearing in photographs'.

Nottingham; and Alan Millard, who had been given a personal chair at Liverpool. These appointments followed Hugh Williamson's appointment as Regius Professor of Hebrew at Oxford the previous year, in succession to James Barr.

Members' Newsletter No. 53 in March 1993 carried news of the appointment of the new General Secretary of the UCCF, the Revd Robert Horn, and also two further obituaries. Howard Marshall wrote about Dr Arthur Skevington Wood, former principal of Cliff College, who had combined scholarship and evangelism. His books on the eighteenth-century Evangelical revival and on Luther showed 'an encyclopaedic knowledge of the original sources and historical judgment of a high order', but he had also spent some years as an itinerant preacher and evangelist. Don Hagner contributed an obituary on Dr George A. Gay, who had completed PhD research under F. F. Bruce and had finally been director of the Hispanic Ministries Programme and associate professor of New Testament at Fuller Theological Seminary.

Re-restructuring

By 1991, the new UCCF Research Council had been in operation for five years and the Whitefield Institute for four, but strains were still appearing in the UCCF structure, particularly in the relationship between the research arm and the UCCF offices in Leicester. The Warden of Tyndale House had already had to face some internal administrative problems in Tyndale House: a backlog of books awaiting classification in the library and some confusion in the subscribers' list for *The Tyndale Bulletin* when it was transferred to a database. He was very grateful for the secretarial work of Heather Richardson beyond her set hours, but he was also facing the administrative burden without a full-time secretary for his own work. But wider administrative problems faced UCCF as a whole, and some proposals for restructuring, prepared by David Monro, were presented by a committee chaired by Peter Bright, the chairman of the UCCF Trust Committee. The Trust Committee had been given a more active role in 1987, coordinating the work of the UCCF Council, which had been the central executive decision-making body of UCCF, and the new Research Council. The proposal of the Bright Committee was that the UCCF Trust Committee would

retire once again to its position as a guarantor and 'back-stop' for
the work of UCCF, and a new UCCF Board would be created. This
would oversee the work of the UCCF Council and the UCCF
Research Council, and eventually IVP and the Professional Groups
would report directly to the Board, leaving the UCCF Council to
concentrate on the original and central focus of IVF/UCCF, the
coordination of the work of the university Christian Unions.

Alan Millard and David Wright, as the chairmen respectively of
the Tyndale House Council and the Tyndale Fellowship Committee,
were invited to a joint meeting of the UCCF Council and the Trust
Committee on 8 August 1991 to discuss the proposals. J. M. V.
Blanshard, Professor of Food Science at the University of
Nottingham, who was now the chairman of the Research Council,
was already included as a member of the Trust Committee. Among
the many practical points discussed on the proposed structure and
its operation, the longest discussion seems to have been concerned
with the relationship between the research arm and the focus which
UCCF had on the work of the Christian Unions in the student
world. In the previous joint meeting of the Council and the Trust
Committee in May, the General Secretary, Robin Wells, had questioned the unified commitment of the Research Council to a new
integrated structure.[23] John Blanshard was able to assure him that
the strengthening of the student work had now been stated to be
one of the primary aims of the Research Council, although there
was variety of views on how far this should influence the activities.
Alan Millard and David Wright both assured the joint meeting that
there was no desire at Tyndale House or in the Tyndale Fellowship
to leave UCCF nor to embarrass the student work in any way. There
was a need to respect the autonomy of the research arm, however,
and it had to be understood that there were different levels of
sophistication between students and theologians. Some things
acceptable to a Biblical Theologian might horrify a good CU executive member. David Wright emphasized that the Tyndale Fellowship
greatly valued its historical links with the UCCF and stood by its

---

23. This had unfortunately appeared erroneously in the minutes as a question
about the Research Council's unified commitment to the student work.

conservative theological position. Alan Millard emphasized that UCCF was the only interdenominational organization where Evangelicals could meet to engage in biblical research and rejected the suggestion from the General Secretary that this could be achieved in a separate organization.

Asked why the Research Council had rejected the idea that the Chief Executive Officer in the new structure (who would be the General Secretary) should also be head of the student ministry, John Blanshard replied that if there were four divisions – the Students Ministries, the Research Council, IVP and the Professional Groups – it would be more natural to have a distinct person who was head over all. David Wright added that that would leave the head of the student ministries free to concentrate on that without being distracted by the other branches. The question of differing levels of sophistication was raised again. Would the Research Council be prepared to accept a Board veto on a publication? Alan Millard responded that the Research Council already had a requirement in its constitution that its work was to be conducted in accordance with the Doctrinal Basis of UCCF and in close association with the work among students in the universities. It should be allowed to continue to operate on trust.

At the end of the meeting the present and retired General Secretaries, Drs Wells and Barclay, were asked to prepare a document in consultation with David Wright and Alan Millard on any differences in the application of the Doctrinal Basis in the theological world and the student world. This document was ready by September 1991 and began from the principle that all the activities and public witness of UCCF should be consistent with the Doctrinal Basis. Speakers at all conferences and other activities had to be those whose beliefs were in accordance with the DB. This principle had been established in the earliest days of IVF to ensure that no drift from the confessional basis led to the IVF's following the same trajectory as the SCM, and the virtual disappearance of the SCM by the late twentieth century demonstrated the wisdom of this. But the question tackled in the document was how this applied to research. The authors concluded that the same principle must apply, but that the same rules need not apply, and argued in favour of a more flexible approach.

When the revised Monro proposal to set up a UCCF Board was presented to the Research Council by Norman Hamilton, the chairman of the UCCF Council, at the RC meeting in September 1991, it was accepted.[24] There was insufficient time to discuss the paper by Wells and Barclay on the application of the Doctrinal Basis, but the Research Council noted the helpful distinction which Dr Barclay had made between the 'consultative' use and the 'declaratory' use of speakers, and accepted the need for responsibility, constraint and sensitivity to the effect of the research work on other parts of UCCF.

But, within two months, members of the Research Council, the Tyndale House Council and the Tyndale Fellowship Committee received a letter from John Blanshard sharing 'the distressing news' that Dr Robin Wells had resigned as General Secretary of the UCCF. The letter went on to explain that he had not been entirely convinced about the closer integration of the two main arms of the Fellowship, the ministry among students and biblical and theological research, and that despite being nominated as General Secretary in the new structure, he felt that he should offer his resignation.

Jubilee

As the Tyndale Fellowship and Tyndale House approached their golden jubilee, they could take some satisfaction in a decade of publishing productivity. In his third report as Warden, presented to the Tyndale House Council the previous year (on 14 July 1990), Bruce Winter had summarized the publishing achievements of the previous decade:

> In the past ten years the former readers, grantees, and Tyndale House fellows have published 351 books, contributed 271 chapters to books,

---

24. One effect of this more unified structure was that the Tyndale Fellowship ceased to have a 'constitution'; it was now to be referred to as their 'Terms of Reference' (TFC minutes, 18 November 1992, minute 15).

written 897 articles for learned journals and a large number of dictionary entries. Thus in the decade of the 1980s on average one book has been published every ten days, one chapter contributed to a book every thirteen days, and one article contributed every four days. Much will have found its way into theological faculties and colleges and on to the shelves of ministers and teachers of God's Word. Seventy-five of these books were 'popular' books, which is an encouraging sign that good biblical scholarship can find its way directly into the hands of all God's people.

He noted that the figures were actually higher, as records did not cover all those overseas who had studied and researched at the House. Four hundred copies of Colin Hemer's book *The Book of Acts in the Setting of Hellenistic History* had now been sold. And the monograph written as part of the Genesis Project by Dr David Tsumura, Professor of Semitic Languages at the University of Tsukuba in Japan, *The Earth and the Waters in Genesis 1 and 2*, had been published by Sheffield Academic Press in August 1989. When the report was forwarded to the Research Council, attention was drawn to an article by John Stott in *Christianity Today* where he attributed much of the health of British Evangelicalism to the work done through the Tyndale Fellowship. The resurgence was 'due more than anything else to the recovery of evangelical, biblical scholarship'.[25]

Family Housing Project
But in his 1990 report the Warden had also presented the greatest need which the House now had if it was to expand its work; namely, residential accommodation for senior visiting scholars:

> Those most affected by our lack of residential accommodation are the married post-doctoral scholars of five to ten years standing who have young children. Their presence on site and the inclusion of their families would make a considerable contribution to Tyndale House. The task of settling families in Cambridge can be time-consuming for visiting scholars.

---

25. John Stott, 'The Remaking of English Evangelicalism', *Christianity Today*, 5 February 1990, 26f.

Planning permission had been given to convert the upper floors of the main House into five flats for married couples, and attempts were being made to secure a block of land across the lane which ran from Grange Road to the Warden's Lodge. In fact, an attempt had been made to buy this land at 15b Grange Road the previous year and the new owner was now asking whether Tyndale House would still like to have it. There was also the possibility that land beside the Lodge would be available. Initial plans had been drawn up by the Fitzroy Robinson Partnership.

By September 1990 the land beside the Lodge was no longer available, but the land at 15b Grange Road had been purchased for £165,000, the architect was being asked to draw up three possible schemes for development and an appeal was envisaged. By February 1991, it was reported to the Research Council that the favoured plan was to convert the present Warden's Lodge into two three-bedroom flats, adding two town houses where there was currently a garage, and to build a new Warden's Lodge with a two-bedroom annexe or granny flat on the new site. Benefactors had expressed interest, and the UCCF Business Advisory Committee had decided to mount a general appeal for funds to cover projects for the Whitefield Institute and the development of the UCCF offices in Leicester as well as the Family Housing Project at Tyndale House. Care had to be taken in the planning to keep the character of the area, but Selwyn College had given permission to use their lane to gain access from Grange Road, so that a new entrance from Selwyn Gardens was unnecessary. The Tyndale Family Housing Project was launched at All Souls, Langham Place, on Wednesday, 18 March 1992. The total cost was to be £800,000. Prof. D. J. Wiseman spoke about the original vision for Tyndale House and John Stott highlighted the unique work of the House in proclaiming and defending the gospel:

> We shall never capture the church for the truth of the gospel unless and until we can re-establish biblical scholarship, hold (and not lose) the best theological minds in every generation, and overthrow the enemies of the gospel by confronting them at their own level of scholarship.

By May 1992, the Warden could inform the Academic Sub-committee of the THC that £405,000 had been raised by way of cash or promises.[26]

By November 1992, Phase 1 of the Family Housing Project was complete and the Warden and his family were able to move into the new Lodge. Phase 2, the renovation of the old Lodge and the construction of two town houses beside it, began. When these were complete, the official opening took place on the Tyndale House Open Day, 15 May 1993. The annual lectures for the Open Day were given by Professor A. R. Millard, Mr Terence Mitchell and Dr Rick Hess on 'Recent Discoveries in Old Testament Times'. Phase 3, the conversion of the three flats in the main House into five, still had to be completed and there was some concern that this be done before the expiry of planning permission.

Jubilee
The golden jubilee of both Tyndale House and the Tyndale Fellowship was celebrated in 1994. Celebrations at the House on the Open Day, 14 May, were attended by 175, and the day finished with a thanksgiving service in the chapel of Selwyn College. Bishop John B. Taylor, Prof. D. J. Wiseman and Prof. H. G. M. Williamson

---

26. The main burden of liaison with the builders was undertaken by the chairman of the Tyndale House Business Committee, J. C. W. Roberts, who was managing director of his family firm, C. P. Roberts. The treasurer of the committee was Vernon Cobb, company secretary of EMESS plc; D. G. Stradling, senior manager at John Laing & Son, and M. W. Middleton, a company director of Cyril Middleton, also served. In addition to the businessmen, other members included S. W. Blake, formerly an Education Officer with Cambridgeshire County Council; the Warden; the chairman of the Tyndale House Council; and the acting General Secretary, Frank Entwistle of IVP. In addition to being a sub-committee of the Tyndale House Council, the Business Committee had also (in the reorganization of 1987) become a sub-committee of the Business Advisory Committee of UCCF, and this had already caused some confusion in lines of responsibility. The BAC was conscious of its responsibility for Tyndale House as a major UCCF asset.

spoke, the Revd F. D. Kidner led the prayers, and Dr Andrew Clarke and Dr George Beasley-Murray read the scriptures.

The Tyndale Fellowship planned a joint conference for the study groups from 4 to 7 July at The Hayes, Swanwick, focusing appropriately on the Bible and taking the theme from a short work of William Tyndale, *A Pathway into the Holy Scripture*. In August 1992, David Wright had written a discussion paper reviewing the developments and prospects of the Fellowship in the light of the approaching jubilee. He had particularly highlighted the need for greater coordination between the study groups and the lack of an integrated theology which resulted from the disciplinary divisions of the academy, which were reflected in the structure of the Fellowship. He suggested that the Fellowship should meet in a single conference every year with enough room on the programme for specialist study-group activity. In his absence on sabbatical during part of 1993, the TF secretary chaired a sub-committee laying plans for such a joint conference for the jubilee. The attempt was made to meet criticisms that the specialist study groups had not been given enough time at the previous two joint conferences. Somehow this need for specialist consultation had to be reconciled with the aim of developing Evangelical thinking on wider theological issues. Historically this can be seen as an attempt to address the tension between 'specialist' and 'generalist' approaches which can be traced back to Martyn Lloyd-Jones's debate with W. J. Martin at the Kingham Hill conference. To some extent it was a debate between biblical scholars and theologians, between long-term detailed biblical research and the need to speak to current issues in theology and ethics. The Jubilee Conference was therefore an experiment in satisfying both needs simultaneously. It was also the first conference attended by associate members.[27]

---

27. An attempt to run a separate conference for associate members the previous November had not proved successful, and it was agreed that associates could attend the joint conference, holding their own meetings during the study-group sessions. The payment of a sizeable cancellation fee to The Hayes for the proposed associates' conference was avoided

Since 1994 was also the five-hundredth anniversary of the birth of William Tyndale, not only was the title taken from Tyndale (*A Pathway into the Holy Scripture*), but also the first plenary session was addressed by Dr Carl Trueman on 'Pathway to Reformation: William Tyndale and the Importance of the Scriptures'.[28] Thereafter plenary sessions took place in the second half of each morning. On Tuesday, 5 July, Dr C. E. Armerding and Dr C. L. Blomberg spoke on 'Critical Issues in Old and New Testament Scholarship for Evangelicals Today'. Carl Armerding (bringing greetings as a charter member of the IBR) addressed the question whether anyone was listening to Old Testament scholarship in an age when the Enlightenment, which had shaped so much their methodology, was giving way to postmodernism. Following John Goldingay (who in turn referred to Hans Frei) he recommended 'story exegesis', with the proviso that it did not require scepticism about historical reality. Craig Blomberg listed twelve themes requiring the attention of Evangelical New Testament scholars, headed by the third quest for the historical Jesus, a synthesis of old and new looks on Paul and the law, a reasoned eclecticism in critical methodology, and the globalization of hermeneutics.

On Wednesday, 6 July, Prof. A. C. Thiselton spoke on 'Authority and Hermeneutics', and in the afternoon, Prof. H. G. M. Williamson and the Revd Morgan Derham spoke on 'The Role of Biblical and Theological Research in the Church Today', Professor Williamson addressing the topic from the viewpoint of the biblical scholar and Morgan Derham, as a former General Secretary of the Evangelical Alliance, from the viewpoint of the church. Tony Thiselton addressed a 'repetitive agenda', which had persisted for a century in Evangelical debates about biblical authority, between the traditions of B. B. Warfield and James Orr. The former was an approach 'from above' and the latter 'from below', and since the

---

when Iain Hodgins, the Bursar at Tyndale House and administrative secretary of the Fellowship, booked The Hayes for the Jubilee Conference.

28. These plenary conference addresses were all published in *A Pathway into the Holy Scripture*, ed. P. Satterthwaite and D. F. Wright (Grand Rapids: Eerdmans, 1994).

1970s, the latter had been represented by Berkouwer, Rogers and McKim and James D. G. Dunn,[29] the former by Harold Lindsell, Carson and Woodbridge, and Wayne Grudem.[30] He argued that the time had come to transcend this polarization, since, as in Christology, neither approach 'from above' or 'from below' was adequate, and the eschatological approaches of Pannenberg and Moltmann to Christology might suggest a way forward on the issue of biblical authority. Had Thiselton put his finger here on the tension we have noted running through discussions in the Biblical Research Committee and the Tyndale Fellowship Committee from the Kingham Hill conference onwards? The Warfield apologetic was certainly introduced into British Evangelicalism by Martyn Lloyd-Jones and championed by James Packer, and it may be equally correct to see the biblical scholars Martin, Bruce and others as standing in the older British tradition of James Orr.

On Thursday, 7 July, a paper by Dr Kevin Vanhoozer on 'The Doctrine of Scripture Today' was presented in his absence. The doctrine of Scripture explained how the Bible was related to the word of God, and he identified three positions: Barth's 'indirect identity'; Barr's 'non-identity'; and the 'Scripture principle' affirming a direct identity between the two. While contemporary theologians tended to construe God's involvement with Scripture in terms of only one biblical genre, he suggested that a more promising approach, overcoming the dichotomy between personal

---

29. G. C. Berkouwer, *Studies in Dogmatics: Holy Scripture* (ET Grand Rapids: Eerdmans, 1975); Jack B. Rodgers and Donald K. McKim, *The Authority and Interpretation of the Bible: An Historical Approach* (San Francisco: Harper & Row, 1979); James D. G. Dunn, 'The Authority of Scripture according to Scripture', *Churchman*, 96 (1982), 104–122 and 201–225.

30. Harold Lindsell, *The Battle for the Bible* (Grand Rapids: Zondervan, 1976); Wayne Grudem, 'Scripture's Self-attestation and the Problem of Formulating a Doctrine of Scripture', in D. A. Carson and John D. Woodbridge (eds.), *Scripture and Truth* (London/Grand Rapids: IVP/Zondervan, 1983); D. A. Carson and John D. Woodbridge (eds.), *Hermeneutics, Authority and Canon* (London/Grand Rapids: IVP/Zondervan, 1986).

and propositional revelation, viewed Scripture in terms of divine communicative acts.

In contrast to earlier joint conferences, the study-group sessions were increased to six in an attempt to meet the complaint that the specialist nature of TF study groups was being lost by joint conferences. The Christian Doctrine group focused on the theme of the conference, the doctrine of Scripture, with papers by G. L. Bray on 'Scripture and Confession: Doctrine as Hermeneutic', I. H. Marshall on 'Systematic and Biblical Theology: Are they Reconcilable?', Nigel Cameron on 'Scripture and Criticism', D. F. Wright on 'Scripture and Evangelical Diversity', T. A. Noble on 'Scripture and Experience' and A. N. S. Lane on 'Sola Scriptura?' These were published along with the plenary session papers in a volume which gave a balanced and innovative diet of Evangelical thinking on one of the key Evangelical distinctives at the end of the twentieth century.[31]

Tyndale Lectures took place each evening. The Old and New Testament Lectures were on Monday evening: Dr Å. Viberg on 'Amos 7:14: A Case of Subtle Irony' and Dr B. Rosner on '"Written for us": Paul's View of Scripture'.[32] Dr N. T. Wright gave the Biblical Theology Lecture on Tuesday evening on 'Justification by Faith: Can we get it right now?'[33] On Wednesday evening, Dr Trevor Hart's Christian Doctrine Lecture, 'The Word, and Words and Witness', was on Barth, and Dr Bruce Winter's Ethics Lecture was on 'Early Christians as Citizens and Benefactors'. Dr Oliver Barclay preached at the final communion service.

Response sheets were available for all members at the conference, and it was clear from the responses that the conference had been a success. The consensus was that there should be triennial

---

31. Satterthwaite and Wright, *A Pathway*, 1994.

32. This paper, directly related to the theme of the conference, was also published in Satterthwaite and Wright.

33. Tom Wright's stimulating paper was followed by an unscheduled period of lively open discussion, and simultaneously a session in which, to mark the jubilee, the TF secretary read a paper on the founding of Tyndale House and Fellowship (substantially the first two chapters of this book).

joint conferences with the same programme structure to allow both specialist discussion and fruitful interchange.[34] This can be seen as a major step towards accommodating the viewpoints of Martin and Lloyd-Jones by balancing the need for specialist scholarship with the need for a 'generalism' which attempts to speak to the major theological issues of the day from a coherent, biblically based theology.

---

34. Members' Newsletter No. 56 (October, 1994) reported on the responses, which the TF secretary reported more fully to the committee on 16 November. Forty-nine response sheets had been returned by TF members, twenty-seven of whom thought that joint conferences should be held every third year, seven thought they should be more frequent, and ten less frequent. (One malcontent thought that they should never be held!) Members were particularly enthusiastic about the contributions of Tom Wright, Tony Thiselton and Craig Blomberg, but that possibly reflected the large attendance of New Testament scholars!

10. RECOGNITION

Wright, Marshall, Taylor and Winter, 1994–2004

By 1994, Tyndale House and the Tyndale Fellowship were operating in a very different world from that of the founders fifty years before. On the international scene the wartime world of the British Empire had given way to years of persistent British economic weakness and the Cold War, and by the early 1990s to economic recovery, the collapse of the Soviet threat and the growth of the European Union. Culturally, however, and in the churches, British links with the English-speaking world remained strong, especially in the Evangelical churches with their missionary vision. The harvest of the sacrificial seed-sowing missions of the nineteenth and early twentieth centuries was evident in a revolutionary change in the balance of world Christianity. The enormous growth of the church in the 'two-thirds world' meant that Christians in Europe and North America were now in the minority.[1] John

---

1. Historians of Christian missions such as Andrew Walls first drew the attention to this revolution, which the myopic British media missed in their comments on world trends at the start of the new millennium.

Stott had played a key role in the development of the Lausanne movement, which brought together in periodic conferences Evangelical leaders from around the world. And it was the representatives of the churches in the 'two-thirds world' who forced the Westerners to recognize that social action and evangelism were equally part of the mission of the church. Stott's continuing concern, seen in the Langham Trust, was for the theological development of strong Evangelical leaders with a solid foundation in theological and biblical studies.[2] At Tyndale House, as we have seen, the growth of world Christianity was reflected in the number of readers from overseas, and Colin Hemer had given this need priority in his legacy. No other institution anywhere in the world fulfilled the role of Tyndale House, and this was also reflected in the number of Americans who came to do research there.

Within the United Kingdom, as in the rest of Europe, the steady erosion of the churches continued as (except for a brief respite in the 1950s) attendance and membership inexorably declined throughout the century.[3] But here, too, as the Evangelical missionary movement was leading to exponential growth overseas, so it was in the Evangelical churches that the great ebbing of the tide was most successfully resisted. Statistically, this was most evident in denominations where Evangelicals were strong, most obviously in the Church of England, but also in Baptist churches. While there were many factors and agencies contributing to increasing Evangelical strength, notably the growth of the charismatic movement and the house churches from the 1960s and

---

Cf. Philip Jenkins, *The Next Christendom: The Coming of Global Christianity* (Oxford: OUP, 2002).

2. Cf. Timothy Dudley-Smith, *John Stott: A Global Ministry* (Leicester: IVP, 2001), especially chapters 7, 'The Lausanne Vision', and 10, 'A Global Ministry'.

3. Compare the new perspective proposed by Callum G. Brown in *The Death of Christian Britain* (London: Routledge, 2001) that the churches were numerically strong and influential until the 'catastrophic and abrupt cultural revolution starting in the 1960s'.

1970s, the growth of the UCCF was one of the most significant. And at the heart of that were the focus on group Bible studies (promoted, as we saw, by G. T. Manley), the emphasis on biblical, expository preaching exemplified by Lloyd-Jones, Stott and many others, and the enormous increase in Evangelical literature, most significantly the production of Bible commentaries and other works of biblical scholarship. It was this productivity, from *The New Bible Commentary* and *The New Bible Dictionary* through the Tyndale Commentaries and on to more advanced works of biblical scholarship, informing the minds of theological students and feeding the preachers who fed their congregations week by week, which was the crucial contribution of Tyndale House and the wider circle of the Tyndale Fellowship. It is no exaggeration to say that it was this hidden, backroom work of the research scholar which, under God, lay behind the work of pastors and evangelists and at the heart of the steady and consistent Evangelical recovery.

Five-year plans

In their jubilee year, Tyndale House and the Tyndale Fellowship were called to rise above the minutiae which absorb the scholar to try to see the strategic picture. It was here that the link with UCCF, sometimes the cause of administrative tension, proved its value by keeping scholarship linked with mission. The new UCCF Board required the three agencies of the Research Council to look ahead by producing five-year plans. The TF secretary wrote to the members:

> Five-year plans perhaps sound more reminiscent of Stalin's USSR than of the UCCF! Yet it is no small part of the vision needed in Christian work to look forward and to try to anticipate the needs of the next few years. To assume that the future will be exactly like the past is to invite obsolescence.[4]

---

4. Members' Newsletter No. 54 (November, 1993).

The Five-year Plan which David Cook drew up for the
Whitefield Institute began with its mission statement

To assist in the training and development of a new generation of
Christian leaders and teachers in theology, ethics and education, and to
help the current generation of Christians apply God's Word to God's
world with theological discernment.

In the light of that, specific objectives were formed for the next
five years, 1993-98. The Whitefield Institute would fund up to five
full-time and ten part-time postgraduate research students, and
between three and six senior researchers aiming at publication.
They would initiate specific writing and research projects on the
model of the Pluralism Project and continue media training and
further education for the staff of Christian organizations and
churches. The main new development would be the creation of
three teams working on the specific projects: a theological team
led by the assistant director, Stephen Williams, focusing initially on
theological anthropology; an ethics team led by the director, David
Cook, focusing on medical and business ethics; and an education
team led by Dr John Shortt, on secondment from Stapleford
House. These teams would address key areas and 'draw together
theologians and practitioners from outside the institute to develop
a strategy and produce academic and practical material in the most
crucial fields'.

Plans for Tyndale House
Bruce Winter's Five-year Plan for Tyndale House, dated 7 January
1993, began with the fulfilment of the original vision of 1942: the
publishing of the specialist articles and books, residential facilities
now extending to married research students, and the publication
of a scholarly journal which now had a circulation of 1,050. But a
new challenge was posed by the move away from the 'Victorian'
model of libraries to the expected 'distance' reading of journals
and books. Would the library become redundant? He argued that
there were reasons why a residential library remained crucial for
Evangelical scholarship. Tyndale House was more than a library;
it was a community where the Christian formation of the next

generation of biblical scholars and their families was a high priority: 'The possession of a degree without a commensurate growth in godliness produces a spiritual dwarf and is out of character with the biblical intention of the transforming nature of Christian truth.' The educative role of a scholarly community where senior scholars could have informal discussion with younger graduates, and where there was scholarly interaction with trends in biblical research, was crucial.

But the spiritual and educative value of the research community at Tyndale House would soon count for nothing if the library did not keep up with technological advances and so was bypassed. The Warden noted that Tyndale House was the first library in Cambridge to secure in 1987 the Ibycus Scholarly Computer and the Wilson disk on bibliographical research; that the link to the University of Cambridge mainframe computer in January 1988 meant that they were accessible to other scholars for the sending and receiving of files from Britain and overseas; and that the computerization of the library's holding had been completed in 1992. These were now all basic tools for a graduate research library.

Backed by such facilities, Tyndale House could engage both in reactive research and in proactive research where Evangelicals could set the agenda. As examples of proactive research, the Warden referred to the Gospels Project of the late 1970s and early 1980s, the production of *Patriarchal Narratives*, and the Acts Project in which Tyndale House was now engaged. But in order to advance the work of research through the library, the implications of change had to be considered. The library was running out of space and they should look at the possibility of buying local property for single scholars, thus releasing the upper floor of the library building for future accessions and reading desks. With the level of technical competence now required of librarians, the present highly competent Librarian might have to be replaced with two: an academic as head librarian and a qualified librarian as assistant. Plans in 1986 to appoint an Assistant Warden had been shelved, and although there was a Research Fellow in Hebrew and Aramaic to complement the Warden's New Testament scholarship, the specific stipulation was that the Research Fellow could not be drawn into administration. The increasing pastoral and administrative demands on the Warden meant that his publishing commitments were behind schedule, and it was now totally unrealistic for him to spend the intended 60% of his time on research. Secretarial and administrative services needed attention: in view of the complexity of the library and the commitment to long-term projects, the UCCF Board should consider whether the UCCF policy on tenure, originally devised for UCCF travelling secretaries, was not inappropriate for the long-term effectiveness of Tyndale House.

Along with the Warden's Five-year Plan there was a twelve-page report by the Librarian, Dr Andrew Clarke, on library trends and their implications for Tyndale House. Drawing on an extended report by the British Library Research and Development Department, he identified major areas of change: computer catalogues, which would enable researchers to produce much broader bibliographies much more quickly; union catalogues, where a group of libraries pooled their individual computer catalogues in a central larger catalogue; computer indexes such as *Religious and Theological Abstracts* and *Religion Indexes*; electronic journals; and electronic books. Electronic journals had already been introduced, specifically the *IOUDAIOS* 'journal', and Tyndale House already made considerable use of electronic books.[5] The Ibycus computer made possible searches of the *Thesaurus Linguae Graecae*, many Latin texts, some Coptic texts, some inscriptions, some papyri, the *Biblia Hebraica Stuttgartensia* and some English Bible versions, and the library also had access to Gramcord, an electronic grammatically tagged text of the New Testament. Quoting the report of the committee appointed to review the provision of library services in the University of Cambridge, Andrew Clarke emphasized the need for a specialist research library like Tyndale House to keep up with developments. Libraries which did not would be left behind.

---

5. Andrew Clarke also commented that computer catalogues would also facilitate basic library housekeeping tasks such as acquisitions, circulation and periodical management; that the Cambridge Union catalogue was already available on the Joint Academic Network (JANET); and that Tyndale House had led the way among British theological libraries by subscribing for the previous two years to the CD-ROM computer indexes.

TF *study groups*

The Five-year Plan for the Tyndale Fellowship was approved by the committee in 1994. After a brief historical introduction, it began from the stated aim of the Fellowship:

> To advance the Christian faith by promoting biblical and theological studies and research and disseminating the useful results of such study and research for the public benefit in a spirit of loyalty to the Christian faith as enshrined in the consensus of the historic creeds, the confessions of the Reformation and the doctrinal basis of the Fellowship.

To further this aim the Fellowship would work through its study groups to 'encourage and support Evangelicals engaged in research and creative thinking in all the major branches of Biblical Studies, Theology and Religious Studies'. It would also 'encourage interaction between these study groups with the intention of promoting a continuing and developing integrated, balanced, comprehensive and contemporary expression of Evangelical theology, securely based on the revelation of God in Holy Scripture'. Six specific objectives came out of that:

1. To strengthen weaker study groups and re-establish a strong Biblical Theology group.
2. To establish a study group in Religious Studies and Missiology to provide mutual encouragement and help for Evangelicals engaged in this crucial area of study.
3. To encourage interdisciplinary cross-fertilization by triennial conferences of the whole Fellowship, beginning with the 1994 Jubilee Conference.
4. To establish a large and active associate membership of graduates and to keep them informed about the progress of research.
5. To improve publicity and recruitment of new members.
6. To encourage members to undertake research in specific areas.

At that point there were officially seven TF study groups. The oldest and strongest of these were the Old and New Testament groups, chaired originally by D. J. Wiseman and F. F. Bruce and now by Gordon Wenham and Howard Marshall. The Biblical

Archaeology group was chaired by Alan Millard, and Tony Lane had just succeeded David Wright as chairman of the Christian Doctrine group. The Biblical Theology group had been in the doldrums for many years; after soldiering on valiantly, the chairman, Roger Beckwith, resigned in 1994. A new proposal came however from Geoffrey Grogan, the retired principal of Glasgow Bible College,[6] to launch a 'Two Testaments' project, and a first meeting took place during the Jubilee Conference, where Dr Desmond Alexander volunteered to act as secretary. This became the new Biblical Theology group. Unhappily, just as that was reviving, the Ethics group decided to go into voluntary liquidation.[7] That was offset, however, by a new group on Philosophy of Religion. Paul Helm had been appointed chairman of that group in 1991 (also being appointed to the chair of History and Philosophy of Religion at the University of London in 1992). Stephen Williams became secretary of the group, and the first meeting, at which Paul Helm delivered the first Philosophy of Religion Tyndale Lecture, took place in 1993.[8]

Another new group was also considered by a working party which reported in June 1993 (Dewi Hughes, Tom Noble and Chris Wright), a group which would combine Religious Studies and Missiology. In June 1994 the TF secretary wrote to Colin Chapman to invite him to become chairman of such a group, and the letter reveals something of the strategic thinking. First, whereas fifty years previously the pressing need had been for Evangelicals to safeguard biblical authority within the church and to pursue Biblical Studies over against liberalism within a largely

---

6. Originally the 'BTI', the Bible Training Institute, the oldest Bible College in the country, and now united with Northumbria Bible College (originally Lebanon Bible College) in Berwick-on-Tweed to form the International Christian College in Glasgow.

7. A short note written by the secretary David Attwood in June 1994 explained that there were only four regular members. A dozen others made occasional contributions, but it was not clear that there was a 'group'. On his resignation as secretary, there was no obvious successor.

8. Since they arranged their dates for 1994 at the 1993 meeting, they met separately from the Jubilee Conference that year.

Christian consensus, now the battle lines were shifting and the need was increasingly to support the mission of the church in a post-Christian culture. Secondly, in the world of education, Religious Studies had overtaken Theology and Biblical Studies in the universities and had replaced them in the schools. Just as the Tyndale Fellowship had supported Evangelical biblical scholars, so now there was a pressing need for Evangelical academic work in Religious Studies to support Christian thinking and mission there. Thirdly, the Pluralism Project had demonstrated the need to have Missiologists and Religious Studies specialists represented at the planning stages and therefore represented on the TF committee. To have such a study group as part of the Tyndale Fellowship would facilitate cross-disciplinary Evangelical discussion. It was clear that the issues which gave rise to the Pluralism Project were not going to go away, and that it followed that it was not just a project which was needed, but a continuing study group.

In the annual report which the TF chairman and secretary gave to the UCCF Research Council in September 1994, Wright and Noble put it like this:

> As Evangelicals become increasingly strong within a shrinking church membership in the nation, it is evident that the defence of the historic Christian faith within the church is becoming less crucial for Evangelicals than its proclamation to the world. In a society which is often perceived to be multi-cultural, Evangelical research into the Study of Religion is likely to be of long-term significance for evangelism. The development of such a group is also seen as a necessary development in the ministry of the Tyndale Fellowship to Evangelical research students (many from the ranks of what is significantly now called RTSF) who undertake research in this area.[9]

But it proved difficult to arrange a consultation of interested people, and it was to be another three years before the group was

---

9. The Theological Students' Fellowship had become the Religious and Theological Studies Fellowship in 1988. For a full account of its changing names see Chapter 1, note 21.

successfully launched. It eventually met for its first conference from 15 to 17 December 1997 in Birmingham, chaired by Colin Chapman and with Dewi Hughes as secretary, and had by then chosen to be the study group on 'Religion, Communication, and Culture'. In addition to the eight study groups (including Ethics), a new group, the Tyndale Fellowship Associates, was also active, with Dr Paul Woodbridge in the chair.

Crisis

Before then, however, Tyndale House had gone through some stormy waters. The problems were not in academic and library affairs, where the five years foreshadowed in the plan were very successful indeed. The Acts Project, with Bruce W. Winter as the series editor of *The Book of Acts in Its First-Century Setting*, and I. Howard Marshall and David W. J. Gill as consulting editors, produced its first and second volumes in 1993 and 1994. Volume 1, *The Book of Acts in Its Ancient Literary Setting*, edited by Bruce W. Winter and Andrew D. Clarke, was published in November 1993 with commendations from Edwin A. Judge and Martin Hengel. David W. J. Gill and Conrad Gempf were the editors of Volume 2, *The Book of Acts in Its Graeco-Roman Setting*, which appeared in July 1994. Volume 3, *The Books of Acts and Paul in Roman Custody*, by Brian Rapske; Volume 4, *The Book of Acts in Its Palestinian Setting*, edited by Richard Bauckham; and Volume 5, *The Book of Acts in Its Diaspora Setting*, by Irina Levinskaya, were all to appear subsequently, published by Eerdmans and Paternoster Press. A volume on the theology of Acts, edited by Howard Marshall and David Peterson, was also published independently of the series.[10]

Library affairs also leaped ahead during the five years covered by the plan. When Andrew Clarke left Tyndale House to lecture in New Testament at Aberdeen in 1995, the *Tyndale House Newsletter* commented: 'He inherited a traditional library and left us with a modern computerized information centre.' Every desk was now linked to the internet and Tyndale House had a page on the World Wide Web.

---

10. I. H. Marshall and D. Peterson (eds.), *Witness to the Gospel: The Theology of Acts* (Grand Rapids: Eerdmans, 1998).

But while academic and library affairs showed excellent progress, the stormy waters were the result of problems in business matters: specifically finance, buildings and administration. In July 1994, as the jubilee was being celebrated, the Tyndale House Council was made aware that the Laing Trust, which had so generously supported the work of the House, was changing its policy somewhat. Its funds were finite and were now being shared more widely, so that the grants to UCCF, the Whitefield Institute and Tyndale House would not be increased in the future beyond the present levels. The Trust saw the maintenance of the library as a top priority, but it was concerned about the relevance of the research to 'the man in the pew'. It was highly supportive of the work of Tyndale House, but felt that the House must do all in its power to raise additional finances. As a consequence of this, an academic policy group was set up to consider whether Tyndale House could gain income through teaching, and it was decided to appoint a Bursar who was also a fund-raiser. By January 1995, however, a long-term financial problem had become an immediate crisis. There was an unexpected deficit for the first six months of the year of £24,800. Also the UCCF Board, which had met the Warden and four members of the Tyndale House Council the previous March, was now asking for a 'clear set of priorities' and raising the question whether Tyndale House could be envisaged as an independent institute. There were also continuing serious problems in the administration office. By July 1995 there was an urgent minute from the Tyndale House Business Committee to the Council recognizing that they had reached a 'crisis':

> In the light of the final outcome of the last financial year the THBC have come to the conclusion that, as at present constituted, Tyndale House is not a viable financial organization without further income being generated.[11]

---

11. The minute actually reads: '. . . have come to the conclusion, as at present constituted, that Tyndale House . . .', but presumably was intended to read as corrected here.

A sub-committee also submitted a confidential report which favoured independence for Tyndale House. The present administrative structures linking it to UCCF seemed incredibly cumbersome and confusing as to where accountability lay. A letter from Howard Marshall took the position that the case for independence had not been established, but that the case for devolution should be explored, and the idea of a local committee was linked to this. Professor Wiseman suggested an additional meeting of the Council in August, by which time the Warden had become totally opposed to the idea of the local committee chaired by a non-academic. The idea was dropped, but it was agreed to continue discussions with the University of Coventry about MA teaching at the House. The chairman of the UCCF Board, Norman Hamilton, attended the next meeting of the THC in January 1996, by which time the difficulties had been compounded by the appearance of extensive mould in the newly built family housing. Problems continued in the business office, and the advisability of transferring the handling of accounts to the UCCF offices in Leicester was raised. The UCCF Board then decided that the situation demanded the appointment of an independent Review Group to consider the whole future of Tyndale House and, in reaction, the Tyndale House Business Committee resigned. D. J. Wiseman had announced his decision to retire from the council, but at the meeting in July 1996 the General Secretary announced that, following the recommendation of the Review Group, the Board had decided to dissolve the Tyndale House Council and reconstitute it.

Eschatology: the fourth joint conference

1997, the year in which the reconstituted Tyndale House Council took office, was also the year of the Triennial Tyndale Fellowship Conference held at The Hayes, Swanwick, on 'Eschatology', a theme which was likely to be a topical one with the arrival of the new millennium. Kent Brower and Mark Elliott edited the volume which included many of the papers given at the conference.[12]

---

12. Kent E. Brower and M. W. Elliott (eds.), 'The Reader Must Understand': Eschatology in Bible and Theology (Leicester: Apollos, 1997), published in the

The editors emphasized the need for preaching on eschatological matters, not leaving them to 'eccentrics and cranks', if the church was to avoid both exaggerated hopes for the present age and the other damaging extreme, 'pie in the sky by-and-by'. Five sections dealt with themes in Biblical Theology, Old Testament, New Testament, Christian Doctrine and Practical Theology. Included in the sixteen papers was one by E. Earle Ellis in memory of John Wenham (who had died the previous year), in which he took up the case for conditional immortality, which had been held by some Cambridge figures at least from the days of Basil Atkinson.[13] Among the other papers were a review by Stephen Williams of a generation of writing on eschatology since Moltmann's *Theology of Hope*, a critique of Moltmann's millenarianism by Richard Bauckham, and a paper on Paul's eschatology by Ben Witherington III.

At the conference David Wright was taken completely unawares by the presentation of a Festschrift edited by Tony Lane to mark his sixtieth birthday: *Interpreting the Bible*, essays written by members of the Tyndale Fellowship.[14] He served a further two years as TF chairman, completing the five years envisaged by the Five-year Plan. Peter Head served as secretary from early in 1995 till the following year, when he became secretary of the New Testament Study Group and was succeeded as TF secretary, after a gap, by Kevin Ellis.

These two books, the Festschrift and the conference papers, joined a stream of other composite volumes, one each year, published as Tyndale House Studies, which 'disseminated' the results of research presented in Tyndale study groups. Beginning with *One God, One Lord in a World of Religious Pluralism* arising from the joint conference of 1991, it also included volumes from the Old Testament group, both edited by Richard S. Hess, Gordon

USA as *Eschatology in Bible and Theology: Evangelical Essays at the Dawn of a New Millennium* (Downers Grove: IVP, 1997).

13. See page 47, note 7. For John Wenham's obituary, see page 260. See also John Wenham, *Facing Hell: An Autobiography 1913–1996* (Carlisle: Paternoster, 1998).

14. A. N. S. Lane (ed.), *Interpreting the Bible: Essays in Honour of David F. Wright* (Leicester: Apollos, IVP, 1997).

J. Wenham and Philip E. Satterthwaite: *He Swore an Oath: Biblical Themes from Genesis 12 – 50* (Paternoster/Baker, 1994)[15] and *The Lord's Anointed: Interpretation of Old Testament Messianic Texts* (Paternoster/ Baker, 1995). The Christian Doctrine study group produced *The Unseen World: Christian Reflections on Angels, Demons and the Heavenly Realm*, edited by A. N. S. Lane (Paternoster/Baker, 1996).

During the 1990s there were more losses of pioneering figures from the ranks of the Fellowship. Sir Norman Anderson and Dr David Broughton Knox died in 1994. *The Times* obituary for Sir Norman traced 'not one distinguished career but two', one in the law and the other in serving the church.[16] His career in the service of Christianity included his missionary service with the Egypt General Mission from 1932; his later presidency of the Bible Churchmen's Missionary Society and the Church Pastoral Aid Society; and his ability as the first chairman of the House of Laity in the General Synod of the Church of England. The writer recalled, too, his Christian witness in facing the loss of all three of his children. Sir Norman had been a familiar figure in Tyndale House during his retirement, working regularly in the library; his children having predeceased him, he left a substantial legacy to Tyndale House.[17]

David Broughton Knox, who had conceived the idea of a residential research library along with W. J. Martin, had been Principal of Moore College, Sydney, for twenty-seven years. At the age of 72,

---

15. This volume was dedicated to D. J. Wiseman in gratitude for his services to Tyndale House and Tyndale Fellowship.

16. *The Times*, Wednesday, 7 December 1994. His legal career included his firsts at Trinity College, Cambridge, being called to the bar, taking silk, his years as Professor of Islamic Law at the School of Oriental and African Studies in the University of London (1954–75) and as Director of the Institute of Advanced Legal Studies, and his election to the British Academy. See also the article by David Goodhew in *Biographical Dictionary of Evangelicals*, ed. Timothy Larsen (Leicester: IVP, 2003), 14f.; and Sir Norman's autobiography, *An Adopted Son* (Leicester: IVP, 1985).

17. See Anderson, *An Adopted Son*, 131–145, where he writes of the 'happiest' years of his life at Tyndale House.

he had gone to South Africa for four years to set up the George
Whitefield College in Cape Town. When John Wenham died in
1996, the obituary in Members' Newsletter No. 59 recalled his particular focus on student ministries through IVF/UCCF and his
pioneering role in the founding of Tyndale House and the formation of the Tyndale Fellowship. Two years later, in December 1998,
Members' Newsletter 65 recorded the deaths of Morgan Derham
and Donald English. Morgan Derham, a former General Secretary
of the Evangelical Alliance, had become a member of the
Fellowship before membership was restricted to researchers.
Making no claim to be an advanced scholar, he attended the Biblical
Theology study groups for many years to help him with his responsibilities as editor of Scripture Union Bible-reading notes, and then,
up to the year of his death, the Christian Doctrine study group. Dr
Donald English had been a leading figure in the Methodist Church,
being twice President of the Methodist Conference, and chairing
the World Methodist Council from 1991 to 1996.[18]

The TF under Howard Marshall

David Wright was succeeded as chairman of the Tyndale Fellowship
in 1999 by Howard Marshall, who retired that year as Professor of
New Testament Exegesis at the University of Aberdeen and was the
current President of the British New Testament Conference. In
2000 the triennial TF conference was held for the first time at
Regents Park Conference Centre at Nantwich in Cheshire, on the
theme 'God's Unfolding Purposes'. The celebration of the new
millennium was an opportunity to focus attention on the birth of

---

18. Dr English had been an IVF travelling secretary and the founding chairman of Conservative Evangelicals in Methodism. His responsibilities as
general secretary of the Methodist Home Mission Division from 1982 to
1995 always made it impossible for him to participate in TF study groups.
Among his many publications, *The Message of Mark* (1992) and *An
Evangelical Theology of Preaching* (1996) particularly give evidence of his
scholarship. See the article by D. R. Owen in *Biographical Dictionary of
Evangelicals* (Leicester: IVP, 2003), 209f., and the biography by Brian
Hoare and Ian Randall, *More than a Methodist* (Carlisle: Paternoster, 2002).

Christ, so the committee planned to explore the significance of the incarnation as the pivot of world history. This invited a focus on God's unfolding purposes; the *praeparatio evangelica* in Israel and beyond; providence and the goal of history; the changing shape of mission; and God's relationship to the historical order.[19] The general secretary of the Evangelical Alliance, the Revd Joel Edwards, preached at the conference service.

Paul Woodbridge succeeded Kevin Ellis as TF secretary that year, and planning began for the 2003 triennial conference, again in Nantwich, on 'Covenant in Bible and Theology'. By the time of that conference the Ethics groups had reappeared in a new form as the study group in Ethics and Social Theology.

University links

In the meanwhile, there had been significant developments at Tyndale House. The Rt Revd John B. Taylor, retired bishop of St Albans, was invited by the UCCF Board to become chairman of the newly constituted Tyndale House Council and took up his duties at the beginning of 1997.[20] The Review Group which had recommended a new TH Council had also recommended the

---

19. Plenary session speakers included Dr Christina Baxter, Principal of St John's College, Nottingham, on 'The Incarnation: Its Significance for History and Humanity'; Dr David Smith, the deputy director of the Whitefield Institute, on 'Change for Good: Renewal, Reformation, Revival, Restoration'; and Dr Henri Blocher of the Faculté Libre de Théologie Évangélique at Vaux-sur-Seine on 'Yesterday, Today, Forever: Time, Times, Eternity in Biblical Perspective'. The Tyndale Lecturers included Dr David Graham of North Berwick (New Testament); Prof. David W. Baker of Ashland Theological Seminary (Old Testament); Dr John Drane of Aberdeen (Religion, Culture and Communication); Prof. Francis Watson of Aberdeen (Biblical Theology); and Dr Carl Trueman, also of Aberdeen (Christian Doctrine).
20. He had been chairman of the Tyndale Fellowship Committee from 1970 to 1972 (see page 147).

abolition of the UCCF Research Council, seeing it as only an 'additional hurdle' between Tyndale House and the UCCF Board, which had the authority to take major decisions. Tyndale House and the Whitefield Institute were to be given direct access to the Board, a recommendation which recognized the weight of Tyndale House in terms of UCCF's total budget and assets.[21] This simpler structure would make for a clearer distinction between the Council, which set policy, and the staff, who were free and responsible to implement it. The Review Group had taken no notice of the place of the Tyndale Fellowship in the revised structure, but in the end it became answerable once again to the Tyndale House Council.

The global significance of Tyndale House
While recommending changes in the structures, the Review Group (three academics, two pastors and two businessmen) had given a resounding vote of confidence to the work of Tyndale House. They endorsed the vision for the future in the Five-year Plan of 1993 and in a more recent paper, Vision 2000. They understood how many Evangelical Christians who did not read learned books might be doubtful about the value of a research institution and might see a course to train pastors, or a television documentary on an ethical issue, or an evangelistic campaign as more 'useful'.

> We believe, however, that to allow this to undermine commitment to the work of the Tyndale House would be a mistake of the highest order.

The case for Tyndale House was then presented under three 'general observations'. The first was 'the need for a recovery of theological nerve or confidence'. In a country where 50% of the population in 1851 went to church every week and which had sent tens of thousands of missionaries around the globe, why was it that there were now more worshippers in non-Christian

---

21. The Tyndale House Council, which had previously met only twice a year, delegating business decisions to the more frequent meetings of the Business Committee, was now to meet four or five times a year, thus effecting a greater integration of academic and business concerns.

religions than active Christians? The Review Group blamed the decline into secularism and paganism on a failure of theological nerve. Liberal theology, dominant in the universities, had taught students to doubt the Bible's authority and relevance. Rapidly changing Western culture demanded more, not less, intellectual competence if historic, confessional Christianity was to be plausibly articulated and defended in the marketplace of ideas. In this cultural context for the mission of the church, Tyndale House with its hard-won reputation for academic rigour was a highly significant resource.

> Evangelicalism needs a centre of academic excellence, with a first-rate library and state-of-the-art IT facilities. It needs a model of theological scholarship conducted within a confessional community. In short it needs Tyndale House.

The second general consideration was the 'trickle-down' effect to the church. Just as medical practice would be compromised if medical research were not pursued, so, if Evangelicals did not engage in front-line theological debate, it would be only a matter of time before pastors and clergy retreated 'into a holy huddle of anti-intellectualism, cultic insularity and fundamentalist separatism'. While not all biblical scholarship was immediately productive in terms of evangelism or preaching or apologetics, the investment of effort (as in medical research) had to have a long-term strategy. Accountability was extremely necessary if resources were not to be wasted, but a preoccupation with the pragmatic concerns of activist evangelism, social campaigning or theological faddishness to the neglect of solid, intellectually rigorous work on the text of the Bible would inevitably make the church vulnerable to further assaults of scepticism.

The third general consideration was the international significance of the work. It was important to realize the influence of Tyndale House in the rest of the world:

> Go to USA or Canada, Australia or Singapore, Japan or India and you will find key evangelical theologians who spent their formative years working for Cambridge doctorates there. The multiplication of this

investment in their theological education through the pastors and scholars they in turn teach in their own countries is huge.

The New Testament department of Trinity Evangelical Divinity School in Chicago was given as an example. Of the six lecturers, five had spent significant time at Tyndale House, and TEDS currently had 4,000 graduates serving around the world. Don Carson was quoted: 'I know of no other Christian institution with comparable global influence for such comparatively little investment.'

The Group endorsed the proposal to initiate a one-year MPhil course which would enable pastors to study for a graduate degree alongside those pursuing an academic career and strengthen the links with the church. The existing staff plus a Deputy Warden, supplemented by one or two outside lecturers could cover the teaching of up to fifteen students. The proposed accreditation with the University of Wales (Bangor) would be financially beneficial to the House, but there were strong reasons to seek a link with the University of Cambridge.

Recognition

The staffing developments at the House made this long-term plan of a link with the university a practical proposition as the old century and the old millennium gave way to the new.[22] Fiona Craig, appointed by the new Tyndale House Council in 1997, brought efficiency to the business office. Dr Peter Williams was appointed as Research Fellow and Affiliated Lecturer in Hebrew and Aramaic in the Oriental Faculty of the University to replace Philip Satterthwaite in 1998. Dr David Instone-Brewer, who had succeeded Andrew Clarke as Librarian in 1995, had the technical expertise required for the computer link to the university. He was therefore appointed Technical Officer when a chartered Librarian was appointed in 1999, combining that with appointment as a Research Fellow in order to relate rabbinic material to the New

---

22. See page 50 for the long-term plan of Bruce, Johnson and Stephens-Hodge in 1944 that Tyndale House should have a relationship to Cambridge similar to that which Pusey House had with Oxford.

Testament through dating procedures which he had developed. This was to be published in six volumes. In October 2002 he reported that the first volume of *Traditions of the Rabbis in the Era of the New Testament* was finished.[23] Dr Elizabeth Magba was the chartered Librarian appointed in 1999, the first in the history of Tyndale House. The following year, 2000, Dr Peter Head came from Oak Hill College to be the Sir Kirby Laing Fellow and Affiliated Lecturer in New Testament in the Cambridge Faculty of Divinity, and in 2001 Dr David L. Baker was appointed Deputy Warden. This was the realization of an intention which was part of the original vision for Tyndale House: that there should be two Wardens, one an Old Testament and one a New Testament scholar.[24] David Baker had been Tyndale Fellowship secretary from 1975 to 1976, and had been a missionary and lecturer in Indonesia for twenty-five years. By 2003, he was reporting that he was finalizing the copyright and layout for the illustrations in his Indonesian publication *Introducing Biblical Archaeology* and starting research on the theme of wealth and poverty in the Old Testament. He had also signed a contract with IVP for a third edition of his book *Two Testaments, One Bible*. Peter Head was working on a book on the history of textual criticism, and Peter Williams had completed a book on Greek variants in the Syriac Gospels.[25]

The Warden's own research continued. The last volume of the Acts Project, of which he was series editor, was published in 1999, and Dr Winter also completed *After Paul Left Corinth: The Influence of Secular Ethics and Social Change* (Grand Rapids: Eerdmans, 2001). He was also considering a sequel which would show how Paul adopted different pastoral approaches to resolving the problems of the Corinthian church. A joint project between Tyndale House and the

---

23. David Instone-Brewer, *Traditions of the Rabbis in the Era of the New Testament* (Grand Rapids: Eerdmans, 2004/5).
24. See Chapter 2, page 44, the fourth point of the Martin–Knox proposal of 1942.
25. Peter J. Williams, *Early Syriac Translation Techniques and the Textual Criticism of the Greek Gospels*, Text and Studies, 2, Third Series (Piscataway, NJ: Gorgias Press, 2004).

University of Samford on New Testament lexicography was also being considered. By 2002 Dr Winter was receiving a Chinese delegation, following his lecture at the opening of the department of Religious Studies in the University of Beijing, and working on *Roman Wives, Roman Widows*.[26] Before the Acts Project was finished, Prof. Martin Hengel was prompting Tyndale House to launch another Gospels Project. It was agreed by the TH Council in 1998 that such a project should be located at Tyndale House under the auspices of The Institute for Early Christianity in the Graeco-Roman World. The Warden also reported to the council that year that a two-volume work in honour of Prof. E. A. Judge, *Ancient History in a Modern University*, had been launched at Tyndale House[27] and that the *Tyndale Bulletin* supplement for that year would be *The Trustworthiness of God*. This fresh approach to the nature of Scripture was edited by Paul Helm and Carl Trueman and, in addition to fourteen chapters by members of the Tyndale Fellowship, had two concluding responses by Colin Gunton and Francis Watson.[28] Two years after the volumes honouring Edwin Judge, the Warden was presented by his own staff with a Festschrift, *The New Testament in its First Century Setting*.[29]

The closer relationship with the University of Cambridge was evidenced not only in the Research Fellows who were also university lecturers, but in a new agreement with St Edmund's College and in two significant visits in 2000 and 2001. At the Tyndale

---

26. Bruce W. Winter, *Roman Wives, Roman Widows: The Appearance of 'New' Roman Women and the Pauline Communities* (Grand Rapids: Eerdmans, 2003). In 2002 Eerdmans also published a second edition of *Philo and Paul among the Sophists: Alexandrian and Corinthian Responses to a Julio-Claudian Movement*.

27. T. W. Hillard (ed.), *Ancient History in a Modern University*, Vols. 1 and 2 (Grand Rapids: Eerdmans, 1998).

28. Paul Helm and Carl Trueman (eds.), *The Trustworthiness of God: Perspectives on the Nature of Scripture* (Leicester: Apollos, 2002).

29. P. J. Williams, Andrew D. Clarke, Peter M. Head and David Instone-Brewer, *The New Testament in its First Century Setting: Essays on Context and Background in Honour of B. W. Winter on His 65th Birthday* (Grand Rapids: Eerdmans, 2004).

House Council in December 1998, the Warden reported an invitation from the Master of St Edmund's College, one of the newer graduate colleges, to enrol senior scholars at Tyndale House as visiting scholars. The college affiliation would be enriching and stimulating, affording contact with colleagues from various disciplines and an exchange of views within a wider academic community. The council agreed that this would be a very positive step and that the Warden should not hesitate to take up the invitation.

The two significant visits were from the Vice-Chancellor and the Chancellor of the University. The Vice-Chancellor, Sir Alec Broers, came for an afternoon visit at the invitation of Bishop Taylor and met some of 'his' twenty-eight graduate students researching for their Cambridge doctorates in Biblical Studies at Tyndale House. He also spoke with two senior scholars visiting the House, Prof. Edwin Judge of Macquarie University and Dr Irina Levinskaya of the University of St Petersburg, a Senior Research Scholar in the Russian Academy of Sciences. He also sat down with the Warden and the Research Fellows to hear each report on his research project.

The following year, 2001, the Chancellor of the University, HRH the Duke of Edinburgh, came to visit what the local paper described as 'Cambridge's best kept secret'. Bishop Taylor gave a short presentation on the history and purpose of the House and Prince Philip talked to the staff and readers about their research and did a 'walkabout' on the croquet lawn, meeting spouses and families. He presented the House with a facsimile of an etching in the Royal Collection, *Moses and the Tablets of the Law* by Marc Chagall, and received a copy of the Cambridge Book of Psalms, especially bound and hand-illuminated. The Prince was also shown a map indicating where former readers of Tyndale House were now serving in universities, colleges, seminaries and churches from Beijing to Brazil and from the UK to the Antipodes.

Both of these unprecedented visits symbolized recognition of the standing of Tyndale House and its great value to the scholarly community in Cambridge. Along with the Pontifical Biblical Institute in Rome and the École Biblique in Jerusalem (as the Warden commented in a newsletter in 2003), it was one of the three major specialist libraries in the world devoted to biblical study and research. Yet there was need for recognition of its value in other circles, for pre-eminently the service Tyndale House offered to the world of scholarship was always secondary, in the view of the founders, to the service it offered to the mission of the church. But as the diamond jubilee of the House was celebrated in 2004, there was a pressing need that Christian people recognize how vital that service was not only to the church in Britain but to the cause of world Christianity.

By 2001, there was an urgent need to expand the library to accommodate the growing book and periodical collection and the continually increasing demand for desks from doctoral and senior researchers in Biblical Studies. At the meeting of the council on 1 October, the Warden reported that the library was oversubscribed by readers and that it was not possible to accommodate all who wished to use it. The rented accommodation was also full and, in fact, there were thirty-two applicants wanting to use the library and the accommodation for the summer of 2002. An Appeals Committee had already been set up to build an extension, and in November 2001 £315,000 had been given or promised. Work started on detailed drawings and tenders were requested from builders with a view to starting construction by September 2002. That had to be delayed, however. By July 2003 almost £500,000 had been given or promised, but the estimates ranged from £1,615,000 to £1,705,000. In 1999 a number of American friends, realizing the unique contribution of Tyndale House to the growth and development of Evangelical seminaries in the United States, formed a company, the American Friends of Tyndale House, to enable fund-raising. By the diamond jubilee in 2004, however, the start of construction was still awaiting substantial grants from donors and trusts.

Prospect

Sixty years after their founding, Tyndale House and the Tyndale Fellowship can celebrate considerable achievements.[30] In addition

---

30. Regrettably, the Whitefield Institute was not fully operational by 2004. After Dr David Cook left Oxford, he was not replaced as Director and no

to what is now a steady stream of works of biblical scholarship produced by the research community at the House, and to the joint volumes produced by the study groups of the Fellowship, and the reference works of IVP,[31] innumerable works have been, and are being, published individually by TF members. Some of these are major works by leading academics, such as the influential work of A. C. Thiselton in hermeneutics;[32] the more recent magisterial contribution of N. T. Wright, now the Bishop of Durham, to questions about the historicity of the New Testament;[33] or, most recently, the New Testament Theology published by I. Howard Marshall.[34] This 'invisible college', as Bruce, Johnson and Stephens-Hodge envisaged it,[35] has produced not only books and articles which shape the thinking of theological students, but whole series of commentaries which continue to inform the preaching in countless churches. Compared with the state of

new grants for research were given. The Whitefield Institute office moved to Tyndale House at the beginning of 2004.

31. In addition to *The New Bible Commentary* (first published in 1953) and *The New Bible Dictionary* (first edition 1962), TF members and the members of the American equivalent, the Institute of Biblical Research, are the core of those who have since contributed to the *New Dictionary of Theology* (1988), the *Dictionary of Jesus and the Gospels* (1992), the *Dictionary of Paul and His Letters* (1993), the *Dictionary of the Later New Testament* (1997), the *Dictionary of New Testament Background* (2000), the new one-volume compendium of the New Testament dictionaries, *The IVP Dictionary of the New Testament* (2004) and the *Dictionary of the Old Testament: Pentateuch* (2003).

32. Most notably, A. C. Thiselton, *The Two Horizons* (Exeter: Paternoster/Grand Rapids: Eerdmans, 1980).

33. See N. T. Wright, *The New Testament and the People of God* (London: SPCK, 1992), *Jesus and the Victory of God* (London: SPCK, 1996) and *The Resurrection of the Son of God* (London: SPCK, 2003).

34. I. Howard Marshall, *New Testament Theology* (Leicester: Apollos, 2004). See also I. Howard Marshall, *Beyond the Bible: Moving from Scripture to Theology* (Carlisle: Paternoster/Grand Rapids: Eerdmans, 2005), which includes responses from Kevin Vanhoozer and Stanley Porter.

35. See page 50.

Evangelical biblical scholarship when Douglas Johnson first called the Biblical Research Committee together in 1938, this is nothing short of a revolution. And in addition to publications there is the influence of members of the Fellowship and former residents of the House who teach in universities, theological colleges and seminaries around the world.[36]

All of this advance in biblical studies has come through a clear determination both to assert the validity of biblical criticism against fundamentalism and to assert the inspiration and infallibility of the Scriptures as the word of God against all forms of liberal theology. Succeeding debates through the decades may have failed to resolve the paradox of these divine-human books, but while Evangelical biblical scholars might be keener to defend the validity of 'unfettered criticism', and Evangelical theologians perhaps keener to assert infallibility, the Tyndale Fellowship and Tyndale House have remained committed to both. And if the Christological paradox of the God-man is taken as a guide, the failure to provide an intellectual resolution of the paradox is what we should surely expect. The intellectual context is also more favourable in that the old assumption that commitment and objectivity are incompatible has largely gone. The advent of so-called 'postmodernity' has led to a new widespread assumption that there is no such thing as 'objective' neutrality and that everyone speaks from a position. In this new context there has been a decline in the prejudice that confessional commitment and open-minded research are incompatible. Being an Evangelical and engaging in research is now more respectable. On the other hand, the new tolerance tends to lead to the idea that there is no such thing as an objectively true position, and that is obviously inimical to the truth claims of the Christian gospel.

Further, although the advance in Evangelical biblical studies has been so remarkable, the wider scene continues to present daunting challenges. In the United Kingdom Evangelical churches are growing, but with growth, the Evangelical movement has developed a wider spectrum. Alongside UCCF, which was the central agency

---

36. See Appendix G for the Tyndale House website, which includes a map showing where former library readers and grantees are serving.

behind Evangelical growth from the 1950s to the 1970s, other Evangelical student organizations now operate in the universities and a revived Evangelical Alliance is the umbrella organization across the Evangelical spectrum. In addition to those who would refer to themselves as 'Conservative Evangelical' and who (with exceptions) would identify with the tradition of Reformed theology, there are those referred to as 'Open Evangelicals' and as 'Charismatic Evangelicals'.[37] The diversity is surely an acceptable price to pay for the growth, but theological clarity and fidelity to Scripture must be vigilantly safeguarded if parts of the spectrum are not to follow the old 'liberal evangelicalism' of the mid-twentieth century into oblivion.

The numerical growth of Evangelical churches in the United Kingdom is certainly encouraging, and it is possible to think that the long decline in total church membership and attendance may be a shaking-out of much conventional and nominal Christianity. If that is true, we may soon see the decline halted and a leaner, fitter church emerge, no longer vitiated by the attempt to adapt the Christian faith to the philosophy and culture of 'modernity' but fully committed to the gospel.[38] But there will still be the challenge to the church to bear its witness in a post-Christian society, where opposition comes not so much from the increasing number of adherents of other world religions as from an aggressive secularism evident particularly in the universities and the media. This may well lead to greater difficulties for confessional theology in the universities and consequently a greater role for independent theological colleges. Like the newly renamed London School of Theology (previously London Bible College), these are likely to

---

37. See *Anvil*, 20 (2003) for a useful collection of articles on the variety now within the Evangelical Anglican tradition: esp. Graham Kings, 'Canal, River and Rapids: Contemporary Evangelicalism in the Church of England', 167–184, followed by articles by Vaughan Roberts on 'Conservative Evangelicals', Christina Baxter on 'Open Evangelicals', and Mark Stibbe on 'Charismatic Evangelicals'.

38. At the beginning of 2005, there are some statistics suggesting the stabilizing of membership and attendance, at least in some parts of the country.

increase in academic stature as they attract an increasing number of committed Evangelical students.

The global church also faces challenges,[39] particularly those associated with poverty and corruption in many countries and the widespread persecution of Christians. There is the challenge of contextualization and the dangers to the church (such as syncretism) which come along with rapid growth. Often there may be the temptation for immature Christians and churches to accentuate spiritual experiences to the neglect of patient study of the Word, or a fundamentalist hermeneutic may lead to an obscurantist attitude to science and a sensationalist tendency to link biblical 'prophecy' with certain political views. As in the first centuries of the Christian era, young churches may be influenced by those Sir Norman Anderson called 'cranks'.[40] The Langham Trust has an impressive commitment to theological education in the 'majority world', and the biblical scholarship of the 'Tyndale school' can provide the resources to ensure that young churches are firmly built on 'the foundation of the prophets and apostles'.

It is clear then that the task of Evangelical biblical scholars will never be at an end. New cultural and intellectual trends in the secular culture of Europe and the English-speaking nations, as well as the dangers facing young churches throughout the world, will continue to demand front-rank biblical research. At present there is no lack of candidates for research who will become the professors and writers of the next generation. But the current lack of funds to provide Tyndale grants for British research students and the difficulty in finding funds for the present projected extension to the Tyndale House library indicate that there is a need for those who share the vision of Sir John Laing to provide the resources. The church at large has evidently not grasped how vital 'Evangelical research' is to continued long-term growth.

To meet the challenges of the twenty-first century, the church is also in desperate need of creative development in Evangelical

---

39. See the illuminating survey of trends and challenges in Alister E. McGrath, *The Future of Christianity* (Oxford: Blackwell, 2002).

40. See page 60.

theology. The word 'creative' may seem a strange one to those who see a virtue in being 'conservative' Evangelicals, but the two concepts are not in fact in opposition. To be 'conservative' is not to be reactionary or obscurantist or to deny all theological development; it is rather to insist that all development in our theology must be true to its source in holy Scripture. It also involves a presumption that our developing thought will be in continuity with the Christian hermeneutic hammered out by the Fathers in the creedal doctrines of Christ and the Holy Trinity and by the Reformers in their doctrines of the atonement and justification by faith.[41] And if the work of the biblical scholar is not simply the defensive and apologetic one of demolishing historical scepticism, but the positive and creative hermeneutical task of understanding the holy Scriptures more fully and deeply, then that necessarily implies that Evangelical theology cannot simply be stuck in the categories of Christian tradition. The authority of Scripture requires that the categories of traditional Systematic Theology must be answerable to our deeper understanding of Scripture.

There is therefore a creative theological task to be done: Christian Theology and Ethics must be developed not only in accordance with Scripture as it is more deeply understood by a faithful Biblical Theology, but also in the context of twenty-first-century culture, not only European culture, but the multiple cultures of the global church. If Evangelical theology cannot do that, it will sink back again into the kind of defensive mindset and cultural irrelevance which characterized it in the early twentieth century and helped to lead to catastrophic church decline in Britain and Europe. On the other hand, if Evangelical theology cannot challenge the increasing popularization of church life, the aping of an increasingly vulgarized Western 'pop' culture with its 'celebrities' and fads and trivialization, then the Evangelical church will become increasingly shallow and vulnerable to pressures to be 'squeezed into the world's mould'.

---

41. See Gerald L. Bray, 'Scripture and Confession: Doctrine as Hermeneutic', *A Pathway into the Holy Scripture* (Grand Rapids: Eerdmans, 1994), 221–235.

There are signs that Evangelical theology can meet the intellectual, cultural and spiritual challenge of today.[42] And to help in that task, the study groups of the Tyndale Fellowship in Doctrine, Ethics, Philosophy of Religion and 'Religion, Culture and Communication' – along with a revived Whitefield Institute – are surely well placed to play a significant role. But, as the founders of the House and Fellowship would surely insist, the creative task must always be done under the authority of holy Scripture. That can surely be promoted by the continuing close association of these study groups with the biblical study groups within the Tyndale Fellowship. Conversely, the theological groups can help to keep the biblical scholars focused on the Christian evangel from which 'Evangelical' theology takes its bearings.

The growth of Evangelical Christianity is evident around the world and is the only hope of the declining Protestant church in secular Europe. But that growth will surely be maintained in the long term only if Evangelicals are committed to the view that passionate proclamation of the gospel in word and action goes hand in hand with biblical and theological research. The need for vision for the creative development of Tyndale House and the Tyndale Fellowship is just as great as it was in 1944.

---

42. As one example of creative Evangelical thinking in theology, see Alister
    E. McGrath, *A Scientific Theology*, Vols. 1, 2 and 3 (Edinburgh & New York:
    T. & T. Clark, 2001, 2002 and 2003).

AFTERWORD

Professor I. Howard Marshall

What this book is really chronicling is a story of two linked entities, twins that were conceived over sixty years ago and formally brought to birth in 1944. One is a wide group of biblical and theological scholars, both in the UK and further afield, who are associated with one another in a Fellowship to support and encourage one another in academic study and writing. The other is a residential library which was created for the benefit of the Fellowship but has inevitably taken its place in the lives of numerous postgraduate students who have lived and worked there. Since the activities of the Fellowship have largely taken place in the highly congenial surroundings of the House, the line between the two is manifestly an indistinct one.

The two institutions, the Fellowship and the House, thus have a common aim: the glorification of God through the encouragement of biblical and theological study at the highest level and the dissemination of the results, both in academic publications and in the mediation of scholarship to the Christian church more widely. Throughout this book we have seen evidences of the sheer amount of material produced, particularly in more recent years, and the

important role it has played in promoting a fuller understanding of
Scripture and Christian doctrine.

My own early development as a Christian believer and student
owes more than I can say to the people who initiated and continued this work. At a time when there was almost nothing otherwise
available to encourage a young Christian to believe that the Bible
was a reliable record of divine revelation, I was immensely helped
by the writings of F. F. Bruce, whose name was noted for future
reference in 1938; his book *Are the New Testament Documents
Reliable?* showed that one could be an evangelical Christian without
intellectual dishonesty, and that the proper way to deal with attacks
on the Bible was not to ignore them but to meet critical scholarship with better scholarship. The fact that he was an Aberdeen
graduate doubtless also had something to do with my appreciation. A Scottish day conference of the Theological Students'
Fellowship in Glasgow at which the speakers were John Wenham
and Andrew Walls (whose names are so prominent in this book)
also stands out as a memorable experience. Round about the same
time came *The New Bible Commentary*, which gave a basic guide to
the whole Bible; it had its shortcomings, but what else could one
expect at that time, at which there was such a tiny number of
people to do scholarly work?

A few years later the plans for *The New Bible Dictionary*, long
promised but long delayed, began to take shape, and this time,
with basic theological training behind me, I was able to share in
the work sponsored by the Fellowship and edited at the House.
This was partly due to my friendship with the organizing editor,
Jimmy Douglas, and to the fact that I had been a student at
Cambridge, where the newly opened Tyndale Library building was
an absolute godsend to a theological student: where else, for
example, could you find a commentary on Isaiah 40 – 55 (one of
the set texts for the Theological Tripos Part II) and know that it
would always be there for consultation because nobody was
allowed to take books out of the Library? Remember that this was
in the era before the provision of scholarly commentaries on
much of the Bible was at all adequate. (Dare I mention, by way of
example, that Kingsley Barrett once told me that it was only after
my commentary on the Greek text of Luke was published that he

felt that he could prescribe Luke as a set text for study in the
Durham New Testament course?) A comparison of *The New Bible
Dictionary* with *The New Bible Commentary* will show the enormous
progress that had been made in something like ten years. Mention
is made elsewhere in this book of the work of Dr Arndt, the
co-translator of what must be the most useful tool for New
Testament study produced in the twentieth century, W. Bauer's
Greek Lexicon. Arndt lectured for the Friends of Tyndale House
on the Lexicon on the day of its publication. That, incidentally, is a
notable example of scholars of rather different theological persua-
sions, the liberal Bauer and the conservative Arndt, working
together to provide a superlative reference book, and demonstrating that scholars of different theological outlooks can and do
cooperate and learn from one another.

From then onwards the stream has become something of a
river. The Tyndale Commentaries on the books of both Old and
New Testaments have been outstanding vehicles for presenting
good scholarship in a format suitable for students and pastors.
The series on Gospel Perspectives brought together specialists in
Gospel study producing original scholarly work that was later to be
summarized in a more popular format by Craig Blomberg.
Alongside them stands the careful study of the historicity of Acts
by Colin Hemer. Then came the major series on The Book of
Acts in its First Century Setting. And these are only some of the
books produced directly under the auspices of the Fellowship and
the House. One cannot begin to list the publications of TF
members and TH residents to which reference is made in this
book. *The Tyndale Bulletin* regularly carries abstracts of doctoral
theses produced within the constituency that demonstrate the creative liveliness of the contemporary younger generation of
scholars. From the same stable has come the growth of the
Whitefield Institute, originally based in Oxford, which has stimu-
lated research and writing in the fields of Theology and Ethics and
perhaps gained rather more publicity because its work is so closely
related to controversial topics in the political and cultural spheres
– although, having said that, one immediately thinks of the wide
influence of Tom Wright as a spokesperson for evangelical
Christianity.

Nor has the effect been confined to this country. The example of the TF and TH stands behind the creation of the Institute for Biblical Research in North America and, more recently, the setting up of a research library in Fort Worth at the instigation of Earle Ellis, himself a frequent and regular visitor to Tyndale House, who felt the need for something comparable in his own country. Similar groups in other parts of the world likewise draw some of their inspiration from what began in Cambridge. It is, of course, an unfinished story. The task of research never ends, and the need to expound and defend the faith once and for all delivered to the Christian church in its Scriptures continues. I share with many in giving thanks for the part played by the Tyndale Fellowship and Tyndale House in this vital work and pray for God's blessing on its future role.

APPENDICES

APPENDIX A
OFFICERS AND STAFF OF TYNDALE
HOUSE AND FELLOWSHIP

Chairmen of the Biblical Research Committee (from 1977 the Tyndale House Council)

1938–42	G. T. Manley
1942–51	F. F. Bruce
1951–57	D. M. Lloyd-Jones[1]
1957–86	D. J. Wiseman
1986–96	A. R. Millard
1997–2004	J. B. Taylor
2005–	A. D. Clarke

---

1. From 1952 to 1954 the name 'Tyndale Fellowship Committee' was adopted and a smaller sub-committee called the 'Biblical Research Committee' was chaired by J. W. Wenham.

Secretaries of the Biblical Research Committee (or Tyndale House Council)

1938–41	H. E. Guillebaud
1941–42	J. W. Wenham
1942–44	S. Barton Babbage
1944–45	L. E. H. Stephens-Hodge
1946–48	J. Stafford Wright
1948–57	D. J. Wiseman
1957–58	G. H. W. Parker
1958–60	G. E. Duffield
1960–65	D. Johnson
1965–78	F. D. Kidner
1977–81	R. T. France
1981–86	M. J. Harris
1987–	B. W. Winter

Wardens of Tyndale House

1946–49	J. N. D. Anderson
1958–60	J. R. Bridger
1961–64	L. L. Morris
1964–78	F. D. Kidner
1978–81	R. T. France
1981–86	M. J. Harris
1987–	B. W. Winter

Librarians

1944–45	L. E. H. Stephens-Hodge
1944–45	H. Chadwick (acting)
1946–49	J. N. D. Anderson (acting)
1948–50	Miss Atkinson (acting)
1952–57	A. F. Walls
1957–58	G. A. Pollard
1958–61	J. D. Douglas
1964–70	A. R. Millard
1970–73	C. N. Hillyer
1973–75	R. T. France
1976–77	G. L. Bray
1978–80	J. G. McConville
1980–82	C. J. Hemer
1982–84	C. C. Broyles
1984–90	D. G. Deboys
1990–95	A. D. Clarke
1995–99	D. Instone-Brewer
1999–	E. Magba

Deputy Warden

2001–	D. L. Baker

Chairmen of the Tyndale Fellowship Committee

Apart from the brief period 1952–54, the Tyndale Fellowship Committee emerged as a distinct committee only in 1961. At that point this name was given to what had been the 'Biblical Research Committee', and that older title was taken by a smaller group of senior academics. Later, in 1977, that senior committee was renamed the Tyndale House Council (see page 167).

1961–62	D. J. Wiseman
1962–64	L. L. Morris
1964–70	A. M. Stibbs
1970–72	J. B. Taylor
1972–86	A. R. Millard
1987–99	D. F. Wright
1999–	I. H. Marshall

Secretaries of the Tyndale Fellowship Committee

1961–65	D. Johnson
1966–69	R. T. France
1969–70	G. J. Wenham
1970–71	D. F. Murray
1971–73	H. G. M. Williamson
1973–75	C. N. Hillyer
1975–76	D. L. Baker
1976–78	C. J. H. Wright
1978–79	J. J. Bimson
1979–83	D. Wenham
1984–89	M. J. Selman
1989–95	T. A. Noble
1995–96	P. M. Head
1997–2000	K. S. Ellis
2000–	P. D. Woodbridge

APPENDIX B
TYNDALE HOUSE LIBRARY

Dr Elizabeth Magba

The Tyndale House Library is not particularly large as academic libraries go, and the physical surroundings are not (yet) as spacious or as modern as we would wish. Sometimes visitors comment on these apparent shortcomings when they first arrive, but after a few hours spent exploring the library's contents their view changes radically. They return to me with remarks such as 'You have just everything I need!' or 'I can't believe that you actually have this book which I've been trying to find for months!' Unlike most academic libraries, our collections are strictly for reference only, not for lending; so the books are always readily available to our readers, not out on loan for weeks at a time. Most of our users also appreciate the fact that all the materials – books, maps and electronic databases – are available close to their desks and are on open access; so there are no long waits while items are brought in from other locations or unlocked from storage rooms in some distant basement. Scholars often seize the opportunity while they are here to browse the shelves in the subjects that interest them and to explore electronic materials with which they are not already familiar. Prof. Hugh Williamson, Regius Professor of Hebrew at the University of Oxford, speaks for many (and not only for Old Testament specialists) when he says: 'The study of the Old Testament requires a combination of many different skills. No library in this country brings together all the tools necessary for this task in so convenient and comprehensive a manner as Tyndale House.'

As we look towards the future, can the Tyndale House library continue to maintain its reputation as the leading biblical studies library in the United Kingdom – and, indeed, as some claim, one of the three most important in the world?

Maintaining the standard of the library collections is, of course, fundamental, and we are continuing to build up our holdings of books and journals. The library currently holds around 40,000 volumes in major European languages and receives more than 200 scholarly journal titles from all over the world. The books include good editions and facsimiles of all major biblical, classical and Near Eastern texts, along with linguistic aids, archaeological material and a valuable map collection.

In recent years, we have focused on trying to complete our collection of facsimile copies of all the major early biblical texts. The most important acquisition has been the facsimile copy of Codex Vaticanus in a limited edition including both Old and New Testaments. The quality of the reproduction is so fine that when we unpacked the crate in which it was shipped to us we thought for one moment that we had the real thing in our possession! The purchase of important material of this kind is possible only through the generosity of our donors.

The selection of books and other library materials is a team effort, carried out at our monthly Library Committee meetings. The committee comprises the Warden, Deputy Warden, Librarian and Research Fellows, each person bringing his or her own expertise to the selection process. The Librarian may also order material in direct response to readers' recommendations; tries to ensure that various subject areas are adequately represented; and struggles to balance the library budget at the end of the financial year.

Like most other academic libraries, we have been adversely affected by rising book prices and especially by large annual increases in the price of academic journals. We have been gradually withdrawing certain journal subscriptions where the content of the publication does not in our judgment contain enough material of importance to Biblical Studies, and especially where the journal is available elsewhere in Cambridge, or on-line. On the other hand, we continue to add new titles, including some of the good biblical studies journals now coming out of the two-thirds world. It should be added that as far as Theological and Biblical Studies journals go, electronic formats have still not rendered paper formats obsolete. It is significant, however, that when we recently compiled on the Tyndale House website a long list of access points to free and subscription on-line journals, we found that the list in effect doubled our current journal holdings – perhaps a sign of the 'Virtual Library' of the future.

As for books, we depend heavily on gifts from our supporters and the generous discounts we receive from many publishers. Some publishers donate books under our Showcase Scheme. The idea, initiated when David Instone-Brewer was the Librarian, is that publishers donate to our library one copy of each academic book in the field of biblical studies. In return, we 'showcase' the books for them, mounting a display of them, along with their catalogues and order blanks. Publishers see this exercise as a useful marketing tool; the readers greatly appreciate the opportunity to see new publications; and the books that we receive relieve pressure on our budget.

One of the keys to the success of any academic library is ease of access to information about its holdings. A major focus in recent years, therefore, has been the enhancement of our web-based catalogue, TynCat. Catalogue records follow standard MARC format, which means that they are compatible with records in most other major academic libraries. In line with the Cambridge University Library, we are currently in the process of moving from UKMARC to MARC21, the new, international standard format for library catalogues.

There has also been a need to improve the level of bibliographical information entered into TynCat and to address the problem of poor (and sometimes non-existent) subject indexing. We use standard Library of Congress subject headings, along with some more detailed headings developed to meet the specialist needs of our

users. Almost all book records now have at least basic subject indexing, and work on improving the standard of subject access is
ongoing. Our records are downloaded periodically to the
Cambridge University Union Catalogue, so that our holdings appear
alongside those of all the other libraries of the university. They are
also, of course, freely accessible worldwide through the web.

One outcome of the wider dissemination of information about
our collections has been a big increase in use of our Postal
Photocopy Service. It is especially satisfying to be able to service
requests from Christian scholars, teachers and missionaries
working in corners of the world where resources are scarce, from
Russia to Africa, from the Philippines to South America. Another
outcome is illustrated by the unexpected arrival on our doorstep
one day of a professor from the Hebrew University in Jerusalem.
It turned out that, back in Jerusalem, he had seen a reference in
our web catalogue to a book that he was unable to find elsewhere.
He was delighted to find it on our shelves, and this positive experience was the beginning of our friendship with him. This kind of
story could be repeated many times, and so the network of scholars connected with Tyndale House grows ever wider.

As we work to ensure that the library remains at the 'cutting
edge' of biblical study and research for the future, we are mindful
that the most important thing of all is to seek and to follow God's
plan for Tyndale House – that unique institution that has taken
shape under his hand over the past sixty years.

APPENDIX C
COMPUTERS AT TYNDALE HOUSE

Dr David Instone-Brewer

Tyndale House library was the first in Cambridge to have all its books on a computer catalogue, and one of the first to make its catalogue available on the web. The catalogue records were upgraded in the 1990s to a very high quality (90% having full MARC standard). They are shared with the University Library Union Catalogue (a joint venture of about 100 libraries in Cambridge) and are also available through Tyndale's own webserver. The cataloguing software (based on Filemaker) and the web database (based on PHP and MySQL) were both written in-house and designed specifically for Biblical Studies and the special facilities of Tyndale House.

Tyndale House was, I believe, the first institution in Europe to have access to the TLG data ('all' Greek texts from ancient times) and had to purchase a special Ibycus computer in order to use it. The House continues to strive to have copies of all current software which is useful for academic research, and sometimes acquires this software before it is publicly released. Some of this is networked, but most is available as a single-terminal licence, so it is loaded on computers in the 'CD Room' (though no data are kept on CDs any more).

Electronic copies of most ancient literature are available, including all Greek literature, inscriptions and papyri; all Latin inscriptions and papyri; all Hebrew and Aramaic texts from rabbinic literature and Qumran; all Ugaritic texts; and many Syriac and Coptic texts. A number of bibliographic resources, such as ATLA and the École Biblique database, supplement the records of Biblical Studies journal articles which were compiled at Tyndale before ATLA began. A very large number of electronic books, especially in the area of Church History, partly make up for the lack of books in this area.

While Tyndale has usually been the first place to employ new Biblical Studies electronic resources, its policy regarding hardware and operating systems has been conservative. New operating systems are not used till they are well established, and hardware is repaired and upgraded many times before it is replaced.

An ethernet network links every desk in the library, with wireless access in residential areas. This gives a fast internet link and access to networked software such as Bible Works and Accordance. Although Accordance is designed for Macintosh computers, it is available to all PCs via emulation software on the network. Macintosh computers became important at Tyndale because they were able to display and print Greek and Hebrew fonts long before PCs, and they have remained important because Accordance is such an important tool.

Tyndale is linked to the University of Cambridge computing resources, which enables it to purchase very fast internet access through JANET (the UK academic network). This also gives access to valuable resources such as datasets which are subscribed to by the University Library for the whole university Wider Area Network to use.

The website contains about 5,000 pages and 1.6 Gb of data, including guides and introductions to the facilities, help pages for users and work by the Research Fellows (which makes up the overwhelming majority of the pages). It is visited by over 100,000 unique individuals per year, who produce millions of 'hits'. Regular e-mails concerning new academic internet resources keep users up to date with technological developments.

Abbreviations

MARC	MAchine Reading Catalogue: a standard format for computer cataloguing
PHP	PreHypertext Processor: a server-based language for writing web pages
MySQL	My Server Query Language: a computer language for reading databases
TLG	Thesaurus Linguae Graecae: a computerized edition of 'all' ancient Greek texts
CD	Compact Disc: a plastic disc holding 650Mb of data in machine-readable form
ATLA	American Theological Library Association bibliographic database of articles
PC	Personal Computer: unusually, denotes one which has a screen of four inches or more
JANET	Joint Academic NETwork: communication infrastructure used by British universities

APPENDIX D
THE TYNDALE LECTURES

Compiled by Douglas Johnson, M. J. Selman and T. A. Noble

Abbreviations

BJRL	*Bulletin of the John Rylands Library*
NT	*New Testament*
OT	*Old Testament*
TynB	*Tyndale Bulletin*
TZ	*Theologische Zeitschrift*
VE	*Vox Evangelica*

Notes

1. Publication details are given where known, but some other lectures may have been published.
2. Those listed as published by Tyndale Press were in the Tyndale Monographs series, which is also listed in Appendix E.
3. The titles of the published article may differ slightly from the title of the original lecture.

4. Douglas Johnson compiled the original list of Tyndale Lectures
   and included it as an appendix to his unpublished history of
   Tyndale House; Martin Selman extended the list to 1988.

Old Testament

Year	Lecturer	Title	Publication
1943	E. Robertson	Samuel and Saul	*BJRL*, 28 (1944), 175–206
1944	N. W. Porteous	The Church in the OT	
1945	D. W. Thomas	'The Prophet' in the Lachish Ostraca	London: Tyndale Press, 1946
1946	J. S. Wright	The Date of Ezra's Coming to Jerusalem	London: Tyndale Press, 1947
1947	F. F. Bruce	The Hittites and the OT	London: Tyndale Press, [1947]
1948	G. C. Aalders	The Problem of the Book of Jonah	London: Tyndale Press, [1948]
1949	W. J. Martin	Stylistic Treatment of Sources	*Stylistic Criteria and the Analysis of the Pentateuch* (London: Tyndale Press, 1955)
1950	D. J. Wiseman	The Literary Environment of Some Early Hebrew Writers	
1951	F. D. Kidner	Sacrifice in the OT	London: Tyndale Press, 1952
1952	J. S. Wright	The Building of the Second Temple	London: Tyndale Press, 1958
1953	H. L. Ellison	The Centrality of the Messianic Idea for the OT	London: Tyndale Press, 1953
1954	D. W. Gooding	Recensions of the Septuagint Pentateuch	London: Tyndale Press, 1955
1955	F. Foulkes	The OT and Theological Study	*The Acts of God: A Study in the Basis of Typology in the Old Testament* (London: Tyndale Press, 1958)
1956	J. A. Motyer	The Revelation of the Divine Name	London: Tyndale Press, 1959
1957	[None]		
1958	E. J. Young	The Son of Man in the Book of Daniel	*Daniel's Vision of the Son of Man* (London: Tyndale Press, 1958)
1959	J. G. S. S. Thomson	The Word of the Lord in Jeremiah	London: Tyndale Press, 1959
1960	R. A. Stewart	The Parable Form in the OT and Rabbinic Literature	

Year	Lecturer	Title	Publication
1961	J. B. Taylor	Some Aspects of Life and Death in the OT	
1962	D. F. Payne	The Creation in the OT	*Genesis One Reconsidered* (London: Tyndale Press, 1964)
1963	K. A. Kitchen	Hittite Hieroglyphs, Arameans and Hebrew Traditions	
1964	H. Jordan	Personal Religion in the OT	
1965	D. A. Hubbard	Wisdom Literature and Israel's Covenant Faith	*TynB*, 17 (1966)
1966	R. T. Beckwith	The OT Canon of Christ and the Apostles	
1967	D. J. A. Clines	The Image of God in Man	*TynB*, 19 (1968)
1967	D. W. Gooding	The Septuagint of Three Reigns	*Textus*, 7, 1–29
1968	A. E. Cundall	The Davidic Dynasty and Sacral Kingship	*VE*, 1969
1969	F. D. Kidner	The Origins of the People of Israel	*TSF Bulletin*, 57 (1970), 3–12
1970	P. C. Craigie	The Poetry of Ugarit and Ancient Israel	*TynB*, 22 (1971)
1971	G. J. Wenham	The Structure of Deuteronomy	
1972	W. J. Martin	Modern Linguistics and Biblical Hebrew	
1973	G. I. Davies	The Wilderness Itineraries	*TynB*, 25 (1974)
1974	P. J. M. Southwell	The Nature of Early Wisdom in Israel	
1975	J. E. Goldingay	The Man of War and the Suffering Servant: The OT and the Theology of Revolution	*TynB*, 27 (1976)
1976	D. F. Murray	The School of Ezekiel? Form and Tradition in the Book of Ezekiel	
1977	H. G. M. Williamson	Eschatology in Chronicles	*TynB*, 28 (1977)
1978	J. Baldwin	Some Literary Affinities of the Book of Daniel	*TynB*, 30 (1979)
1979	R. P. Gordon	David's Rise and Saul's Demise: Narrative Analogy in 1 Samuel 24 – 26	*TynB*, 31 (1980)
1980	D. W. Gooding	The Literary Structure of the Book of Daniel and its Implications	*TynB*, 32 (1981)

Year	Lecturer	Title	Publication
1981	L. C. Allen	Psalm 73: An Analysis	*TynB*, 33 (1982)
1982	J. G. McConville	Priests and Levites in Ezekiel	*TynB*, 34 (1983)
1983	K. Aitken	The Oracles against Babylon in Jeremiah 50 – 51: Structures and Perspectives	*TynB*, 35 (1984)
1984	T. D. Alexander	Jonah and Genre	*TynB*, 36 (1985)
1985	R. W. Cowley	Technical Terms in Biblical Hebrew?	*TynB*, 37 (1986)
1986	D. C. T. Sherrifs	'A Tale of Two Cities': Nationalism in Zion and Babylon	*TynB*, 39 (1988)
1987	C. C. Broyles	Pre-exilic Liturgical Forms and Motifs in Isaiah 40 – 55	
1988	D. T. Tsumura	Ugaritic Poetry and Habakkuk 3	*TynB*, 40.1 (1989)
1989	M. J. Selman	The Kingdom of God in the Old Testament	*TynB*, 40.2 (1989)
1990	P. P. Jenson	Creation, Call and Cult: The Theme of the Priestly Writing	
1991	J. J. Niehaus	The Central Sanctuary – Where and When?	*TynB*, 43.1 (1992)
1992	G. P. Hugenberger	Samson: A New-Old Interpretation	
1993	M. J. Paul	Our Attitude to Culture: A History of the Exegesis of Genesis 4:17–24	
1994	Å. Viberg	Amos 7:14 – A Case for Subtle Irony	*TynB*, 47.1 (1996)
1995	M. D. Carroll R.	The People of God among the Nations: A Literary Reading from Latin America	*TynB*, 47.1 (1996)
1996	R. Schultz	Unity and Diversity in Wisdom Theology? A Canonical and Covenantal Perspective	*TynB*, 48.2 (1997)
1997	D. I. Block	Ezekiel's Eschatological Vision with Special Reference to the Gog Magog Oracle (Ezek. 38 – 39)	K. E. Brower & M. W. Elliott (eds.), *The Reader Must Understand* (Leicester: Apollos, 1997)
1998	P. Barker	The Theology of Deuteronomy 27	*TynB*, 49.2 (1998)

Year	Lecturer	Title	Publication
1999	T. Renz	Proclaiming the Future: History and Theology in Prophecies against Tyre	
2000	D. W. Baker	The Wind and the Waves: Biblical Theology in Protology and Eschatology	
2001	L. Wilson	Letting God Be God: Exploring the Fear of God Motif in Genesis	
2002	P. Johnston	Figuring out Figurines	*TynB*, 54.2 (2003)
2003	D. C. T. Sheriffs	Perseverance and Perpetuity – the Human Need for Continuity: Old Testament and Near Eastern Reflections	*TynB*, 55.1 (2004)
2004	P. Pitkänen	Ethnicity, Assimilation and the Israelite Settlement	*TynB*, 55.2 (2004)

New Testament

Year	Lecturer	Title	Publication
1942	F. F. Bruce	The Speeches in the Acts of the Apostles	London: Tyndale Press [1943]
1943	B. F. C. Atkinson	The Theology of Prepositions	London: Tyndale Press [1944]
1944	E. K. Simpson	Words Worth Weighing in the Greek NT	London: Tyndale Press [1946]
1945	F. Davidson	Pauline Predestination	London: Tyndale Press [1946]
1946	P. W. Evans	Sacraments in the NT	London: Tyndale Press, n.d. [1947]
1947	A. M. Stibbs	The Meaning of the Word 'Blood' in Scripture	London: Tyndale Press [1948]
1948	F. D. Coggan	The NT Basis of Moral Theology	London: Tyndale Press [1948]
1949	N. B. Stonehouse	The Areopagus Address	London: Tyndale Press [1949]
1950	A. Cole	The New Temple	London: Tyndale Press [1950]
1951	E. M. Blaiklock	The Christian in Pagan Society	London: Tyndale Press [1951]
1952	J. R. W. Stott	The Biblical View of the Kingdom of God	

Year	Lecturer	Title	Publication
1953	J. W. Wenham	Our Lord's View of the OT	London: Tyndale Press, 1953
1954	L. Morris	The Wages of Sin	London: Tyndale Press, 1957
1955	D. Guthrie	The Pastoral Epistles and the Mind of Paul	London: Tyndale Press, 1956
1956	A. E. Guilding	The Relation of St John's Gospel to the Ancient Jewish Lectionary	
1957	E. A. Judge	Social Obligation in the New Testament	'The Social Pattern of Christian Groups in the First Century'
1958	J. N. Birdsall	The Bodmer Papyrus of the Gospel according to St John	*The Bodmer Papyrus of the Gospel of St John* (London: Tyndale Press, 1960)
1959	R. P. Martin	Study in Philippians, ch. II, vv. 5–11	*An Early Christian Confession* (London: Tyndale Press, 1960)
1959	E. M. Blaiklock	Rome in the NT	London: IVF, 1959
1960	E. M. B. Green	The Authenticity of II Peter	*2 Peter Reconsidered* (London: Tyndale Press, 1960)
1961	H. N. Ridderbos	St Peter's Sermons in the Acts	*The Speeches of Peter in the Acts of the Apostles* (London: Tyndale Press, 1962)
1962	R. E. Nixon	The Exodus in the NT	London: Tyndale Press, 1963
1963	I. H. Marshall	The Parables	*Eschatology and the Parables* (London: Tyndale Press, 1963)
1964	R. S. Wallace	Word and Deed	
1965	S. S. Smalley	New Light on the Fourth Gospel	*TynB*, 17 (1966)
1966	A. C. Thiselton	Eschatology and the Holy Spirit in I Corinthians	
1967	J. T. Tabor	The Purpose of the Acts of the Apostles	
1968	D. R. Hall	Pauline Church Discipline	*TynB*, 20 (1969)
1969	C. N. Hillyer	First Peter and the Feast of Tabernacles	*TynB*, 21 (1970)
1969	R. N. Longenecker	Biblical Exegesis in the Apostolic Period and Today	*TynB*, 21 (1970)
1970	M. J. Harris	2 Corinthians 5:1–10: Watershed in Paul's Eschatology	*TynB*, 22 (1971)
1971	D. Wenham	The Synoptic Problem Revisited: Mark 4:1–34	*TynB*, 23 (1972)

Year	Lecturer	Title	Publication
1972	G. N. Stanton	The Theology of the Q Material in the Gospels	'The Christology of Q', in B. Lindars and S. S. Smalley (eds.), *Christ and Spirit in the New Testament: In Honour of C. F. D. Moule* (Cambridge: CUP, 1975)
1973	E. E. Ellis	'Knowledge' and 'Wisdom' in 1 Corinthians	*TynB*, 25 (1974)
1974	J. D. G. Dunn	Romans 7:14–25 in the Theology of St Paul	*TZ*, 31 (1975)
1975	J. W. Drane	Theological Diversity in the Letters of St Paul	*TynB*, 27 (1976)
1976	D. R. de Lacey	Image and Incarnation in Pauline Theology – a Search for Origins	*TynB*, 30 (1979)
1977	M. M. B. Turner	Jesus and the Spirit in Lucan Perspective	*TynB*, 32 (1981)
1978	N. T. Wright	The Paul of History and the Apostle of Faith	*TynB*, 29 (1978)
1979	B. M. Metzger	Some Basic Questions concerning the NT Canon	
1980	F. Lyall	Legal Metaphors in the Epistles	*TynB*, 32 (1981)
1981	D. A. Carson	Understanding Misunderstandings in the Fourth Gospel	*TynB*, 33 (1982)
1982	H. J. B. Combrink	The Structure of the Gospel of Matthew as Narrative	*TynB*, 34 (1983)
1983	D. R. Carnegie	The Hymns in Revelation: A Survey of Theories	
1984	P. R. Jones	Paul – the Last Apostle (1 Cor. 15:8)	*TynB*, 36 (1985)
1985	J. F. Maile	The Ascension in Luke-Acts	*TynB*, 37 (1986)
1986	R. Riesner	Bethany beyond the Jordan (John 1:28): Topography, Theology and History in the Fourth Gospel	*TynB*, 38 (1987)
1987	S. Motyer	Righteousness in John and Paul: Diversity and Unity	
1988	C. C. Caragounis	Kingdom of God, Son of Man and Jesus' Self-understanding	*TynB*, 40 (1989)

Year	Lecturer	Title	Publication
1989	B. Capper	Baptists and Ascetics: Reflections on the Career of the Beloved Disciple	
1990	B. W. Winter	Religious Pluralism in I Corinthians 8 – 10	*TynB*, 41.2 (1990)
1991	G. R. Beasley-Murray	The Resurrection and the Parousia of the Son of Man	*TynB*, 42.2 (1991)
1992	G. Grogan	The *argumentum ad hominem* in the Epistles of Paul	
1993	C. Gempf	The Imagery of Birth Pangs in the NT	*TynB*, 45.1 (1994)
1994	B. Rosner	'Written for Us': Paul's View of Scripture	P. Satterthwaite & D. F. Wright (eds.), *A Pathway into the Holy Scripture* (Grand Rapids: Eerdmans, 1994)
1995	P. Towner	Pauline Theology or Pauline Tradition in the Pastoral Epistles? The Question of Methodology	*TynB*, 46.2 (1995)
1996	M. E. W. B. Thompson	The Holy Internet: Communication between Churches in the First Century	
1997	K. E. Brower	'Let the Reader Understand': Mark and Eschatology	K. E. Brower & M. W. Elliott (eds.), *The Reader Must Understand* (Leicester: Apollos, 1997)
1998	A. Clarke	'Imitate Us': Paul's Model of Leadership	*TynB*, 49.2 (1998)
1999	S. Hafemann	Eschatology and Ethics: The Future of Israel and the Nations in Romans 15:1–13	*TynB*, 51.2 (2000)
2000	D. Graham	AD 2000? The Prospects and Possibilities of Recovering the Historical Jesus in the New Millennium	
2001	P. Trebilco	'What Name Shall We Give Ourselves?' The Issue of Self-identification in Some Areas of NT Christianity.	*TynB*, 53.2 (2002) and 54.1 (2003)

Year	Lecturer	Title	Publication
2002	P. M. Head	The Early Manuscripts of John	
2003	E. Adams	The Coming of the Son of Man in the Gospels	*TynB*, 56, (2005)
2004	P. Oakes	Wrestling with the Context: Considering the Places of Archaeology, History, and the Social Sciences in Interpreting the NT	

Biblical Archaeology

Year	Lecturer	Title	Publication
1955	D. J. Wiseman	The Exile: A Study of the Archaeological Evidence	
1956	F. F. Bruce	The Teacher of Righteousness in the Qumran Texts	London: Tyndale Press, 1957
1957	K. A. Kitchen	The Joseph Narrative and its Egyptian Background	
1958	T. C. Mitchell	Archaeology and the First Chapters of Genesis	'Archaeology and Genesis 1 – 11', *Faith and Thought*, 91 (1959)
1959	C. de Wit	The Date of the Exodus	*The Date and Route of the Exodus* (London: Tyndale Press, 1960)
1960	[None]		
1961	A. R. Millard	Archaeology and the Life of Jesus	
1962	T. C. Mitchell	The Philistines	
1963	J. A. Thompson	The Ancient Near Eastern Treaties and the OT	London: Tyndale Press, 1964
1964	[None]		
1965	[None]		
1966	A. R. Millard	A New Babylonian 'Genesis' Story	*TynB*, 18 (1967)
1967	T. C. Mitchell	Ancient South Arabia and the OT	
1968	H. A. Hoffner	Contributions of Hittitology to OT Studies	*TynB*, 20 (1969)
1969	[None]		

Year	Lecturer	Title	Publication
1970	E. M. Yamauchi	The Evidence for Pre-Christian Gnosticism	in E. M. Yamauchi, *Pre-Christian Gnosticism: A Survey of the Proposed Evidences* (London: Tyndale Press, 1973)
1971	M. E. J. Richardson	Ugaritic Influence on Biblical Exegesis	*TynB*, 24 (1973)
1972	J. P. Kane	The Tomb where Jesus Lay: Evidence from Material Remains	
1973	C. J. Hemer	Alexandrian Troas	*TynB*, 26 (1975)
1974	M. J. Selman	The Patriarchs and their Social Environment	*TynB*, 27 (1976)
1975	J. Ruffle	The Wisdom of Amenemope and its Connection with the Book of Proverbs	*TynB*, 28 (1977)
1976	K. A. Kitchen	Proverbs and Wisdom Books of the Ancient Near East: The Factual History of a Literary Form	*TynB*, 28 (1977)
1977	D. J. Wiseman	Archaeology and the Book of Jonah	*TynB*, 30 (1979)
1978	[None]		
1979	C. J. Davey	Temples of the Levant and the Buildings of Solomon	*TynB*, 31 (1980)
1980	J. J. Bimson	King Solomon's Mines? A Reassessment of Finds in the Arabah	*TynB*, 32 (1981)
1981	[None]		
1982	P. C. Craigie	Ugarit, Canaan and Israel: Cultural Similarities and Differences	*TynB*, 34 (1983)
1983	E. A. Judge	Cultural Conformity and Innovation in Paul: Some Clues from Contemporary Documents	*TynB*, 35 (1984)
1984	A. R. Millard	Sennacherib's Attack on Hezekiah	*TynB*, 36 (1985)
1985	D. T. Tsumura	Ugaritic Poetry and Habakkuk 3	
1986	C. J. Hemer	Reflections on the Nature of NT Greek Vocabulary	*TynB*, 38 (1987)
1987	H. G. M. Williamson	The Governors of Judah under the Persians	*TynB*, 39 (1988)

Year	Lecturer	Title	Publication
1988	T. C. Mitchell	Crafts and Technology in Biblical Times	
1989	P. W. L. Walker	The Holy Places of the Incarnation: Fourth Century Attitudes	P. W. L. Walker (ed.), *Jerusalem Past and Present in the Purposes of God*
1990	G. H. R. Horsley	The Inscriptions of Ephesus and the Testament	
1991	D. W. J. Gill	Behind the Classical: Religious Pluralism in the Roman East	A. D. Clarke & B. W. Winter (eds.), *One God, One Lord in a World of Religious Pluralism* (Cambridge: Tyndale House, 1991)
1992	[None]		
1993	B. Van Elderen	The Rise and Development of Early Christianity	*TynB*, 45.1 (1994)
1994	J. Woodhead		
1995	[None]		
1996	[None]		
1997	D. W. J. Gill	Rome, Rivalries, and Riots: Threats to Urban Life in the Greek Cities of the Roman East	
1998	B. W. Winter	The Imperial Gods and the First Christians	
1999			
2000			
2001			
2002			
2003	S. Sherwin	'I am against You': Yahweh's Judgement on the Nations in its Ancient Near Eastern Context	*TynB*, 54.2 (2003)
2004	D. Swanson	The Nature of Biblical Authority at Qumran	

Biblical Theology

Year	Lecturer	Title	Publication
1950	C. Van Til	The Christian Revelation and Modern Thought	*The Intellectual Challenge of the Gospel* (London: Tyndale Press, 1950)
1951	R. V. G. Tasker	The Biblical Doctrine of the Wrath of God	London: Tyndale Press, 1951
1952	A. M. Stibbs	The Finished Work of Christ	London: Tyndale Press, 1952
1953	J. Murray	The Covenant of Grace	London: Tyndale Press, 1954
1954	J. I. Packer	Christ our Righteousness	
1955	E. F. Kevan	The Evangelical Doctrine of Law	*Keep His Commandments: The Place of Law in the Christian Life* (London: Tyndale Press, 1964)
1956	P. E. Hughes	Scripture, Myth and History – an Examination of Rudolf Bultmann's Plea for Demythologisation	*Scripture and Myth* (London: Tyndale Press, 1956)
1957	G. Walters	The Intercession of the Spirit	
1957	G. E. Ladd	The Place of Apocalyptic in Biblical Religion	
1958	R. A. Finlayson	Man's Spiritual Responsibility – its Nature and Extent	
1959	M. R. Gordon	An Examination of the Doctrine of Final Perseverance	
1960	L. Morris	The Biblical Doctrine of Judgment	London: Tyndale Press, 1960
1961	H. M. Carson	The Doctrine of Eternal Punishment	
1962	M. H. Cressey	'God is Love' as a Norm for Theology	
1963	C. Brown	The Challenge of Barth's Christology	
1964	E. A. Russell	John the Baptist and Jesus	
1965	A. Willingale	Time in the Bible	
1966	C. H. Pinnock	A Defence of Biblical Infallibility	*A Defense of Biblical Infallibility* (Phillipsburg, NJ: Presbyterian & Reformed, 1967)
1967	R. T. France	The Servant of the Lord in the Teaching of Jesus	*TynB*, 19 (1968)

Year	Lecturer	Title	Publication
1968	G. W. Grogan	The OT Concept of Solidarity and its Importance for NT Theology	
1969	R. E. Davies	Christ in our Place: The Contribution of the Prepositions	*TynB*, 21 (1970)
1970	J. W. Charley	The Enigma of Man: A Study of Man's Nature and Fulfilment	
1971	W. Stott	This is the Day: A Study in the Biblical Theology of the Lord's Day	R. T. Beckwith & W. Stott (eds.), *This is the Day: The Biblical Doctrine of the Christian Sunday in its Jewish and Early Church Setting* (London: Marshall, Morgan & Scott, 1978)
1972	C. Brown	History and the Believer	C. Brown (ed.), *History, Criticism and Faith* (Leicester: IVP, 1976)
1973	J. I. Packer	What Did the Cross Achieve? The Logic of Penal Substitution	*TynB*, 25 (1974)
1974	D. B. A. Milne	The Idea of Sin in Twentieth Century Theology	*TynB*, 26 (1975)
1975	O. M. T. O'Donovan	Towards an Interpretation of Biblical Ethics	*TynB*, 27 (1976)
1976	K. Runia	What is Preaching according to the NT?	*TynB*, 29 (1978)
1977	H. Blocher	The Fear of the Lord as the 'Principle' of Wisdom	*TynB*, 28 (1977)
1978	S. H. Travis	The Value of Apocalyptic	*TynB*, 30 (1979)
1979	R. J. Bauckham	The Delay of the Parousia	*TynB*, 31 (1980)
1980	G. L. Carey	The 'Lamb of God' and Atonement Theology	*TynB*, 32 (1981)
1981	W. L. Lane	Covenant – the Key to Paul's Conflict with Corinth	*TynB*, 33 (1982)
1982	R. W. L. Moberly	God Incarnate: Some Reflections from an OT Perspective	*TynB*, 34 (1983)
1983	J. P. Baker	Biblical Attitudes to Romantic Love	*TynB*, 35 (1984)

Year	Lecturer	Title	Publication
1984	P. Wells	The Humanity of Scripture Considered in the Light of the Covenant Concept	
1985	J. B. Webster	The Imitation of Christ in Recent NT Theology	*TynB*, 37 (1986)
1986	R. T. Beckwith	The Unity and Diversity of God's Covenants	*TynB*, 38 (1987)
1987	A. Nordlander	Paul and the Law in Contemporary Debate	
1988			
1989	L. McFall	Jesus the Terminus of the OT Genealogies	
1990	D. A. Carson	Reflections on Christian Assurance	
1991	G. L. Bray	The Image and Likeness of God	*TynB*, 42.2 (1991)
1992	C. H. H. Scobie	Israel and the Nations: A Biblical Theology of Missions [An Essay in Biblical Theology?]	*TynB*, 43.2 (1992)
1993	M. J. Evans	A Plague on Both Your Houses: Cursings and Blessings Reviewed	
1994	N. T. Wright	Justification by Faith: Can We Get It Right Now?	
1995	D. Instone-Brewer	Three Weddings and a Divorce: The Covenant of God with Israel, Judah and the Church	*TynB*, 47.1 (1996)
1996	R. T. France	The Writer to the Hebrews as a Biblical Expositor	*TynB*, 47.2 (1996)
1997	G. Grogan	The OT Concept of Solidarity as Applied in the Inaugurated Eschatology of the Epistle to the Hebrews	*TynB*, 49.1 (1998)
1998	D. Alexander	Royal Expectations in the Books of Genesis to Kings	*TynB*, 49.2 (1998)
1999	P. W. L. Walker	The Land in the NT	
2000	F. Watson	The Coherence of the Canon: Rethinking Biblical Unity	*TynB*, 52.2 (2001)
2001	C. E. Armerding	Did I Ever Ask for a House of Cedar? T. D. Alexander & S. J. Gathercole (eds.), *Heaven on Earth: The Temple in Biblical Theology* (Carlisle: Paternoster,	

Year	Lecturer	Title	Publication
		2004) The Contribution of 2 Samuel 7 and 1 Chronicles 17 to the Theology of the Temple	
2002	R. W. L. Moberly	How May We Speak of God? A Reconsideration of the Nature of Biblical Theology	*TynB*, 53.2 (2002)
2004	G. Beale	The Inauguration of the Eschatological Temple in Acts 2	

Historical Theology

Year	Lecturer	Title	Publication
1957	G. C. B. Davies	The First Evangelical Bishop – Some Aspects of the Life of Henry Ryder	London: Tyndale Press, 1958
1958	[None]		
1959	A. S. Wood	Luther's Principles of Biblical Interpretation	London: Tyndale Press, 1960
1960	R. J. Coates	Eucharistic Sacrifice – an Historical Survey of the Doctrine	
1961	R. N. Caswell	Calvin's Doctrine of Ecclesiastical Discipline	
1962	T. H. L. Parker	*Supplementa Calviniana* – an Account of the Manuscripts of Calvin's Sermons Now in Course of Preparation	London: Tyndale Press, 1962
1963– 1975	[None]		
1976	A. N. S. Lane	*Sola Scriptura* in Recent Roman Catholic Theology	
1977	[None]		
1978	D. F. Wright	The Evangelical Doctrine of Scripture in Britain in the Twentieth Century	*TynB*, 31 (1980)
1979	[None]		
1980	P. Toon	A Critical Review of John Henry Newman's Doctrine of Justification	

Year	Lecturer	Title	Publication
1981	J. Atkinson	Luther and the Wittenberg Disputations 1535–36	*TynB*, 33 (1982)
1982	G. L. Bray	The *Filioque* Clause in History and Theology	*TynB*, 34 (1983)
1983	N. M. de S. Cameron	Inspiration and Criticism: The Nineteenth Century Crisis	*TynB*, 35 (1984)
1984	[None]		
1985	C. A. Baxter	Barth – a Truly Biblical Theologian?	*TynB*, 38 (1987)
1986	J. E. Colwell	A Radical Church? A Reappraisal of Anabaptist Ecclesiology	*TynB*, 38 (1987)

Christian Doctrine

The change of designation of this lecture series followed the combining of Historical Theology and Systematic Theology in the 'Christian Doctrine' Study Group in 1984 (see page 204).

Year	Lecturer	Title	Publication
1987	T. A. Noble	Gregory Nazianzen's Use of Scripture in Defence of the Deity of the Spirit	*TynB*, 39 (1988)
1988	M. A. Noll	Revival, Enlightenment, Civic Humanism and the Development of Dogma: Scotland and America, 1735–1843	*TynB*, 40.1 (1989)
1989	G. Keith	Our Knowledge of God: The Relevance Debate between Eunomius and the Cappadocians	*TynB*, 41.1 (1990)
1990	R. Tudur Jones	'Union with Christ': The Existential Nerve of Puritan Piety	*TynB*, 41.2 (1990)
1991	R. Kearsley	Greek God and Christian Christ? The Impact of Theology on Christology in Cyril of Alexandria	*TynB*, 43.2 (1992)
1992	T. Bradshaw	John Macquarrie's Doctrine of God	*TynB*, 44.1 (1993)
1993	L. Osborn	Entertaining Angels: The Place of Angels in Contemporary Theology	*TynB*, 45.2 (1994)
1994	T. Hart	The Word, the Words and the Witness: Proclamation as Divine and Human Reality in the Theology of Karl Barth	*TynB*, 46.1 (1995)
1995	A. E. McGrath	An Evangelical Response to Pluralism	

Year	Lecturer	Title	Publication
1996	R. Kreider	The Nature of Conversion in the Early Centuries of the Church	*TynB*, 47.2 (1996)
1997	R. J. Bauckham	Must Christian Eschatology be Millenarian? A Response to Jürgen Moltmann	K. E. Brower & M. W. Elliott (eds.), *The Reader Must Understand* (Leicester: Apollos, 1997)
1998	K. Vanhoozer	Effectual Call or Causal Effect: Summons, Sovereignty and Supervenient Grace	*TynB*, 49.2 (1998)
1999	M. Davie	'Dead to Sin and Alive to God – Penal Substitution Revisited', *SBET*, 19.2 (2001)	
2000	C. R. Trueman	A Man More Sinned Against than Sinning? The Picture of Martin Luther in Contemporary New Testament Scholarship: Some Casual Observations of a Mere Historian	
2001	M. W. Elliott	Luther's Bible and Authority	
2002	G. J. Williams	Was Evangelicalism Created by the Enlightenment?	*TynB*, 53.1 (2004)
2003	P. M. Bassett	Wesley's Covenant Service	
2004	J. W. Ward	Apprehending the Mystery of the Ascension of Jesus Christ	

Christian Ethics

Year	Lecturer	Title	Publication
1988	S. N. Williams	The Limits of Hope and the Logic of Love on the Basis of Christian Social Responsibility	*TynB*, 40.2 (1989)
1989	E. Storkey	A Search for Intimacy	
1990	F. W. Bridger	Towards an Evangelical Theology of Power	
1991	C. J. H. Wright	The Ethical Authority of the OT: A Methodological Survey	*TynB*, 43.1 (1992) & 43.2 (1992)
1992	N. Biggar	Should Public Institutions be Christian?	
1993	D. G. Peterson	Worship and Ethics	

Year	Lecturer	Title	Publication
1994	B. W. Winter	Early Christians as Citizens and Benefactors	*Seek the Welfare of the City: Christians as Benefactors and Citizens* (Carlisle: Paternoster/Grand Rapids: Eerdmans, 1994)
1995			
1996			
1997	J. Chaplin	Can a Modern State be 'Christian'?	

Philosophy of Religion

Year	Lecturer	Title	Publication
1994	P. Helm	Eternal Creation	*TynB*, 45.2 (1994)
1995	R. Sturch	Divine Knowledge: Comparisons and Contrasts with the Human	*TynB*, 47.1 (1996)
1996	S. N. Williams	Dionysius against the Crucified: Nietzsche *contra* Christianity	*TynB*, 48.2 (1997) & 49.1 (1998)
1997	[None]		
1998	C. Bartholomew	Derrida and Babel: The Challenge of Deconstruction for Biblical Interpretation	*TynB*, 49.2 (1998)
1999	H. Bunting	Ethics and the Perfect Moral Law	*TynB*, 51.2 (2000)
2000	P. Roche	Knowledge of God and Alvin Plantinga's Reformed Epistemology	
2001	J. Jedwab	Metaphysics and Trinity	
2002	H. Cunningham	The Idea of General Equity in the Westminster Confession of Faith	
2003	D. Hill	Language, Truth and Scripture	
2004	O. Crisp	Problems with Perichoresis	

Religion, Culture and Communication

Year	Lecturer	Title	Publication
2000	J. Drane	Keeping Faith and Reimagining the Gospel: Missiological Challenges for the Church and Theology in Post-modern Culture	

Year	Lecturer	Title	Publication
2001	J. A. Kirk	The Confusion of Epistemology in the West and Christian Mission	*TynB*, 55.1 (2004)
2002	B. Stanley	Conversion to Christianity: The Colonization of the Mind	
2003	C. Chapman	Dispensing with Dispensationalism	
2004	P. Riddell	From Death to Judgment: Islamic Perspectives from Classical Arab and Malay Texts	

John Wenham Lectures

Year	Lecturer	Title	Publication
1995	D. A. Carson	An Assessment of Contemporary Evangelicalism	
1996	B. W. Winter	The Church versus the People of God	
1997	C. Blomberg	Eschatology and the Church	*Themelios*, 23.3 (June 1998)
1998	G. L. Bray	Present Trends in Biblical Interpretation	Published as 'Rescuing Theology from the Theologians' Theology', *Themelios*, 24.2 (February 1999)
1999	D. Smith	Transforming the World 2000	Published as 'Junction or Terminus? Christianity in the West at the Dawn of the Third Millennnium', *Themelios*, 25.3 (June 2000)
2000	C. Trueman	Those Who Can Do: Those Who Can't Teach Church History	
2001	P. F. M. Zahl	Mistakes of the New Perspective on Paul	*Themelios*, 27.1 (autumn 2001)
2002	C. Trueman	Theology and the Church: Divorce or Remarriage?	*Themelios*, 28.3 (summer 2003) and *The Wages of Spin* (Mentor, 2004)
2003	D. F. Wright	Children, Covenant and Church	*Themelios*, 29.2 (spring 2004)
2004	D. Macleod	Discerning Heresy and False Teaching in the Church	

APPENDIX E
TYNDALE MONOGRAPHS

A number of the monographs in the First Series are undated and the dates given here are therefore approximate.

First series

1. F. F. Bruce, *The Speeches in Acts* [1943]
2. J. S. Wright, *The Date of Ezra's Coming to Jerusalem*, 1947
3. J. Murray, *The Covenant of Grace*, 1954
4. D. W. Thomas, *The Prophet in the Lachish Ostraca*, 1946
5. F. F. Bruce, *The Hittites and the Old Testament* [1947]
6. G. C. Aalders, *The Problem of the Book of Jonah* [1948]
7. F. D. Kidner, *Sacrifice in the Old Testament*, 1952
8. B. F. C. Atkinson, *The Theology of Prepositions* [1944]
9. E. K. Simpson, *Words Worth Weighing in the Greek New Testament*, 1946
10. F. Davidson, *Pauline Predestination*, 1946
11. P. W. Evans, *Sacraments in the New Testament* [1947]
12. A. M. Stibbs, *The Meaning of the Word 'Blood' in Scripture* [1948]
13. F. D. Coggan, *The New Testament Basis of Moral Theology* [1948]

14. N. B. Stonehouse, *The Areopagus Address* [1949]
15. A. Cole, *The New Temple* [1950]
16. E. M. Blaiklock, *The Christian in Pagan Society* [1951]
17. C. Van Til, *The Intellectual Challenge of the Gospel* [1950]
18. R. V. G. Tasker, *The Biblical Doctrine of the Wrath of God* [1951]
19. P. E. Hughes, *The Divine Plan for Jew and Gentile*, 1949
20. R. V. G. Tasker, *The Gospel in the Epistle to the Hebrews*, 1950
21. H. L. Ellison, *The Centrality of the Messianic Idea for the Old Testament*, 1953

Second series

1. H. P. V. Nunn, *The Fourth Gospel*, 1946
2. A. M. Stibbs, *The Finished Work of Christ*, 1952
3. J. W. Wenham, *Our Lord's View of the Old Testament*, 1953
4. D. W. B. Robinson, *Josiah's Reform and the Book of the Law*, 1951
5. D. W. Gooding, *Recensions of the Septuagint Pentateuch*, 1955
6. Leon Morris, *The Wages of Sin*, 1957
7. W. J. Martin, *Stylistic Criteria and the Analysis of the Pentateuch*, 1955
8. E. F. Kevan, *The Evangelical Doctrine of the Law*, 1951
9. D. Guthrie, *The Pastoral Epistles and the Mind of St Paul*, 1956
10. P. E. Hughes, *Scripture and Myth*, 1956
11. A. M. Stibbs, *God Became Man*, 1957
12. F. F. Bruce, *The Teacher of Righteousness in the Qumran Texts*, 1957

Third series

1. J. N. Birdsall, *The Bodmer Papyrus of the Gospel of John*, 1960
2. J. S. Wright, *The Building of the Second Temple*, 1958
3. A. S. Wood, *Luther's Principles of Biblical Interpretation*, 1960
4. J. A. Motyer, *The Revelation of the Divine Name*, 1959
5. G. C. B. Davies, *The First Evangelical Bishop*, 1958
6. F. Foulkes, *The Acts of God*, 1958
7. E. J. Young, *Daniel's Vision of the Son of Man*, 1958
8. C. de Wit, *The Date and Route of the Exodus*, 1960
9. J. G. S. S. Thomson, *The Word of the Lord in Jeremiah*, 1959

10. E. M. B. Green, *2 Peter Reconsidered*, 1961
11. J. S. Wright, *The Date of Ezra's Coming to Jerusalem*, reprinted 1958
12. R. V. G. Tasker, *The Gospel in the Epistle to the Hebrews*, second edition, 1956

Fourth series

1. H. N. Ridderbos, *The Speeches of Peter in the Acts of the Apostles*, 1962
2. J. Murray, *The Covenant of Grace*, second edition, 1956
3. T. H. L. Parker, *Supplementa Calviniana*, 1962
4. R. E. Nixon, *The Exodus in the New Testament*, 1963
5. I. H. Marshall, *Eschatology and the Parables*, 1963
6. D. F. Payne, *Genesis One Reconsidered*, 1964
7. A. S. Dunstone, *The Atonement in Gregory of Nyssa*, 1964
8. J. A. Thompson, *The Ancient Near Eastern Treaties and the Old Testament*, 1964

APPENDIX F
'THE TYNDALE FELLOWSHIP FOR BIBLICAL RESEARCH'

F. F. Bruce

F. F. Bruce, 'The Tyndale Fellowship for Biblical Research,' *Evangelical Quarterly*, 19 (1947), 52–61. Reproduced with permission.

In May 1938 some senior members and friends of the Inter-Varsity Fellowship of Evangelical Unions met in the house of one of their number in London to consider how best the reproach of obscurantism and anti-intellectual prejudice might be removed from Evangelical Christianity in England. How far this reproach was justified is a question outside the scope of this paper; at any rate, it was widely believed that Evangelicals were afraid of scholarship, especially biblical and theological scholarship, and Evangelicals in England did not always act in such a way as to explode this belief. In this respect, of course, there was a considerable difference between English and Scottish Evangelicalism. One ordinand in the 1920's, who is now on the staff of a theological college, was strongly urged by an eminent Evangelical clergyman not to read for theological honours in one of the ancient English universities; and when he disregarded this and other warnings, the oddity of a confessed Evangelical pursuing such a course earned for him in Evangelical circles the title of 'The Theologian'. Most happily, the precedent he established was followed by others. But the situation left much to be desired when these men met to consider it in 1938.

After some discussion, they constituted themselves as the Biblical Research Committee, loosely attached to the Inter-Varsity Fellowship. The object of this Committee was from the first to endeavour by all possible means to promote sound Biblical scholarship among Evangelical Christians in England. Contact was made with probable sympathisers throughout the British Isles, as well as in Europe and America, and a few men who were interested in certain fields of Biblical scholarship were encouraged to pursue these interests and produce work which might help to remove the reproach of unscholarliness from English Evangelicalism. One or two major works of Biblical scholarship undertaken at that time are now in course of publication.

The outbreak of war in 1939 augured ill for the schemes of the infant Committee, but in fact those schemes grew and fructified during the war in a measure beyond what could have been hoped. By the summer of 1941 sufficient progress was made to encourage the Committee to convoke a Conference of sympathisers from all parts of Britain to consider further plans. This Conference met at Kingham Hill, Oxfordshire, two or three weeks after Hitler's attack on Russia; and those who were present will not readily forget it. The Conference profited greatly by the wise and experienced advice of that true father in God, the late Principal Donald Maclean of Edinburgh, who had played a leading part in the resurgence of Scottish Evangelicalism twelve years previously, when he and his colleague, the late Professor J. R. Mackay, inaugurated THE EVANGELICAL QUARTERLY. It was at this Conference, incidentally, that the first steps were taken towards ensuring the continued witness of the QUARTERLY under its present constitution.

Among the decisions reached at Kingham Hill the three most important were (1) to hold an annual Summer School, (2) to found two annual lectures in Biblical studies, one for the Old Testament and one for the New, and (3) to secure a residential centre and library for Biblical research.

Arrangements were made at once to hold a Summer School the following year, and held it was, despite many unfavourable conditions arising from the war, at St. Deiniol's Library, Hawarden, North Wales. The stimulating intellectual atmosphere at St. Deiniol's showed those who attended something of the value of such a residential centre, and encouraged them to do their best to secure one of their own. Very few attended the first Summer School, but at least it was a beginning, and those who came found the time by no means wasted as they read 1 Samuel in Hebrew and Galatians in Greek. Larger numbers attended the Summer Schools of 1943 and 1944, which were held at Wadham College, Oxford; and the 1945 Summer School was held in our own residential centre, Tyndale House, Cambridge (of which more anon), to study the problems of the Fourth Gospel for the first week and the Biblical Doctrine of the Church for the second week. The latest Summer School was held there in July 1946, having as special subject for the first week 'The Relation between the Testaments' and for the second week 'The Authority of the Bible'. At these Summer Schools, as well as on other occasions, we have benefited greatly by the help of friends from Scotland and Ireland – it may not be invidious to mention Professors G. T. Thomson and A. M. Renwick of Edinburgh, and the Rev. W. C. G. Proctor of Trinity College, Dublin.

After careful deliberation, it was decided to call the two annual lectures founded as a result of the Kingham Hill discussions 'The Tyndale Lectures' in Old and New Testament studies. The first two were delivered at Oxford in December 1942, and two more have been delivered each Christmas vacation since then. Among our Old Testament lecturers we have had Dr. W. J. Martin of Liverpool and Professors E. Robertson (Manchester), N. W. Porteous (Edinburgh), and D. Winton Thomas (Cambridge); among the New Testament lecturers have been Dr. Basil Atkinson, Mr E. K. Simpson, Professor Francis Davidson, and Principal P. W. Evans. Some of these lectures have been published in pamphlet form: *Samuel and Saul*, by E. Robertson; *The Theology of Prepositions*, by B. F. C. Atkinson; *Words Worth Weighing in the Greek New Testament*, by E. K. Simpson; *Pauline Predestination*, by F. Davidson; *'The Prophet' in the Lachish Ostraca*, by D. W. Thomas;

The Date of Ezra's Coming to Jerusalem, by J. S. Wright; *The Speeches in the Acts of the Apostles*, by F. F. Bruce.[1]

It was necessary, of course, to find an audience for these Tyndale Lectures; they were therefore held during the Annual Conference of the I.V.F. Theological Students' Fellowship, which regularly meets during the Christmas vacation, and a number of senior men came together for a day or two in the same place, primarily to hear the Tyndale Lectures, but also for further papers and discussions. The Biblical Research Committee therefore decided to convene a Conference each Christmas vacation, to spend three or four days discussing a given topic. In the Christmas vacation of 1944–1945, for example, the topic was Biblical Interpretation; in 1945–1946, Biblical Eschatology; in 1946–1947, Biblical Anthropology.

The need for a residential centre was increasing all the time, and at last, in September 1944, we were able to secure the excellent freehold property at 16, Selwyn Gardens, Cambridge, to which the name 'Tyndale House' was given. The name of William Tyndale is one in which no one party or section of English-speaking Christendom has a special interest; he and his work are our common heritage. And – rather strangely – Tyndale's name had not been already appropriated by a learned foundation, as those of Wycliffe, Ridley, and others had been. Tyndale House was first used for its proper purpose when the Conference convened by the Biblical Research Committee met there in January 1945, and it was solemnly dedicated to God for that purpose on the afternoon of January 2, at a simple service in which the Rev. G. T. Manley, Professor G. T. Thomson, and Dr D. Martyn Lloyd-Jones took part.

When Tyndale House was acquired, a library was ready to be housed in it. From the time of the Kingham Hill Conference onwards, some of us had been collecting books suitable for Biblical and theological research. The heavy expenditure thus entailed was most generously defrayed by a Christian gentleman of

---

1. All published by the Tyndale Press, 19 Bedford Square, London, W.C.1, except *Samuel and Saul*, which was published by the John Rylands Library, Manchester.

long-range spiritual vision, whose anonymity must be preserved at his own desire. Now, Tyndale House contains a library of several thousand volumes, on which the Biblical scholar's eye rests with fond and envious delight. It is strictly a residential library, so that volumes cannot be lent out. It is mainly intended for the use of people who come to stay for longer or shorter periods at Tyndale House in order to carry out some form of Biblical research, though its facilities are also at the disposal of residents in Cambridge who wish to consult the volumes in Tyndale House. Colonel J. N. D. Anderson, O.B.E., M.A., LL.B., late of Egypt and Cyrenaica, a Cambridge graduate and Semitic scholar, has recently been appointed Resident Warden and Librarian.

As a result of the Summer Schools and Winter Conferences, a larger group of interested men and women was gradually forming round the Biblical Research Committee as its nucleus. It was plainly desirable that this group should be more definitely integrated, and at the first Conference held in Tyndale House (January 1945) it was constituted as the Tyndale Fellowship for Biblical Research. This Fellowship is linked with the I.V.F. in that the I.V.F. Biblical Research Committee is also the Council of the Tyndale Fellowship, and its theological outlook is that expressed in the I.V.F. Doctrinal Basis. Its object is to maintain and promote Biblical studies and research in a spirit of loyalty to the Christian Faith as enshrined in the consensus of the Historic Creeds and Reformed Confessions, and to re-establish the authority of Evangelical scholarship in the field of Biblical and theological studies.

Among its activities the Tyndale Fellowship endeavours (1) to encourage younger scholars to engage in Biblical research, along linguistic, historical, archaeological or theological lines; (2) to call attention to and to examine contemporary research bearing upon the right understanding of the Bible; (3) to urge the claims of Biblical studies to a permanent and influential place in the national system of education; (4) to create opportunities for intercourse and co-operation between those who have at heart the objects which the Fellowship desires to promote, and to co-operate with similar bodies among the English-speaking nations and on the European Continent and elsewhere.

Membership of the Tyndale Fellowship is open to all persons of either sex who are in sympathy with its objects and wish to take an active part in Biblical Research. Members are kept in touch with the affairs of the Fellowship by means of the quarterly *Tyndale Bulletin* and circulating portfolios devoted to various branches of Biblical and theological studies. They are encouraged to contribute to theses studies by writing monographs or theses for higher degrees, by reading papers at Conferences, Summer Schools or Reading Parties, by contributing articles to appropriate periodicals, and so forth. Several articles appearing from time to time in THE EVANGELICAL QUARTERLY have been first composed to read at meetings of the Tyndale Fellowship.

But an important question is sometimes raised. While the Tyndale Fellowship confesses its desire to remove the stigma of obscurantism from English Evangelicalism, is it in fact free from obscurantism itself? Does not its acceptance of the I.V.F. Doctrinal Basis commit it *ipso facto* to an unprogressive 'Fundamentalism' (to employ what Principal Maclean aptly called 'a refined theological swearword'!)? Are not its conclusions in the field, say, of Biblical criticism, prescribed and settled in advance? The answer is, unreservedly, No.

As for its acceptance of the I.V.F. Doctrinal Basis, that is simply a summary, in untheological language, of the Protestant faith as exhibited in its chief formularies. The Basis has frequently been criticised for explicitly predicting 'infallibility' of Holy Scripture as originally given, as well as its divine inspiration and supreme authority in all matters of faith and conduct. But *Evangelical Belief*, the official interpretation of the Basis, explains this 'infallibility' to mean 'that the Scriptures themselves, in their proper sense, never lead astray the soul who is sincerely seeking truth' (1st edition, p. 10).[2] The words, 'in their proper sense',

---

2. The use of the term 'infallibility' has been bedevilled by the dogma of Papal Infallibility. The I.V.F. Doctrinal Basis probably took it from the *Westminster Confession of Faith*. The word is strictly equivalent to Gk. ἀσφαλεια, used in Luke i. 4 (translated 'certainty' in A.V. and R.V.); and the interpretation quoted above from *Evangelical Belief* gives the precise

necessarily imply that each part of the Bible must be viewed in the light of the whole, and that the Old Testament must be read in the light of the New.[3] There is nothing obscurantist in this position.

Admittedly, the Tyndale Fellowship has its presuppositions and its distinctive point of view. It is committed to the Catholic Evangelical Faith.[4] Few, if any Biblical scholars, whether working singly or in groups, approach their studies without presuppositions of any kind. Those who say or think that they do, very often betray in the event that their presuppositions, even if unsuspected by themselves, are none the less real. It is much better to be aware of one's presuppositions and bias, and to acknowledge them frankly, as allowances can then be more easily made for them.[5] Some Biblical critics, on the other hand, while professedly pursuing their research with unbiased minds and scientific methods, have in fact proceeded on the assumption that the supernatural may be discounted. They were at liberty to make this assumption if they wished, of course; if we disagree with what our opponents say, we readily defend their right to say it; but it would have been better if their anti-supernaturalist premises had been explicitly admitted by themselves and understood by their hearers and readers. A curious situation arose when, towards the end of last century, devout Christian scholars in Scotland and England accepted conclusions reached in Biblical criticism from rationalist premises by Continental scholars. When Dr James Begg

---

meaning of the term. Later on the same page we read: 'By using the word "infallibility" in reference to Holy Scripture, we mean that it is in itself a true and complete guide, and requires no external correction either by Church or Tradition.'

3. Of course, it is also true that the New Testament must be read in the light of the Old, but in a slightly different sense of the phrase.

4. This does not mean, of course, that we have not the soundest reason for holding this Faith in the first place!

5. 'Prejudices that are recognized as such are generally harmless; the unrecognized ones are the dangerous ones' (A. D. Ritchie, *Civilization, Science and Religion* [1945], p. 12).

described to Thomas Carlyle the development of such a situation among some Scottish theologians, the sage of Chelsea, no devotee of the Reformed Faith himself, thundered: 'Have my countrymen's heads become turnips, that they think they can hold the premises of German unbelief and draw the conclusions of Scottish Evangelical Orthodoxy?' It is a good thing to know what our premisses are, to acknowledge them openly, and to see to it that our conclusions stand in some sort of rational relationship to them.

It is helpful to contrast the position of the Tyndale Fellowship with that of Roman Catholic Biblical scholarship. Roman Catholic scholars have, of course, their special presuppositions and preferences; that is but natural, and we have no fault to find with it, the more so as they freely avow them. But the Papal authorities are not content to leave well alone and trust their scholars not to reach conclusions at variance with the premisses of their faith. The growth of the Modernist movement in the Church of Rome led to the establishment by Pope Leo XIII in 1901 of the Pontifical Biblical Commission, which in many cases prescribes the limits within which Roman Catholic Biblical scholars may operate. A reference to Dr E. J. Kissane's scholarly work on Isaiah, for example, will show the learned author's pains to show that his view of the composition of that book does not transgress the limits prescribed by the Biblical Commission.[6] The late Abbot Chapman, in the introduction to his book *Matthew, Mark and Luke* (1937), related the steps by which he exchanged his earlier view of the priority of Mark for his later one of the priority of Matthew. We do not question that he really did change his mind through further study of the evidence as it appealed to him; but his arguments would carry greater weight if the Biblical Commission had not previously laid down the priority of Matthew as a conclusion not to be gainsaid. Or, when Mgr. Ronald Knox in his new translation of the New Testament says that while the passage about the Three Heavenly Witnesses in 1 John v. 7 does not occur in any good Greek manuscript,

---

6. E. J. Kissane, *The Book of Isaiah*, Vol. ii (1943), pp. lviii f.

'the Latin manuscripts may have preserved the true text', we wonder what he would have said had he been left free to exercise his own judgment in the matter.

No such conclusions are prescribed for members of the Tyndale Fellowship. In such critical *cruces*, for example, as the codification of the Pentateuch, the composition of Isaiah, the date of Daniel, the sources of the Gospels, or the authenticity of the Pastoral Epistles, each of us is free to hold and proclaim the conclusions to which all the available evidence points.[7] Any research worthy of the name, we take it for granted, must necessarily be unfettered.

Evangelical Christians must, once and for all, give the lie to the common idea that they are afraid of scientific research. If the idea were true, it would say little for the strength of such people's personal faith. But it must not even *seem* to be true. Of course, if our premises are intellectually untenable, the sooner we know it the

---

7. Thus, if in this QUARTERLY different views of the common authorship of the Fourth Gospel and the Apocalypse have been aired by two members of the Tyndale Fellowship – Mr Beasley-Murray in Vol. xviii (1946), pp. 185 f., and the present writer in Vol. xvi (1944), pp. 107 ff. – it is simply because we differ as to which side the weight of the evidence comes down on. Or, when Mr Nunn, in his recent Tyndale Fellowship publication (reviewed on p. 79), maintains the Apostolic authorship of the Fourth Gospel, it is purely because the evidence he adduces points so irresistibly to that conclusion. We may contrast the situation in which a Roman Catholic scholar like M. J. Lagrange finds himself. At the beginning of his *Évangile selon saint Jean* (1925), he says: 'L'Église catholique a rangé parmi les livres canoniques les évangiles selon Matthieu, Marc, Luc et Jean. Le quatrième évangile a donc été écrit sous l'inspiration de l'Esprit-Saint. Pour nous c'est un dogme, ce n'est pas une question. Ce n'est pas non plus une question de savoir s'il a eu pour auteur le disciple bien-aimé, Jean, fils de Zébédée. Ce point est fixé par la tradition ecclésiastique' (p. vi). In our view, the inspiration of the Fourth Gospel is sufficiently clear even to a reader endowed with the slenderest spiritual discernment, while its authorship can be determined only by considering the internal and external evidence.

better; but if we are convinced that our position is impregnably secure, then we shall welcome all the light that science and scholarship have to throw upon it, whether coming from friendly or from hostile quarters, in order that it may be *seen* to be impregnably secure. The early Christians challenged the closest scrutiny of their claims: 'this thing', they gladly asserted, 'was not done in a corner'. We wish to be of their spirit. Our desire for our contemporaries, as Luke's for Theophilus, is that they may know the certainty – in the proper sense of the word, the *infallibility* – of the Christian message as they read or hear it.

From the outset, the Biblical Research Committee and the Tyndale Fellowship have emphasised the importance of the linguistic side of Biblical study. Sound theology must be based on sound exegesis, and sound exegesis on a sound text; and to establish and understand a sound text we require a thorough acquaintance with the original languages. And a thorough acquaintance with these requires some knowledge at least of other languages which influenced them. The New Testament idiom cannot be properly understood without some knowledge of Hebrew and Aramaic, and the intensive study of these Old Testament languages leads one into such other languages as Sumerian, Akkadian, Hittite, Hurrian, Egyptian, Persian, and Arabic. We desire to be worthy followers of the Reformers in our insistence on the primacy of the strict grammatico-historical exegesis of Scripture, and we emphasise the necessity of laying a stable foundation for this exegesis, and discourage the taking of short cuts. Though this policy may not show such immediate results as some would like to see, we believe that the results, when they come, will be the more enduring.

It has been pointed out that the success of the Evangelical Revival two centuries ago was all the greater because the intellectual tenability of Christianity, scouted by the Deists, had been re-established for many, in terms which appealed to the eighteenth-century mind, by Bishop Butler. There will be the greater hope for evangelism in this century if people in general can be rationally persuaded that Evangelical Christianity has nothing to do with pseudo-conservatism that fears to face the facts of Biblical or any other science lest it should find its position undermined. A sane and cogent Biblical theology can be presented in terms which, on the one hand, acknowledge the revelation of God recorded in Holy Writ and, on the other, cannot be assailed as unscientific, illogical or obscurantist. The Tyndale Fellowship desires to play its part in preparing the way for such a presentation. It is no friend of the irrationalism popular in some modern theological circles.

The need for renewed efforts in Biblical and theological study in the British Isles in these post-war years is all the greater because of the eclipse – temporary, we may well pray – of these studies in Germany. When we contemplate the magnificent wealth of contributions to Biblical research made over so many years in Germany, it is with a sense of appalling loss that we learn that, at the time of writing, not one periodical devoted to Biblical or theological learning is being published in that land. Fortunately, we cannot say that none is being published in the German language, for we have to welcome the new *Theologische Zeitschrift* edited in Switzerland by Professor K. L. Schmidt; but this can go only a small way to repair the loss. There may be some people who view with equanimity or even satisfaction this eclipse of German scholarship in the Biblical field as in so many others; but the Tyndale Fellowship is of another mind. There have indeed been tendencies from time to time in German Biblical scholarship which did not commend themselves to Evangelical thought;[8] but its present sorry plight can be regarded as nothing less than a calamity for the whole world – though not such a calamity as its plight under a triumphant Hitlerism would have been, for then the hope of an early and vigorous resurrection, which we may now indulge, would have been slender indeed.

On these and other grounds we feel we have reason to hope and believe that the Tyndale Fellowship may have 'come to the kingdom for such a time as this'; and we confidently look for the

---

8. Those who have talked and written, especially during the recent war, as if all Biblical and theological study in Germany were affected by rationalistic tendencies, seem never to have heard of such giants as Zahn and Schlatter!

sympathetic interest of all who have at heart the revival of the full-orbed historic Evangelical Faith, and invite the co-operation of those like-minded who desire to pursue the paths of Biblical scholarship to the glory of God and the blessing of their fellows.[9]

---

9. Those who would like further information are invited to apply to the Secretary of the Tyndale Fellowship, the Revd J. Stafford Wright, M.A., Senior Tutor, Oak Hill College, Southgate, London, N.14. In addition to an entrance fee of 5s., members pay an annual subscription of 7s. 6d. or a life membership of £4. The subscription includes the subscription to *The Tyndale Bulletin*, the private memorandum printed for the information of members; and membership carries with it specially favourable terms for residence at Tyndale House. For terms of residence at Tyndale House and further information about the House and Research Library, apply to the Warden, Col. J. N. D. Anderson, Tyndale House, 16 Selwyn Gardens, Cambridge. A leaflet dealing with the financial support of the enterprise may be obtained from Dr. D. Johnson, General Secretary of the I.V.F., 39 Bedford Square, London, W.C.1.

APPENDIX G
THE TYNDALE WEBSITE

The Tyndale website was launched by Andrew Clarke in 1995, when there were only a few thousand websites in the world, and Cambridge University had the world's only webcam that monitored the staff coffee pot. David Instone-Brewer transformed it into 'Doorway to Biblical Studies', providing a quick route to the valuable material hidden away on the web, as well as a home for thousands of pages of resources for biblical scholars.

Valuable content was gradually added, mostly from the publications of Tyndale research fellows, including:

- Divorce and Remarriage Papyri from 400 BCE to 500 CE
- Illustrations for Dr Bruce Winter's books
- Catalogue of Greek New Testament papyri
- Tyndale Font Kit – keyboards, fonts and texts for biblical languages

Other valuable work from outside Tyndale House was also hosted, including:

- Biblon2000 – NT Greek text variants that can be swapped into the base text
- Scripture translations – comparisons of over 100 English translations

Like most modern institutions, the website provides information for visitors about accommodation, travel, local facilities, links to individuals, visual tour, and introductions to peculiar Cambridge customs – presented with distinctly British dry humour.

The Tyndale House Library catalogue was available through the Internet via the Cambridge University Library from 1994, but TynCat (the Tyndale web Catalogue) was born in 2003. This has become a very flexible and powerful search tool for biblical studies, linking the library collection to online versions of the books, price comparisons and scholarly reviews.

Tech@Tyndale was introduced in 1999 as an email bulletin to help biblical scholars keep up with the fast pace of new technologies. The address list has grown to include a significant proportion of serious scholars in the world, and highlights advances in software and websites.

The Bible text has always taken advantage of the latest technology, from the codex, to the printed book, to computer disc and now the web. The Tyndale website aims to provide easy access to the best of it.

www.TyndaleHouse.com

INDEX OF NAMES

Bevin, Ernest, 60
Biggar, N., 308
Bimson, J. J., 166, 170, 173, 284, 301
Birdsall, J. N., 297, 312
Black, M., 162
Blaiklock, E. M., 52, 107, 296f., 312
Blake, S. W., 240
Blanshard, J. M. V., 235–237
Blocher, H., 261
Block, D. I., 295
Blomberg, C. L., 178, 197, 206, 208f.,
    242, 245, 277, 310
Boettner, Loraine, 53
Bolster, G., 72
Booth-Clibborn, Catherine, 4, 23
Boyd, R. L. F., 169
Bradshaw, Miss A., 161, 197
Bradshaw, T., 214, 307
Bray, G. L., 161, 164, 187, 203, 225,
    244, 273, 283, 305f., 310
Brencher, J., 144
Bridger, F. W., 308
Bridger, J. R., 99, 103, 107–109, 123,
    282
Bright, P., 234
Broers, Sir Alec, 267
Bromiley, G. W., 15, 33–35, 38, 40, 42,
    45, 48f., 56, 63f., 71f., 78
Broughton Knox, D., 33f., 36, 38, 41f.,
    83, 259
Brower, K. E., 257, 299
Brown, Callum G., 247
Brown, Colin, 303f.
Broyles, C. C., 197, 205, 283, 295
Bruce, F. F., 11, 30, 32f., 38, 40–43,
    46–49, 51–56, 58f., 63, 65–68, 70,
    72–74, 78f., 82–85, 89, 95f., 102f.,
    108, 110–114, 116f., 119–121,
    126–130, 133, 135–138, 147, 149,
    152f., 155, 158, 162, 167–169, 175,
    178f., 184, 190, 202, 218f., 223,
    231f., 234, 243, 252, 264, 269, 281,
    293, 296, 300, 311f., 314, 317
Brunner, Emil, 56, 64, 71
Buchanan, C., 144
Buckton, J. W., 56, 83, 91, 100f.
Bultmann, R., 129
Bunting, H., 309
Burden, 199

Burleigh, J. H. S., 41, 90
Butler, J., 323
Buxton, Alfred, 23
Buxton, Barclay, 23
Buxton, Godfrey, 23, 35, 48

Cachet, L., 219
Cailliet, Professor and Mrs E., 84
Callaghan, James, 150
Calvin, John, 73, 76, 78, 122, 202
Cameron, N. de S., 183, 202, 244, 307
Cameron, W. J., 104
Campbell, R. J., 25
Capper, B., 299
Caragounis, C. C., 298
Carey, G. L., 128, 139, 163, 178, 202f.,
    208, 229f., 304
Carlyle, Thomas, 321
Carnegie, D. R., 298
Carr, D., 94, 187
Carroll R., M. D., 295
Carson, D. A., 162, 208, 217, 243, 298,
    305, 310
Carson, H. M., 111, 114, 303
Caswell, R. N., 93, 306
Catchpole, D. R., 132f., 139, 175
Catherwood, J., 94
Cawley, F., 53
Chadwick, Henry, 58f., 84, 283
Chagall, M., 267
Chaplin, J., 309
Chapman, Abbot, 321
Chapman, C., 224–226, 253, 255, 310
Charley, J. W., 304
Chemnitz, M., 95
Chew, J., 219
Christie, Agatha, 100
Churchill, Sir Winston, 99
Clark, R. E. D., 85
Clark, S. C., 84f.
Clarke, A. D., 226, 241, 251, 255, 264,
    266, 283, 299
Clines, D. J., 140f., 152, 294
Coad, F. Roy, 68
Coates, R. J., 306
Cobb, Jack, 29
Cobb, V., 169, 172, 190f., 204, 240
Coggan, F. D., 23, 45, 63, 229, 296, 311
Cole, A., 296, 312